Killing JFK:

50 Years, 50 Lies

From the Warren Commission to Bill O'Reilly,
A History of Deceit in the Kennedy Assassination

Dr. Lance Moore

©2013 Sky-Fy Publishing
All Rights Reserved
ISBN: 978-1492248170
www.Sky-Fy.com

For Melissa, Amanda and Karlin:
Hoping you will one day have an honest government.

Early Praise for *Killing JFK: 50 Years, 50 Lies*:
"Finally, a well-written, witty, and factual overview of the case that examines both the big picture and all the important details in the mosaic—without getting lost in a morass of tangential information. This is an important book that clearly demonstrates why the JFK assassination case is still relevant, unsolved, and intriguing. Whether an expert or a beginner on the subject, you will find yourself rereading many passages and marveling at the wealth of information that clearly indicates a conspiracy in the Kennedy murder. Moore's work also serves as a terrific counter-assault towards several prominent apologists of the official story.

Not just "Recommended": *Highly* recommended!"

—Vince Palamara, author of ***Survivor's Guilt: The Secret Service and the Failure to Protect President Kennedy***

Table of Contents?

A neat, linear order does not fit the content and design of this book. It is not organized into standard chapters, but rather is composed of fifty sections: 50 lies with 50 rebuttals. Also, we anticipate many readers will purchase the Kindle (electronic book) version, which puts pagination in flux. Therefore, there is no Table of Contents. Each section is like a piece of a jig-saw puzzle and could be examined in isolation, yet the big picture does not become clear until all the pieces are in view. What this means is that we hope the reader will pardon the format and read straight through in a few sittings, eager for the landscape view.

The sections are, however, clearly numbered and identified by topic (i.e. *Lie Number x*), and all sources are footnoted in numerical order, with the works cited at the end of the document as "Endnotes."

Note: the "Warren Commission" will be abbreviated "WC" in this book; most quotes are from the 1992 Barnes and Noble special summary edition of *The Warren Commission Report*, similarly abbreviated *WCR*.

Thanks to: family and friends who encourage my writing (you know who you are), and to Gaynor, for invaluable editing and proofing. *~Love, L*

Read other books by Dr. Moore at www.Sky-Fy.com
or at Amazon.com
Available in softcover and Kindle

For anyone new to the topic:

At half past noon on Friday, November 22, 1963, a "flurry" of shots rang out as the Presidential motorcade coasted through a city park, Dealey Plaza, and a wounded Texas Governor Connally cried out, "They're going to kill us all!" Then the world changed: President John F. Kennedy's head flew backward and exploded.

An hour later, Lee Harvey Oswald was arrested and charged with murder. Before the weekend was over, Jack Ruby strolled into the Dallas Police station and shot Oswald at point-blank range. The sudden death of the suspect, and the conflicting press reports (some using the word "assassins," plural), prompted the new President, Lyndon Baines Johnson, to establish a Presidential investigation, now known as the Warren Commission. LBJ's handpicked group spent a year investigating, only to conclude that just two bullets had caused half-a-dozen wounds on two men as well as damage to the car: "The shots which killed President Kennedy and wounded Governor Connally were fired by Lee Harvey Oswald,"[1] who "acted alone."[2]

This conclusion, however, flies in the face of nearly every page of their own 26-volumes of evidence.

Killing JFK: 50 Years, 50 Lies:

Fifty years ago, on the morning after the fatal shooting of our young President, two men were already on the phone conspiring to place the blame onto a "patsy," Lee Oswald.[3] Their cover-up would not be perfect; although they knew White House phone conversations were recorded[4], they were not guarded enough with their words. During the Watergate scandal, we learned of the existence of an archival **White House tape-recorder** that had not only ensnared Nixon, but also reveals a conspiracy of concealment by his predecessor, LBJ. The same tape-recorder tells us that within 24 hours of the assassination, the freshly-ascended President Johnson heard troubling news from FBI Director J. Edgar Hoover:

```
"We have up here the tape and the photograph of the
man who was at the Soviet embassy [in Mexico], using
Oswald's name. That picture and the tape do not
correspond to his voice, nor to his appearance.  In
other words, it appears that there is a second person
who was at the Soviet embassy down there."[5]
```

Johnson and Hoover were smart men and understood the implications of this news: **someone had been impersonating this loser "nobody," Lee Harvey Oswald**, just weeks before the assassination. Contrary to the **Warren Commission** (henceforth abbreviated "**WC**") that "Oswald acted alone," to speak of a "second person" spells CONSPIRACY in loud letters. Yet, look how casually LBJ responded to Hoover's news: the normally-inquisitive Johnson merely changed the subject. He knew better than give Hoover a direct order, by phone, to cover up the Mexico hoax. And it wasn't necessary. Lyndon had already ensured that his close friend, Edgar, was on his side. How? First, by pouring the Johnson sycophantic-charm on his longtime neighbor (Hoover and LBJ had lived for years just three houses apart in a D.C. suburb). Second, by promising Hoover a long reign as Master of his FBI domain via an extraordinary Executive Order that would lift what would have been his mandatory retirement the next year. He owned Hoover. So neither LBJ nor Hoover made any attempt to convey to the Commission this earth-shaking news of an impostor. In short order, all the tapes regarding the matter (both the CIA's Mexico City bug tapes and this particular White House phone tape) were erased. Fortunately for history, a printed transcript of the damning conversation survives and surfaced in the nineties. Ask yourself: *Why was this shocking evidence of an Oswald* *impersonator, and the ensuing conspiracy to conceal it by LBJ and Hoover, never reported widely in the press?* The question is no longer, "Did they lie?" The question is, "Why are so many denying it?"

Before we continue, we address two more prefatory questions: "Why write yet another book about the JFK assassination, when hundreds already exist on the topic? And does the topic have any real relevance for our time?"

Why It Matters

50 years later, it still matters. The shooting of our young, visionary President was a violent *coup* that derailed our nation's direction. Politics and policies were altered, and we continue to pay a price for it. To understand our future, we must uncover the secrets of our past, secrets that began the moment Jack and Bobby Kennedy tried to rein in the Mafia, the CIA, the FBI, and the military moneymen. The guilty parties may now be dead, but history still demands accountability for their crimes of murder and the abrogation of democracy. We cannot have a secure and true democracy with such a poisonous conspiracy hidden in dark corners. Spiders may die quickly, but they leave enduring webs... and offspring.

To be good citizens, we must know the truth. Unfortunately, most of the books on the subject meander through five or six hundred pages filled with trivialities. Thus I offer this abridged version of the substantial facts—avoiding wild speculations and extraneous details—to offer a clear view of how **our government and our media continue to lie to us.** I also present a bit of new information here, but more significantly, this report focuses concisely on the key truths, rather than majoring in minor "red herrings." And in particular, using a **new lens** for that focus, we apply the principle of **Occam's Razor** (see Lie Number 10).

O What a Tangled Web We Weave,
When First We Practice to Deceive

We also learn from the LBJ White House tapes that he did not establish an investigatory commission (the WC) in order to find the truth. Johnson's goal, within days of occupying the Oval Office, was to block Congress or other government agencies from starting aggressive investigations. Hoover would have loved to have kept the investigation within his department (and the FBI Director initially questioned LBJ's gambit of a bipartisan commission). But Johnson knew he could not sell an FBI-only investigation, as there were already widespread calls for major investigations by both the Senate and the House. So he put in place a bipartisan commission that appeared unbiased, but that was, in reality, dominated by LBJ's hand-picked people intent on finding nothing but a lone gunman. And that is what they did—even though it required quite a few detours around the facts, and left telltale signs of a cover-up. **The convoluted work-arounds of the WC and its defenders created more questions than answers.** Their explanations require explanations, their defenses require defense, their complex machinations and fabrications require another layer of lies.

To be a fair-minded judge, take note that disinformation is an oft-used tool of the CIA. Silly and confusing disinformation abounds in this case. For that reason, I built these 50 points on the most indisputable, irrefutable evidence, much of which is found in the very pages of the *Warren Commission Report* (WCR). Considering the advantages the conspirators had in government resources, their cover-up was sloppy. They let some truth slip out. They are caught in the tangled web of their own lies... a drama fit for Shakespeare. The government and media has spun far more than fifty strands of deception, but these verified 50 facts will be enough to convince you: **Oswald was not a lone assassin.**

The 50 Lies

These 50 Lies may seem randomly ordered, but it can be no other way: **this is a complex, interwoven case and cannot be mapped out in a linear fashion.** This is algebra, not simple arithmetic. A thousand-piece jigsaw puzzle that only makes sense when assembled into a big picture. A cross-woven web, not a single thread. To use our Shakespearean spider metaphor, "Where do we start unraveling a tangled web of practiced deceit?" So allow me to start with a look ahead at Lie Number 50, before we circle back to Lie Number 1... in part to alert the reader that we cannot number these lies in order of importance. Each lie's rebuttal crosses with another, to weave our counter-case *in toto*, not piecemeal.

The "50th Point" also answers a foundational question: "If there *is* a conspiracy, was it just a few rogue nuts or mobsters... or does it reach to the highest levels of government?" Jumping to answer the 50th Lie may ruin the suspense, but 'tis best that I "show my hand" as to the direction of this book: the facts herein ultimately point to something bigger than a handful of historically-insignificant Mafioso. Means, motive, opportunity— along with hundreds of pieces of evidence and witnesses—all add up to a **politically-motivated assassination and a government cover-up**. The name of the man who fired the fatal bullet is far less important, for our times, than the political ramifications of our first several Lies, which show: *our government cannot be trusted*.

Lie Number 50: The Impersonators: Was "someone... impersonating Secret Service agents, indicating a conspiracy? Most of the witnesses [to impersonators] later admitted they were mistaken."
~Gerald Posner in *Case Closed*

No, Mr. Posner, most of the witnesses did not "admit" they were mistaken... that is a lie. In fact, quite a few witnesses who had reported run-ins with fake Secret Service or a fake Oswald *cannot* admit they were mistaken, because they are dead! (Yes, mysterious murders, accidents and suicides befell those who spoke up about impostors.) The once-secret tape of Hoover admitting to Johnson that someone impersonated Oswald at embassies in Mexico is irrefutable proof that the trick of impersonation was employed by the conspirators. When so-called "debunkers" rejected this now-indisputable fact, **they failed a litmus test of intellectual honesty**. The test of open-mindedness is in how you react to the overwhelming evidence pointing to the activity of impostors in the JFK case. At least Posner admits that *if* impostors were involved, that would be proof of conspiracy. So those who claim Oswald acted alone have painted themselves into a corner: they have no choice but to dismiss those who encountered impersonators as merely "mistaken." An honest person reads the words from the Hoover-to-LBJ tape and responds, "What!? Why would someone pretend to be Oswald?" But others just ignore this, as it challenges their comfortable belief that our institutions are trustworthy.

The official investigators should have delved deeper into the evidence regarding a fake Oswald and a fake Secret Service agent. Instead, we find the WC, the House Special Committee and the debunkers doing the opposite: rather than dig deeper, they throw dirt on top of this body of evidence. They bury it with attacks on witness credibility, selective reporting of facts, and gerrymandered explanations.

Posner, like the Commission before him, can gin up an explanation for any single point of suspicion, but a problem emerges as their explanations begin to be self-contradictory. We find that their strained explanation for one problem then contradicts their explanation for another, much like the arcade game, "Whac-A-Mole," where when you squash one mole with a rubber mallet, it causes another mole to pop his head up. As we shall see, the standard with which they dismiss the witnesses/evidence indicating conspiratorial impostors at work is a standard later abandoned when they marshal other witnesses to defend their own claims.

It is a pivotal point: **if Oswald were a lone, disassociated nut, no one would have impersonated him**. But if there were plans to frame him, to make him appear to be a commie plotting with Castro, then we would not be surprised to find someone loudly pretending to be Lee Oswald at the Soviet and Cuban embassies in Mexico... which is exactly what happened, as we learned from the White House tapes and from what remains in the CIA records.

In addition to the hard evidence of Oswald impersonations, we have strong eyewitness testimony of another form of impersonation: men with **counterfeit badges** on the scene in Dealey Plaza. Several people reported seeing suspicious men behind the Grassy Knoll fence within two minutes of the shooting—men who claimed to be law enforcement and/or Federal agents, flashing badges. But every government agency (WC, House committee, FBI and Secret Service) agreed that not a single agent or officer was present in that area in those earliest moments... with one exception. Ironically, the exception—veteran Dallas Police Patrolman Joe M. Smith— encountered an impostor himself. Officer Smith had been standing near the Texas School Book Depository (TSBD) during the motorcade, yet heard no shots coming from that building in particular. He was instead immediately directed by a woman to look for a gunman behind the fence and bushes of the Grassy Knoll. He gave the following testimony to the WC—damning evidence not found in the widely-read single volume summary, but buried in the 26-volumes:[6]

Officer SMITH: "...this woman came up to me and she was just in hysterics. She told me, "They are shooting the President from the bushes." So I immediately proceeded up here [Smith pointed to a chart present at the hearing. WC interrogator Wesley Liebeler then confirmed the chart location as the parking lot behind the fence. Smith continued.] I was checking all the bushes and I checked all the cars in the parking lot."

Mr. LIEBELER. "There is a parking lot in behind this grassy area back from Elm Street toward the railroad tracks, and you went down to the parking lot and looked around?"

Officer SMITH. "Yes, sir; I checked all the cars... and checked around the bushes. Of course, I wasn't alone. There was some deputy sheriff with me, and... one Secret Service man when I got there.... I pulled my pistol from my holster, and I thought, *this is silly, I don't know who I am looking for*, and I put it back. Just as I did, he showed me that he was a Secret Service agent."

Mr. LIEBELER. "Did you accost this man?"

Officer SMITH. "Well, he saw me coming with my pistol and right away he showed me who he was."

Mr. LIEBELER. "Do you remember who it was?"

Officer SMITH. "No, sir; I don't--because then we started checking the cars [again]."

~~

It is well-established that the only Secret Service agents in Dealey Plaza from 12:30-1:00 pm were in the motorcade, headed to Parkland Hospital—a fact confirmed by Secret Service Chief James Rowley and his agents in their own Commission testimonies. Officer Smith not only knew what a Secret Service badge and ID looked like, he also examined the badge closely enough to notice that the so-called "Agent" had dirty fingernails. Thus we know that within sixty seconds of the fatal shot, a man behind the Grassy Knoll fence was carrying fraudulent Secret Service credentials, either because he had just shot the President, or because he was in league with the one who did, helping him escape. In retrospect, it was the perfect getaway plan. The same blind trust in government that causes some to accept the Warren Commission Report (WCR) is also what caused Officer Smith to not question this fake "government agent."

Smith was not the only witness to encounter mock-agents in the Knoll parking lot after the shooting, before any real Federal agents arrived there. And others reported that *before* the shooting, the mock-agents had asked them to leave the area—which explains why the crowds were packed like sardines everywhere on the parade route *except* Dealey Plaza. So there is no justification for calling this experienced officer "mistaken" about seeing a badge and hearing the words "Secret Service." His testimony is corroborated (see below); it was a face-to-face encounter in broad daylight with vivid details ("dirty fingernails"); he had no motive for lying and did not equivocate; he confirmed his 1964 sworn testimony in later years. After time to reflect, Officer Smith regretted his own blind acceptance of the impostor's ruse: "I should have checked that man closer, but at the time I didn't snap on it.... He looked like an auto mechanic... he had dirty fingernails... a sports shirt and sports pants... it didn't ring true for the Secret Service. [But] at the time we were so pressed for time... and he had produced correct identification, and we just overlooked the thing."[7]

Even Dallas Police Chief Jesse Curry found the account to be proof of an impostor, saying in 1977 that the Secret Service Agent encountered by Officer Smith "must have been bogus—certainly the suspicion would point to the man as being involved in the shooting since he was in an area immediately adjacent to where the shots were...."

Witnesses to "Impersonating an Officer of the Law":

•**Jean L. Hill** is not considered to be the best of witnesses; her recollections seem shaky and inconsistent. Critics ridiculed her because she had thought she had seen a small white dog in the limo (but it turned out to be either a white lamb puppet, or white flowers, depending on which film/photo you look at, which someone had given the First Lady. The "Lambchop or flowers" debate is the kind of trivia people like David Von Pein love to foment. It is irrelevant: the photos obviously show *something* that could have appeared to be a small white poodle). Debunkers cite Hill's minor discrepancies in order to discredit *all* eyewitnesses in general. A tactic of critics is to dismiss an entire page of testimony simply because a witness was mistaken about one small aspect of the event. Even the worst of witnesses may still have a golden kernel of truth. Good investigators are willing to pan for gold; lazy investigators glance at the stream and say, "There's nothing of value in that creek!" The bigger point here is that Jean Hill's account **does match Smith's at key spots.** She told the WC of a suspicious man running from the TSBD parking lot, and of a uniformed impostor on the Grassy Knoll.[8] Why did they dismiss her, and the impostor scenario, so quickly? As we shall see, Hill's testimony on this matter does not stand alone; Posner's lie that *no one corroborated this* is challenged by **a dozen** who saw men behind that fence consistent with what Officer Smith experienced:

•**Malcolm Summers**, who ran immediately up the Grassy Knoll, was stopped by what he thought was a Federal agent, and sounds similar in description:

```
"We were stopped by a man in a suit and he had an
overcoat over his arm... I saw a gun under that
overcoat. And he [said], "Don't you all come up here
any further, you could get shot, or killed," one of
those words. A few months later, they told me they
didn't have an FBI man in that area. If they didn't
have anybody, it's a good question who it was."[9]
```

•**Ed Hoffman** reported seeing two men there whose actions match those of Officer Smith and the impostor: "A police officer came around the north end of the fence. He saw and confronted the suited man. The policeman held his service revolver in both hands.... The suit man held both arms out to his side, as if to gesture, 'it wasn't me. See, I have nothing.' Then the suit man reached inside his coat and pulled out something and showed it to the police officer. The officer relaxed...."[10]

- **Lee Bowers, Jr.**, watching in the train observation tower behind the parking lot, saw two strangers near the wooden fence during the shooting, and one matched the description of the casually dressed man stopped by Officer Smith: "One man, middle-aged, or slightly older, fairly heavy-set, in a white shirt, fairly dark trousers."[11]
- **The House Special Committee** added more corroboration: "After the assassination, several witnesses stated they had seen or encountered Secret Service agents behind the stockade fence situated on the Grassy Knoll area and in the Texas School Book Depository."[12]
- **Post Office employee J.C. Price** signed an affidavit stating that immediately after the shots he saw a man running from the parking area with something in his right hand. He said the man wore "a white dress shirt, no tie and khaki colored trousers... He had something in his hand."
- **Sam M. Holland** told the WC that, having seen puffs of smoke arise behind the Knoll fence, he ran behind it *immediately* after the shots and saw muddy footprints, proving that someone had been standing behind the fence. And he mentions finding "agents" in the parking lot.
- **James Simmons** stood near Holland and corroborated his testimony.
- **D.V. Harkness, Ronald Fischer** and **Joe Marshall Smith**, cited in the House investigation, all spoke of an encounter with an "agent"—Joe Smith even viewed his fake credentials.[13]
- **Deputy Sheriff Roger Craig** also bumped into a man who identified himself (falsely) as a Secret Service agent. Craig was

quite emphatic and specific about this encounter.[14]

Why did Posner and the WC so quickly dismiss the presence of impostors when we have over a dozen witnesses, several in law enforcement, telling us it happened? Besides the lie that Officer Smith was uncorroborated and mistaken about his encounter with an impersonator,[15] another attempt by debunkers to explain away this red flag is to claim Smith had encountered an off-duty Army Intelligence officer (though Smith knew the difference between a "Secret Service agent" and an "Intelligence Agent"). Vincent Bugliosi proposed in his book, *Reclaiming History*, that the "agent" Smith met was an Army Intel agent named James W. Powell... even though Powell's testimony places him on the other side of the Plaza at that time. Moreover, Powell did not carry a badge.

Others suggest Smith bumped into Secret Service Agent Lem Johns, who had momentarily jumped from one of the cars in the motorcade. However, neither Powell's nor Johns' testimony places them standing beside a car in the parking lot, and neither encountered an officer pointing a gun at them, and both were wearing a tie while Officer Smith's "agent" was not. All of this demonstrates the irrational desperation of debunkers like Vincent Bugliosi and John McAdams. When they must use lies (and insults) to defend previous fabrications, they lose all credibility. Another liar: FBI Special Agent James P. Hosty stated that Frank Ellsworth, an ATF agent, had been in the Grassy Knoll area, and for some reason had identified himself to someone as a Secret Service agent. But the House Committee deposed Ellsworth, who denied Hosty's allegation. Hosty, we will learn, is the FBI agent who knew Oswald worked in a building overseeing the motorcade route, yet warned no one. Hosty also destroyed a note from Oswald days before the shooting, an obstruction of justice for which he was never penalized.

The cover-up is almost as crucial a question as the killing. At the end, we will return to wrap things up with *Lie Number 50, Part 2*, but now we are back to the top of the circle, with *Lie One*: the Warren Commission obfuscation.

Lie Number 1: You Can Trust Us: "Truth is our only client here." ~Chief Justice Earl Warren, at the start of the Commission's investigation in 1964, saying the American people deserved the whole truth.

While some members of the WC had good intentions, such as Congressmen Richard Russell and Hale Boggs, the record shows from the outset that Earl Warren, Allen Dulles, Gerald Ford and others were interested in speed and simplicity of verdict, not in exposing the truth. Let's look at the facts—without yet speculating about ulterior motives. We know that:

• White House audio tapes and FOIA documents now reveal that President Johnson had encouraged investigators to move quickly in scapegoating Oswald as a lone nut. On a tape, just seven days after Dallas, LBJ and Hoover further discussed the need for a quick resolution; their conversation showed no concern for an honest investigation, only a desire for a rapid whitewash.[16]

• Johnson put the fear of God into Justice Warren, urging him to tread carefully when examining secrets, with the excuse that revealing too much of Oswald's Russian connection might lead to "thermonuclear war" with the USSR. LBJ used a similar excuse (that digging too deep might start a war) in badgering Sen. Richard Russell to serve on the WC. On phone tapes LBJ asked Russell to be "my man on the investigation." Russell resisted being LBJ's lackey, and accused his friend the President of trying to manipulate him to rubber-stamp the FBI's pre-determined version of the one-gunman theory.

- At one of the earliest meetings of the WC, they divided the investigation into various categories. Area II was assigned the task of finding "the identity of the assassin." *The assassin*, singular—i.e. the patsy Oswald. Despite ample evidence that there may have been two shooters, the investigation was framed as a search for a singular culprit... before it even began.[17]
- Rather than release all of its findings, the WC gave most of the files to the National Archives, knowing the records would be sealed for 75 years. The Kennedy autopsy photographs and X-rays were deeded separately to the National Archives under the strictest conditions for secrecy. Later, new laws would force the release of many (though not all) documents, but critics saw a pattern of frequent and heavy redaction: documents were blacked out at various spots (and no one knows how many documents were shredded, never archived at all). **One cannot claim to serve "truth" while hiding the facts for 75 years.** The documents that *have* been uncovered, and other information gleaned by FOIA requests over the last five decades, have repeatedly proven the voluminous WC Report to be biased, inaccurate, and misleading.
- **President Kennedy had fired Allen Dulles from his job as CIA Director, yet LBJ appointed him to the small, elite panel of WC commissioners.** This was an egregious error, the equivalent of having a police detective—let's call him *Allen Fox*—appointed to the investigative committee for the murder of a police chief— let's call him *Chief Jack Henhouse* — despite the fact that just before the murder, Chief Henhouse had announced his plans to fire Detective Fox. No surprise then that the House Select Committee on Assassinations (HSCA) would later learn that the CIA had hidden documents, skewed facts, and lied about their nefarious activities—including the fact that the CIA ran assassination plots against other world leaders.[18] We also see **Dulles, at an early formative meeting of the WC,**

already trying to convince the Commissioners that Oswald was a lone assassin. In Executive Session on December 16, 1963... just three weeks after Oswald had been suspiciously silenced by Jack Ruby), ex-CIA Director Dulles handed out copies of the book, *The Assassins,* by Robert J. Donovan. It chronicled seven previous assassination attempts on Presidents, and Dulles said to his fellow Commissioners, "You'll find a pattern running through [this book] that I think we'll find in this present case." The pattern Dulles referred to, he went on to say, was not of a "plot" but of a lone-nut assassin. Commissioner John McCloy argued with him: "The Lincoln assassination was a plot." Dulles retorted: "Yes, but one man was so dominant, it almost *wasn't* a plot."

Why was Dulles so insistent on pushing the "lone gunman theory" when the investigation had barely begun? And why would an intelligent man like Dulles try to argue that the plot to kill Lincoln had not been a plot? The investigation had hardly begun, the WC had not called a single witness, some Commissioners were seriously raising the possibility of a second gunman, and yet here we find Allen Dulles beginning his pre-determined "attorney's summation" to the jury: *Ladies and gentlemen of the jury, I think you see a pattern here... a single, crazy assassin. Case closed.*

Once critics began crying "cover-up," Justice Warren defensively replied it was absurd to believe so many upstanding leaders and government agencies would have lied. Absurd or not, many *did* lie, so Warren's statement begs the question: *Why did they lie?*

Not everyone was in on a murderous conspiracy. Some buried the facts, believing it was best for national security; some whitewashed the failures of their particular departments/agencies for career protection; some turned a blind eye out of ignorance or misguided patriotism; some were duped by the nefarious conspirators; some had received physical threats and silently cowered in fear. But in sum, the Commission showed little desire to tell the American people the whole truth. *Truth* was not their client. Expediency was.

Lie Number 2: Rely on the FBI: "We can rely upon the reports of the various agencies that have been engaged in investigating the matter, the F.B.I., the Secret Service, and others." ~Chief Justice Earl Warren

In the seventies, both the House Special Committee and the Senate-appointed Church Committee found that the JFK-related work of the FBI, CIA and Secret Service was seriously flawed, and that important facts had not been forwarded to the WC by those agencies.[19] Rather than excuse the WC, this bears another question: If the Warren Commissioners had truly been independent investigators in search of truth, why would they blindly trust those agencies, especially when red flags were flying from the start—such as rumors that Oswald had been an FBI or CIA informant? The FBI was *the* key investigative agency from the moment the shots were fired in Dallas, yet they had made a huge mistake in failing to surveil a known Soviet defector (Oswald). It was apparent on day one that they were hiding things. The WC knew it almost immediately.

Commissioner Gerald Ford inadvertently revealed this failure —and the bias of the Commission— in the first page of his book, *Portrait of the Assassin*. Ford wrote in detail of the WC's consternation in hearing a "dirty rumor" that Oswald might have been a paid informant for the FBI. In the once-secret Minutes from one of the WC's earliest meetings, we learn how they dealt with this information. Ford and Dulles showed no concern about the ramifications of the accusation. They had no way, initially, of knowing whether or not it was true, yet instead of pursuing what it might say about the trustworthiness of the FBI, the concern was how to clean-up and cover-up the "dirty rumor" (the phrase used by Ford to describe it). The greatest concern of the commissioners was not *investigation*, but *public relations*. FBI Director Edgar Hoover had persuaded Ford to inform him of the WC's proceedings and to help do damage control for the FBI's mistakes. Within hours of the assassination, before a shred of evidence was collected, Hoover had announced the official story: *Oswald was a lone nut... no conspiracy.* The WC made accidental "honest mistakes," but the record shows that Dulles, Ford and others on the Commission had made a conscious choice to do a "public relations spin," not a true investigation.

The Commissioners were not the lone culprits in the cover-up: later revelations show how elements in the FBI and CIA, and to a lesser degree the Secret Service and Dallas police and sheriff's departments, altered and/or buried the facts.

We will see more specifics on this in other sections. The reader may here ask why I begin with, and emphasize with redundancy, these points about bias and cover-up. Two answers: first, the ongoing pattern of collusive cover-up, the expansive complicity of government in the whitewashing of dark truths, is what makes the JFK issue relevant and still timely; second, knowing this prepares the reader to be cautious in equating "evidence" with "proof" merely because the government says so. Skepticism is in order, and in this case, paranoia in pursuit of truth is no vice.

Lie Number 3: Unbiased Investigators: "We... presumed [Oswald] innocent until proven guilty.... The Commission [did not function] as a prosecutor determined to prove a case...."
~*The Warren Commission Report* Foreword, p. xiv

Yes, Lies One through Three may seem redundant. They do overlap. Yet these are three distinct points that beg for clarity as we try to answer **the key question: "Can we trust our government?"** Was the government cover-up intentional, and how far did the intentionality extend? Any open-minded reading of the *WCR* shows not only a PR "spin," but also **a deliberate cover-up, a one-sided argument *designed* to paint Oswald as a lone assassin**. Early in the process, this fact became apparent to two of the WC's own lawyers, Joseph Ball and Wesley Liebeler. Ball complained that the WC was resting much of its case on "utterly unreliable" witnesses, but most of his report was ignored and deleted from the final report. Similarly, Liebeler complained that the *WCR* "read like a brief for the prosecution." His complaint, too, fell on deaf ears.[20] So the foreword of the *WCR* was a lie; they did exactly what they claimed they would *not* do: function as a prosecutor. The Commissioners and their counsels not only acted as prosecutors, they acted as *corrupt* prosecutors. They railroaded Oswald. They never presumed innocence, and they never seriously considered the evidence of accomplices. The WC was eager to convict a corpse so that embarrassing questions would not be asked of the living.

An easy-out for politicians has been to admit—as the House Select Committee did— "Oh, there may have been other men involved in the plot with Oswald... but we had no way to sort that out." Nonsense. The FBI and CIA had enormous resources. The Secret Service had already begun to investigate assassination plots in Chicago, Miami and Tampa *before* the Dallas tragedy. Respectable, private citizens were able to discover a mountain of evidence implicating others, so why would the government not pursue these leads with its unlimited resources?

Examples will follow that prove how the WC, and elements in

the FBI, CIA, and the Dallas police department, altered records and hid photos, twisted testimony, dismissed witnesses, crafted misleading summaries, and made illogical conclusions in opposition even to their own recorded "facts." The ironclad proof of this will be in Lie Number 19, regarding the head wounds. But let's first consider examples in the category of **disregarding eye witness testimony**... our next Lie.

Lie Number 4: Witnesses Not Credible: "Many people who witnessed the assassination... or were present in the area were a major source of ...contradictory information."
~*The Warren Commission Report*, Appendix 12

False rumors and careless eyewitnesses must be sorted out in a case such as this. But in their rush to judgment, the WC wildly *understated* the value and accuracy of eyewitnesses. They tagged "many witnesses" as "contradictory," when in fact, the opposite was true: most of the witness testimony (especially from Dealey Plaza) was consistent with the reality of November 22nd: two shooters. The witnesses were not *self*-contradictory... **most only contradicted the pre-determined, official version of just three shots coming from a single shooter.** The Commission selectively highlighted testimony that supported their "Oswald did it" case, and called contrary witnesses "not credible" without offering sound reasons. The WC discounted the testimony of the best witnesses, even that of law enforcement experts like **Secret Service Agent Clint Hill and Deputy Sheriff Roger Craig**. Craig stated that WC Counsel David Belin "changed my testimony fourteen times when he sent it to Washington."

Eyewitness identification of a stranger's face, a *suspect,* can be notoriously wrong. But the WC accepted questionable "ID's" of Oswald while rejecting more reliable testimony from those who ID'ed non-Oswald suspects, like those who saw a gunman behind the Grassy Knoll fence. It would be easy for a witness to confuse Oswald's face with another young man with similar build, complexion and hair... yet they rest their case on Howard Brennan's *can't-tell-if-he's-crouched-or-standing*, waffling long-shot ID of Oswald. **Objects are more reliably described than faces**: seeing a rifle vs. *not* seeing a rifle is a fact that is hard to mistake. In Dealey Plaza, the witnesses had no motive to lie, they were sober, they saw events in broad-daylight, and usually had corroborative testimony. Many had made statements to the news media, or written down notes, within hours of the event—fresher memories than the average court witness.

The WC failed to treat sworn testimony as "evidence," despite the fact that legal textbooks at the time defined "sworn testimony of witnesses" as the number one form of acceptable "trial evidence." Indeed, the very word *evidence* comes from Latin words (*e videns*) that literally mean "from what was seen." For example, the WC stated repeatedly there is "no evidence" that Oswald knew Ruby, but actually, evidence of the Oswald-Ruby connection is contained in the very pages of the *WCR*: more than once, eyewitnesses testified they saw the two together, it admits. You may not *believe* the witnesses, but if the Commissioners were as honest and unbiased as they claimed, the statement would at least read "no *credible* evidence." (In Lie Number 33 will see even more proof of the Ruby-Oswald connection.)

The **WC disregarded over 60 witnesses** who heard more than three shots and/or heard a gunshot from the Grassy Knoll (at the right front of JFK, as opposed to the much more distant School Book Depository behind him). Over and over, the WC labeled witnesses as "not credible," without any explanation—

simply because they were contrary to the official "one gunman" story. Cooperative, but contrary:

• **William and Gayle Newman**, with children in their laps, were interviewed on WFAA-TV within 30 minutes of the shooting—memories fresh and unaffected by the later propaganda that would push a "one-shooter, sixth-floor" theory. They were standing about ten feet away from JFK at the time of the fatal shot—the closest witnesses outside the limousine. Young William Newman spoke sincerely and articulately as he described what he and his wife had seen and heard: a shot that came from "directly behind" them, "back up on the knoll," near the pergola where it meets the fence (they stood a few yards downhill from there). Gayle Newman also referred to "the Grassy Knoll," which her husband described as "a mound of ground near the garden, on top of the hill." He did *not* say it came from the pergola or the garden, as one debunker claims... just near it. In fact, when the newsman asked specifically if a shot had come from the Triple Underpass (also called the viaduct), Mr. Newman answered: "No, not on the viaduct itself, but on top of the hill." Later that afternoon, Newman would add in a sworn statement: "The [President's] car sped away and everybody in that area had run up on top of that little mound." He later added that his word "everybody" included officers with guns, so evidently he was not the only one convinced a shot had come from the top of the Grassy Knoll. For no reason, the WC ignored the unequivocal reports by the Newmans.[21]

• We previously mentioned **Ed Hoffman**, who said he saw a man in a blue suit fire a rifle from behind the Grassy Knoll stockade fence. Because Ed was hearing impaired, his testimony was disregarded as "inconsistent"—a failure of interpretation, not of message.

• **Dolores Kounas** stood across the street from the TSBD, and said shots came from "the vicinity of the viaduct," which means the Underpass and the knoll that rises up to it.

•**Phil Willis** (well-known for having snapped some of the clearest photos of the tragedy) stated on video in 1988 that the WC refused to listen objectively to his testimony. He reported later that "all they wanted to hear about" was that he, Willis, had heard "three shots and three shots only," and only from the Book Depository. [22] In his testimony, Willis had clearly stated, "I am very dead certain that [the shot] that took the president's skull off had to come from the right front [the Grassy Knoll area], and, I'll stand by that to my death." Like so many witnesses contrary to the official story, Willis was confident in his testimony, so emphatic as to state, "I would swear on my mother's grave" the shot had blown out the back of JFK's head, and "I will believe that 'til the day I die." You won't find that statement in his testimony recorded in the *WCR*... but you can watch Willis speak here on the video "*The Men Who Killed Kennedy: The Killing of a President*," and read it in La Fontaine's book (see Endnotes).

•**Deputy Roger Craig** saw Oswald a few feet away, outside the Texas School Book Depository, and then spoke with him in custody... but the WC called him a liar. Instead, they trusted a man on a faraway sidewalk six floors down to I.D. the shooter (Brennan, whose flawed observations are explicated in Lie Number 36). The WC also gave credence to Charles Givens, the only eyewitness from within the Depository who claimed to have seen Oswald on the sixth floor (where the "sniper's nest" was found). However, Givens had changed his story, which normally would be a reason to dismiss a witness; Givens had first gone on record with the FBI on 11-22-1963 saying he had seen Oswald in the *first* floor "domino room" (reading a newspaper), not on the sixth... and first said he not seen him with a gun, yet later altered his story.[23] Why, then, did the WC deem Givens' changeable testimony credible, and the Sheriff's as not?

- **Oswald's mother** testified that her son had travelled to Russia as a U.S. double-agent, but the WC said her testimony was "not credible," and instead accepted the inconsistent testimony of his wife, Marina, a Russian who could barely speak English and who had received generous cash "gifts." No reason is given as to why they trusted a Russian over an American during the height of the Cold War. Marina lied under oath (about the Hidell name, among other things). Yet the WC relied heavily on her testimony. (Years later, Marina confessed on Oprah Winfrey's TV show that she never believed Oswald was the killer, but had felt pressure to say otherwise. She feared if she had not cooperated with the government, she would be deported. She has now stated on camera, "I know Lee was innocent.") The WC also never mentioned in its more public statements this testimony of Robert Oswald regarding his brother: "The Lee Harvey Oswald that I knew would not have killed anybody." Despite the WC public "spin" to the contrary, Lee's family believed he was a government agent.
- Dozens of contrary witnesses were not called upon by the WC, such as **Acquilla Clemons**, who went against the grain in saying that she had seen a killer who did not match Oswald's (in reference to the slaying of Officer Tippit... see Lie Number 27), and **Cheryl McKinnon**, a spectator standing on the Grassy Knoll, who had seen "puffs of white smoke still [hanging] in the air in small patches" behind the Grassy Knoll fence.

Conversely, the WC Assistant Counsel David Belin portrayed as unimpeachable the few witnesses able to pick Oswald out of a line-up. This is even more egregious when we learn that the line-up was rigged. Oswald looked bruised and unkempt when they stuck him in the line-up. Witness William Whaley told the WC: "You could have picked him out without identifying him by just listening to him because he was bawling out the policeman, telling them it wasn't right to put him in line with teenagers and all that... they were trying to railroad him."²⁴ (Also see above regarding Brennan's so-called I.D. of LHO.)

Deputy Sheriff Roger Craig said something quite interesting about WC Counsel David Belin: "When Belin interrogated me... he would ask me certain questions and whenever an important question would come up... he would have to know the answer beforehand. He would turn off the recorder and instruct the stenographer to stop taking notes. Then he would ask for the question, and if the answer satisfied him, he would turn the recorder back on, instruct the stenographer to start writing [typing] again, and he would ask me the same question, and I would answer it. However, while the recorder was off, if the answer did not satisfy him... he would turn the recorder back on and instruct the stenographer to start writing again and then he would ask me a completely different question." This manipulative behavior was reported by other WC witnesses, and Craig's experience is also confirmed by how often in the *WCR* minutes we find Belin or Allen Dulles stopping the eyewitness' testimony. They would then ask for an "off-the-record" chat before resuming the stenography, without any explanation on the record as to the nature of the interjection. Witnesses who testified in ways that pointed away from Oswald as the lone shooter were discredited or slandered by Belin, without substantiation.

College professor John McAdams runs a website for "debunking" JFK evidence. He continues a Commission tradition of insulting and attacking eyewitnesses, citing "wild, wacky, and often downright bizarre elements in their testimony." As an example, he deemed Sam Holland an unreliable witness by quoting Holland's statement, "after Kennedy was shot, Jackie jumped up and tried to get over in the back seat to him." While this description is inaccurate (there *were* three rows of seats, but Jackie was already seated in the far back seat), reasonable persons, from certain angles and distances, might well have described Jackie's movements in that way. She did indeed "jump up and tried to get over," though not into another back seat but onto the trunk lid. With eyes glued on Jackie's movements, without paying attention to the configuration of the limo seating, one could describe the scene in this manner and yet still be a reliable witness in every other regard. We would not call on Holland as a reliable witness to the question, "How many seats were in the limousine?" But the fact that he saw gun smoke on the Grassy Knoll is a specific piece of testimony that is not impugned by his mistaken notion that Jackie was trying to climb over into a non-existent backseat; the smoke does not seem to be an imaginative figment sparked by some other event or movement —especially considering that his observation was corroborated by others who smelled smoke in the same vicinity.

McAdams and the WC are guilty of throwing the baby out with the bathwater by using one unrelated mistake in one portion of an eyewitness' description to discredit and discard his entire testimony—despite the many cases where the rest of the testimony is consistent with other witnesses. Let us say, for example, that six people testify they saw a brown elephant in their neighborhood. Our investigation reveals that a circus had been in town and a grey elephant had temporarily escaped. We would not then say, "These people are nuts! There was no brown elephant in town that day!" No, we would rightly assume that the sunlight filtered through the trees and the elephant's color appeared brownish, or even that the eyewitnesses were just plain wrong about that detail... but we would rightly conclude that they indeed saw the grey circus elephant wandering down their street. We have several witnesses who saw or smelled gun smoke near the hilltop fence, and many witnesses who heard a shot from there, and some who even saw a man with a gun there... so collectively we have a compelling case for a Grassy

Knoll shooter (even before we add in other proofs of frontal entrance wounds on JFK). But the "debunkers" and the WC—with a clear agenda to frame Oswald—find some flimsy reason to discredit each of those 20-plus witnesses part and parcel. They would deny the existence of the entire elephant in the neighborhood simply because some witnesses mistakenly called him brown instead of grey.

Now, do we still need to evaluate eyewitness testimony with a healthy skepticism? Yes. And in particular with flaws that are relevant to a specific fact. If *two* elephants had escaped the circus—one grey and one brown—and we were trying to determine *which* one was in the neighborhood of our six witnesses, obviously we would then be more concerned about the issue of their eyesight in terms of color distinction. If we learned that all six were color-blind, they would be worthless in determining which elephant was where (though of course, they still saw an elephant). Ironically, this is a point where McAdams and the Commission suddenly care nothing of event-specific eye-testimony flaws. The location of Oswald **in the sniper's nest rests solely on one man**, Howard Brennan, and his faulty eyesight (see Lie Number 36). Was he able to discern that the man he saw in the shaded window, from six floors down and across the street, was Oswald? All other evidence implicating Oswald is shaky and debated but even if we accept that the gun and bullets belonged to Oswald, that does not prove the gun was not stolen and used by someone else (especially since the conspirators' goal was to frame him). So to place Oswald with that gun in that window, we only have Brennan, and Brennan was completely wrong in saying the man was standing when he fired. Then he could not identify Oswald in the first line-up. So we have sound reasons to doubt Brennan's observational and eyesight ability at that distance. I don't doubt that he saw *a* man there, and I have no reason to doubt he saw a gun-barrel extend out of the window. But we cannot accept that his long-distance glimpse of a shadowy figure would be enough to positively I.D. Oswald's face based on that one tenuous observation—again, six floors down and across a street. Yet, the Warren Commission, Bugliosi, McAdams, and Posner all embrace Brennan, but prejudiciously dismiss dissonant witnesses and blithely accept questionable ones —when they bolster the lone-nut theory.

The remaining 46 Lies will be more concise than this one, but we must repeat this key point: **as the reports from the FBI, CIA and the autopsy all grew more inconsistent and problematical, the testimony of solid eyewitnesses should have been given *more* weight, not *less*.** Early on in the investigation, the failures, equivocations and inconsistencies among the Federal investigative agencies should have prompted the Commission to turn to independent investigators. Rather than *discount* the testimonies of ordinary bystanders, of local doctors and of local (Texas) law enforcement, the WC should have *spotlighted* their testimony.

Forgive the redundancy, but we must revisit these facts in proving the WC's manipulation of testimony and their lack of objectivity. Our point here is to show deliberate obfuscation of testimony, which leads to the next lie....

Lie Number 5: Location, Location, Location: "There is no credible evidence that shots were fired... from any other location."
~the *WC Report,* p. 19

"The majority of Dealey Plaza witnesses said shots came from behind the President, in the direction of the School Book Depository Building."
~David Von Pein

Many of the witnesses—including those riding in JFK's limo— and news reporters had spoken of more than three shots, more than one assassin, and of shots from places other than Oswald's workplace. WFAA-Radio in Dallas, within minutes of the shooting, referred to "the knoll on which the assassin was apparently situated." Although newsman Pierce Allman had been standing at the Book Depository when the shots rang out, sights and sounds drew him toward the Knoll. He stated on the same early WFAA broadcast, "I ran up the knoll... foolishly" chasing the assassin along with other newsmen and police..." TV news broadcasts showed law enforcement racing up the Grassy Knoll, believing a sniper had been behind the wooden fence—a reasonable assumption since that spot was far closer for a marksman than to be six floors up, 90 yards away.

The historical record refutes debunker David Von Pein's lie (above): **the majority of eyewitnesses at Dealey Plaza or in the motorcade reported hearing shots from locations other than, or in addition to, the sixth-floor of the Texas School Book Depository (TSBD)**. Writer Harold Feldman tallied the reports of 121 eyewitnesses in the *WCR* and found that 38 gave "no clear opinion" as to the directional source of the shot, 32 thought the shots came from the TSBD building, and **51**, the highest category, thought the shots came from the Grassy Knoll. The "no clear opinion" does not rule out the Grassy Knoll, and some witnesses heard shots from *both* locations. When we more closely examine testimony, and add in those whose testimony did not make it into the WC Report, we do find that the majority of witnesses would fall into the category of "locations other than or in addition to the TSBD." For example, **James L. Simmons** told the FBI "it sounded like it came from the left and in front of us, towards the wooden fence" (i.e. the top of the Knoll). But the FBI changed his testimony to state that the shots came from "the direction of the Texas School Book Depository." **When**

carefully reviewed, we find that over sixty witnesses conflict with the lone gunman theory.[25]

You can't kill 60 witnesses. So what could the conspirators do? Ignore some. Re-word or re-interpret the testimony of others. Kill a few, threaten a few and hope others get scared into the "official story." The main tactic of the Warren Commission was to call most of the witnesses stupid: *They can't distinguish distant echoes from an actual shot!* If the goal of the WC had been to find truth, they would have performed a simple test: blindfold the witnesses, re-position them in the same positions of that fateful day, fire separate but randomly-ordered shots from the sixth floor of the Depository and then fire shots from the Grassy Knoll. Then quiz the witnesses individually on the direction of each shot and what echoes they heard. But no such test was done (years later, the House Committee used *microphones* to test acoustics in Dealey Plaza and determined there was most likely a fourth shot from the Grassy Knoll). This author stood in Dealey Plaza, and with a lifetime experience in acoustics and a degree in electronics (Dean's List in Electrical Engineering), I could distinguish the difference in the sound and directionality of echoes versus original sounds. But an untrained individual could do as well. The Knoll area is acoustically "soft" (trees, grass and rough wooden fence), while the Depository is "hard" (concrete and glass). If the TSBD had been the only sound source, the loudest echoes would be those reflecting from concrete structures: the Triple Underpass and the concrete Pergola. But those locations are *not* where the majority of ear-witnesses heard shots. Those standing exactly midway between the TSBD and those structures by the Grassy Knoll might have some "echo confusion," but the vast majority of other witnesses expressed confidence in locating the directionality of shots. They could tell the difference between an initial bang and its echo. **James Tague**, for example, was emphatic: a shot came from the

Knoll, and it was **not an echo**. The WC interrogating attorney, Wesley Liebeler, tried to lead the witness. Read verbatim from the *WC Report, Vol. VII*, p. 557:

```
Mr. Liebeler. Do you think that it is consistent with
what you heard and saw that day that the shots could
have come from the sixth floor of the Texas School
Book Depository?
Mr. Tague. Yes.
```

[He was answering a hypothetical, that the shots *could have* come from the TSBD... but Tague had already stated that his "impression" was that the shots came from near the "monument," which adjoins the Grassy Knoll.]

```
Mr. Liebeler. There was in fact a considerable echo
in that area?
Mr. Tague. There was no echo from where I stood. I
was asked this question before and there was no echo.
```

It bears repeating: if the shots attributed to a second gunman had merely been an echo from "Oswald's gun," those echoes would more likely have come from the hard reflective surfaces of the concrete railroad overpass *directly in front* of the President's car —not from the soft Grassy Knoll, front *right*. Yet not a single Secret Service agent believed any shots came from the Overpass. **Agent Clint Hill** testified that he heard the last shot coming from the "right" of JFK: the Grassy Knoll. "It was right, but I cannot say for sure that it was rear, because... it had a different sound."[26] Just before that, Agent Hill had referred to the *first* shot as coming from "my right rear." So Clint Hill was able to distinguish the first shot (from his right *rear*, the TSBD) from later shots that came just from his right (i.e. the Grassy Knoll area). After all, the car had moved parallel to the Grassy Knoll area by then, so the best way to describe the fatal shot from his spot was from the right, not from the front (which would have been the Overpass). No one on the Commission paused to explore this line of questioning; they changed the subject immediately.

Similarly, **Secret Service Agent Paul Landis**, standing on the opposite running board from Hill, reported what he saw: "My reaction at this time [of the fatal head shot] was that the shot came from somewhere towards the front, but I did not see anyone on the overpass, and looked along the right-hand side of the road," the area near the Grassy Knoll.

Who could ask for more "credible" evidence than the report of the agents **nearest Kennedy, trained in firearms, accustomed to the noise of gunfire?**

Witnesses contrary to the WC "official story" included policemen, deputy sheriffs, Secret Service agents, and most of the bystanders. Even many of Lee Oswald's fellow-workers *at* the TSBD thought at least one or more shots came from the Grassy Knoll—this is a salient point, since they were closest to the "lone gunman" in their own building.

Add to the sheer numbers of **ears**, we even have **eyes** that *saw* evidence of a Grassy Knoll shooter:

•Eyewitness **Lee Bowers** was located in the railway tower overlooking the parking lot behind the Grassy Knoll fence. He testified that at the moment of the shots, he **saw** something "out of the ordinary, which attracted my eye for some reason...." The WC interrogator cut him short. He later explained further, in an interview with Attorney Mark Lane, that what he'd seen was "a flash of light" at the fence." (Blast from a gun muzzle?) He also saw nearly "50 officers" rushing into the area behind the Grassy Knoll fence. Debunkers try to cast doubt on Mark Lane's work, but in a *filmed* interview, Bowers clarified that "there was a flash of light... which caught my eye in this immediate area on the embankment... a flash of light or smoke or something." (Bowers was killed a few months after his WC testimony in a strange, single-car accident.)[27]

•**Gordon Arnold** said in a TV interview that a man identifying himself as a government agent chased him out of the area behind the fence on the grassy knoll shortly before the shooting. Arnold then walked to another nearby spot near the triple overpass and **saw** a uniformed man with a rifle leaving the fenced area above the Grassy Knoll.[28]

•**Ed Hoffman** stood at the on-ramp of the Stemmons Freeway (near the railroad triple overpass), looking down on the motorcade and with a good view of the wooden stockade fence. Hoffman **saw** two men with guns there, and one of the men, who wore a bluish suit, fired a rifle from behind that fence. Because Ed was hearing impaired, his testimony was at first not recorded correctly by the FBI, thus later was disregarded as "inconsistent" —a failure of interpretation, not of message. He was a very credible witness but had initially could not find a policeman who could read sign language, and then later remained quiet because his father did not want his "deaf mute" son to get involved. (Debunkers hate Arnold and Hoffman, but I challenge the reader to actually watch to the video interviews with these witnesses… quite compelling.)

•**S. M. Holland and Richard C. Dodd**, bystanders near or on the Underpass, both **saw** a puff of smoke near the stockade fence atop the Grassy Knoll. Dodd is on record stating that his testimony to the FBI at the time clearly said "the shots—the smoke—came from behind the hedge on the north side of the plaza" (i.e. the Grassy Knoll).[29]

These and others *saw* as well as *heard* a second gunman (of literally, the smoking gun), yet the WC disregards all contrary witnesses and offers no explanation as to how an echo could "smoke" (Holland and Dodd) or cause a "flash of light" (Bowers).

Another hint of a cover-up by the Commissioners is found in the wording of their "Appendix," in which they try to dismiss "false rumors." The *WCR* Appendix reads:

"THE SOURCE OF THE SHOTS: There have been speculations

that some or all of the shots aimed at President Kennedy and Governor Connally came from the railroad overpass...."

Yet **very few witnesses specifically named the Overpass** structure as a source of shots; the *majority* pointed to the Grassy Knoll area (and sometimes referred to the Overpass/Underpass *area* when, in fact, they meant the Grassy Knoll sloping up to it… the Underpass being the specific, adjacent landmark to the vague "grassy hill," it is not surprising the two are used interchangeably). The vast majority pointed to either the Knoll or the Book Depository... neither of which was mentioned in the Appendix's attack on false rumors. The WC set up the Triple Overpass as a "straw man" argument, easy to knock down.

As we shall see, substantial evidence proves that shots came from an additional location. If Oswald fired at all, he did not fire the fatal shot; the final, gruesome, head-exploding shot could not have come from a full-metal-jacket bullet fired from behind JFK on the distant sixth floor via an old and inaccurate WWII-surplus rifle (more on the gun later). Whoever the sniper in the TSBD was, he did not act alone.

By now you have discovered that each "Lie" overlaps and leads to the next. That is the nature of this complicated case....

Lie Number 6: Oswald Could Do It Alone:

"Oswald assassinated President Kennedy, acting alone and without advice or assistance."
~*The Warren Commission Report*, Appendix 12
Oswald took "the bus to and from target practice, and indeed to and from the murder scene itself." [referring to an alleged attempt on the life of General Edwin Walker]
~Bill O'Reilly, *Killing Kennedy*, p. 159

The lie that Oswald was a solo act has been repeated as recently as 2012—in Bill O'Reilly's book, *Killing Kennedy*, and in Gerald Behn's apologetic for the Secret Service, *The Kennedy Detail*. These books still spout flimsy claims, still paint Oswald as the crazy, lone gunman. Why is an intelligent newsman like O'Reilly so ill-informed? Or does he have an agenda, charged with protecting the *status quo*?

Whatever Oswald's role may have been, **the evidence is overwhelming that Oswald did not fire the last shot, and would have missed if he had.**

According to Marina (who may have been paid or manipulated to make this claim), Oswald attempted to shoot General Edwin "Ted" Walker, a rabid anti-communist. But even as O'Reilly and others cite the Walker incident as "proof" that Oswald was capable of murder, they ironically and inadvertently remind us that he was: **a) not a great shot** (he missed Walker at an easy distance of 40 feet with all the time in the world to aim)[30] and **b) not able to pull off the crimes alone**. *Two* men in a car were reported leaving the scene of the Walker crime. Oswald, with no driver's license or car, had no way to get to that crime scene nor to a shooting range for target practice with his new-to-him rifle. O'Reilly claims (without any footnotes/references) that Oswald did so many times, via city bus! This is pure speculation. No one actually saw Oswald on a bus carrying a rifle; if he did go to a shooting range to practice, it would have required a car, and thus an accomplice (Oswald had no car or license). Marina claimed that on one occasion she saw him headed to the levee with his rifle wrapped in a raincoat ...but we have no record of Oswald shooting a gun there.

His scope was out of alignment, and there is no way Oswald could have learned to compensate for it, or align the scope, without taking the Mannlicher-Carcano rifle to a shooting range or a gun-shop... hard to do when you don't have a car or an accomplice with a car.

Nevertheless, we are told that on November 22nd, Oswald hitched a ride to work with his friend, Wesley, so that he could smuggle the gun into the TSBD in a paper bag. Wesley Frazier said the package fit between Oswald's cupped hand and armpit, yet the rifle was too long for that, nor would it fit in the bag— even disassembled. We must also accept that Oswald made two amazing, on-target shots within 3 seconds, even though he missed an easy shot on Walker with plenty of time, *and* missed the first easy shot on JFK when the limo was a stone's throw from Oswald's building. We are asked to believe he made a "lucky" perfect shot on the final attempt, **hitting a six-inch moving target at 260 feet**. How lucky a shot? The U.S. Army's Ballistics Research Laboratory had three Master Marksmen attempt it; they were rated higher than Oswald's best Marine "Sharpshooter" rating. In other tests, a better scope and rifle was used, but this test at least used the same actual Carcano rifle/scope that allegedly shot the moving target: Kennedy. But this test used *fixed* targets. The marksmen were given four attempts each to duplicate Oswald's "luck." The result: a total of twelve shots *all* missed the target at 240 feet.

In 1967, *CBS News* re-enacted the shooting at the H. P. White Ballistics Laboratory with a moving target... but without the curves and slope that would make it a truly accurate test... and not with Oswald's flawed Carcano, but with a better weapon. In this easier test, only *one* very skilled marksman replicated the accuracy and timing claimed of a TSBD sniper on November 22nd. Here's the punch line: that Master Marksman, Howard Donahue, doubted that Oswald could have pulled off the feat.

The bulk of witnesses and evidence indicate another shooter in lieu of, or in addition to, Lee Oswald: witnesses described two men on the sixth floor, two men at Tippit's shooting, two men at General Ted Walker's shooting (one described as a "short" and "heavy-set" man; the other as a dark complected "bald" or balding man).[31] It does seem that accomplices were "advising" Oswald: not to assist him, but rather to make sure he would fit their frame. The WC had only one answer for the enigma of Lee Harvey Oswald: he was crazy and solitary. But herein we will show otherwise: he was smart (although his troubled upbringing made him a poor student, he had above-average intelligence ...even O'Reilly concedes this). Lee was a calculating ex-Marine who wanted badly to be a spy or double-agent; not a loner, but instead, known to associate with a wide variety of strange characters from across the political spectrum.

The WC claims that, rather than having assistance, this lone nut was the "luckiest" assassin in history: he just happened to have bought a sniper-rifle and a pistol, from different sellers, that both were shipped to him on March 20, 1963... before the public knew that JFK would come to Dallas seven months later. Just one month before the shooting, he "luckily" landed a job at a tall building overlooking the motorcade route—before the route was announced. An extraordinarily-lucky shooter might have succeeded in killing Kennedy from that sixth floor with three fast shots from a clunky old rifle... but Oswald, ironically, was one of the most *unlucky* men in the world. He was not, however, stupid. A smart (but lone) shooter would have not put six floors of distance between him and his target and trapped himself high in a building; he would have disguised himself; he would have used a better gun with an aligned sight; he would have not left his palm print on the rifle; he would have made an escape plan (Oswald had no car, no bag packed, and left his money on his wife's dresser). Thirty minutes after the "lucky shot," Oswald instantly reverted back into the "unluckiest" man on earth: based on the vaguest of descriptions, he was (allegedly) questioned by a policeman in a remote neighborhood, then spotted by a suspicious shoe clerk (based on *no* description), quickly arrested, then unlucky enough to become the only criminal ever shot to death *inside* the Dallas Police headquarters by a civilian! He seems to have had someone helping him or conspiring with him in every place he lived in the years leading up to November 22nd. The record shows that Oswald was smart in some ways, naive in others, and often assisted by a guardian angel (getting him in and out of Russia with ease, for example)... but **after the shots were fired at 12:30 pm, he became very unlucky... and very alone**... with the exception of the men who shadowed him in order to silence him. Our next two Lies look deeper at the question of accomplices and a wider conspiracy.

Lie Number 7: Lyndon Johnson's foreknowledge: "I was startled... Agent Youngblood turned in a flash, immediately after the first explosion... I was pushed down by Agent Youngblood."
~Lyndon Baines Johnson, memo to the WC

"President Johnson [was] wrongly smeared by the conspiracy theorists.... The History Channel has distorted history beyond recognition."
~LBJ cohort Jack Valenti

Hollywood mogul Jack Valenti, Gerald Ford and other defenders of the LBJ legacy attacked the History Channel program, "The Men Who Killed Kennedy," for its compelling testimonies which indicate foreknowledge by Johnson. But the defenders (all who have a stake in that false legacy) fail to address the multiple pieces of evidence against LBJ. They never offer any specific or substantive rebuttal. And no one has offered any believable explanation why Johnson had starting ducking *before* the shots hit JFK.

It is highly suspicious that the Vice-President was crouching down even before the first shot rang out, and as the second shot was fired he had already ducked out of sight. **No one else, not even trained Secret Service agents, moved their bodies before the second shot**... heads turned, that's about it. Even more damning is the fact that Johnson lied about his quick duck. We might be persuaded he had ESP-precognition and lightening-fast reflexes and let it go at that... except for the fact that LBJ perjured himself on this important matter to the Warren Commission.

The proof? A picture paints a thousand words. Carefully examine the photograph called "Altgens 6," one of the most famous newspaper photos of the shooting. Examine the original, full AP photo in full resolution, not the smaller, cropped version publicly released. I'll describe it here for your convenience, but view it for yourself; don't let the naysayers describe it for you. See it here: www.jfkassassinationforum.com/Unger_Altgens6.png[32]

Some claim to see an "object" they say is either LBJ or the Secret Service Agent on top of him in the backseat. I see no such object in the photo... but forget subjective Rorschach interpretations. If Youngblood had been pushing him down at this point, we would not only see it clearly, we would certainly observe a puzzled or alarmed look on the faces of the driver or Ladybird. **Instead, they are smiling at the crowd and calm.** This is obvious. Here's what we can plainly see in the Altgens photo: the foreground is the Presidential limo, in which we see John Kennedy has just been shot. On its bumper, we see the Secret Service car, in which a few of the agents have turned their heads to discern if it was shots or backfire—but not a single body has reacted, no one has jumped from the running boards. Just behind the Secret Service car, look to the Vice-Presidential car in the far right background. In the front seat is a driver, and beside him is Secret Service Agent Rufus Youngblood (mostly obscured by a motorcycle cop in the foreground, his shoulder and part of his head are fuzzily visible). Invisible in the back seat is the man who would become President in a matter of seconds... left-to-right in the photo (as the car is facing us) should be Lyndon, Lady Byrd Johnson, and Senator Yarbrough. Or as one might describe the car seating in terms of "driver's side" and "passenger's side," Vice-President Johnson was seated on the far passenger's side of the car's back seat.

Wait, you say, *I can't see LBJ. I just see the crowd beside and behind the car... he must not be in that car.* **But he was, in fact, in that car**, and that photo was taken two seconds after the first shot. **Johnson has already ducked out of sight**, down beneath the car-window level and behind the passenger's seat-back. Youngblood is *about* to reach around and push LBJ down further and then climb over the seat to shield the Vice-President with his body (an action which earned the Agent a medal). But he's not had time to react yet. Johnson, however, has already reacted to the first shot... in less than two seconds time, he has disappeared from view—and the angle of the photo is such that we *should* be able to see the Vice-President clearly, *had* he been sitting anywhere near upright. To repeat: before any other person in the motorcade reacted fully, LBJ had ducked, and the only other reactions seen were a few heads turning toward the Depository, where the first or second shot rang out. No one else in the motorcade had moved positions, no one had time to go beyond thinking, "Is that a firecracker?" or "I wonder if that's gunfire?" Governor Connally, an experienced hunter, was one of a very few inclined to believe it was indeed gunfire... yet his reaction was merely to turn his head around, and that quick action had *only just begun* in this Altgens photo. Johnson, and Johnson alone, had ducked completely out of sight. In the context of all we know about LBJ, it is clear: he did not have cat-like, super-hero reflexes... he was a man "in the know," anxious and ready for what he knew would be shots.

And there are plenty of other clear and inarguable facts to prove that LBJ ducked. Those around him testified that LBJ had already begun slouching in the seat, on Houston Street, before they rounded Elm Street. On Houston, we can briefly see the back side of LBJ already starting to slouch just as his car comes in sight of the TSBD. Lyndon was the tallest person in the car, but in the Orville Nix home movie and for a split second in the Robert Hughes home movie, we can see LBJ's head and shoulders were the lowest in the car... even lower than Ladybird, seated on the same seat! But that's the last glimpse we get of him until they arrive at Parkland. There were half a dozen movie cameras and perhaps fifty still cameras, including several professional photographers, on Houston and Elm that day, and **not a single one of them captured the face of our Vice-President in Dealey Plaza**. Several of the movie camera films are missing frames right at the very moments where Johnson's car comes into their view (Elsie Dorman's, Tina Towner's, Nix's, Hughes'). Before the first shot rang, just as the Presidential limo was turning onto Elm ahead of him, he was slouched down, and then leaned over further, down and forward toward the middle of the front seats, listening to the radio or walkie-talkie. We are expected to believe Johnson's cover story: that he, a master politician, visiting his own state, was more intent on bending over to listen to the radio rather than to smile and wave at his fans and voters.

Our suspicions (and I credit author Phillip Nelson for his careful work on this) can be confirmed by the Warren Commission testimony and the Altgens photo. The WC Report tells us that when Youngblood pushed Johnson down, Ladybird ducked too. But she is *not* ducking in the Altgens photo. She is, as stated, still smiling... obliviously grinning at the crowd, not reacting to the fact that her husband is ducking, because he had already been slouching down before they even made the turn. Or perhaps "duck" is the wrong poultry. "Chicken" describes his actions more accurately. A coward who was afraid of a stray bullet, or fearful the CIA might double-cross him... but without a bit of concern for his wife's safety.

Just as Lyndon Johnson was the only one who reacted simultaneously with the shots, he is also **the only one who had a different version of the events in his car**. How did he explain this? By controlling the questions and the answers. He never allowed himself to be questioned or cross-examined by the WC. Vincent Bugliosi whined (in his *Reclaiming History*) that witnesses weren't cross-examined by the WC... another lie. Witnesses were sworn in before the Commission and, in most cases, questioned vigorously by one or more attorneys. LBJ was the one key witness NOT cross-examined—because he was not even called to testify. He answered no questions. He sent a carefully-crafted written statement in which he claimed Agent Youngblood had instantly leapt over the front seat and pushed him down. But in the Altgens photo, taken before Youngblood had time to get to the rear seat, we do not see any sign of Youngblood's body atop the President, protruding up into sight as it would have had to be. We know from the Agent's testimony that he was *beginning* to react by looking around, but was still seated upright in this photo, mostly hidden—except for the edge of his left shoulder—from the camera's view, obscured behind the motorcycle officer. The camera's angle on Johnson's seat, however, is such that, were he seated upright, we would be able to see him.

Study the photo. Please do not trust Johnson's explanations, or the debunker's lies about this. Read the testimony for yourself, here: www.jfkassassination.net/russ/testimony/youngblo.htm or go to a public library and read the Warren Commission Report.[33] Youngblood testified that he heard a shot and thought it was a firecracker (the Commission says "explosion," but he later clarified that the notion of a harmless firecracker first crossed his mind). He had no real reaction at that point, except to glance around. After the second "explosion," Youngblood realized it was likely a shot, so he then began to reach his left hand back to Johnson. In previous photos of their car, such as in the Nix film, we can see that LBJ was indeed seated directly behind Agent Youngblood, close to the right-hand car door because Ladybird was seated in the middle beside her husband. In the front seat, no one is seated in the middle, which allows us a clear view of where LBJ should be. After the Altgens photo was snapped, the WCR tells us a curious thing happened: Youngblood, reaching backwards and around his seat to the backseat occupant is not only able to reach LBJ with his left hand (try this in your car and you'll see how hard it is), but finds the VP has already shifted positions. The agent's hand was able to reach LBJ's now bent-over tall shoulder. Next, Youngblood says,

```
"I hollered 'Get down!', and then looked around again
and saw more movement, and so I proceeded to go to the
back seat."
```

    Johnson tries to credit the SS Agent with an even quicker response, saying Youngblood instantly leapt on top of him, pushing him down. But the testimony of others and the photo tell a different story: Johnson was *already* crouched down and was moving the upper torso of his lanky body further down and toward the center of the car *before* Youngblood had time to twist and force Johnson down further. It was a full second before Youngblood yelled, looked around again, and only then moved up out of his seat to shield the Vice-President. From the WCR we read:

```
SPECTER: "Which hand did you use in hitting the Vice
President's shoulder [pressing it downward]?"
Mr. YOUNGBLOOD. "My left, sir."
Mr. SPECTER. "And which shoulder of the Vice President
did you hit?"
Mr. YOUNGBLOOD. "His right, because I turned this way.
```

```
I turned to my left, with the hand out, and then came
into his right shoulder."
```

LBJ's *right* shoulder!? Arlen Specter doesn't bite on this curious fact: had Johnson not already moved, Youngblood's hand would have first reached the back seat passenger's *left* shoulder. Instead, Specter ignores that oddity and presses on with a new question, about the agent's movements to shield his ward. Youngblood makes things even clearer in reply:

```
YOUNGBLOOD: "Well, the Vice President says that I
vaulted over. [But] it was more of a stepping over.
And then I sat on top of him, he being crouched down
somewhat."
SPECTER. "And what were the positions of the other
occupants of the back seat at the time you sat on the
Vice President?"
Mr. YOUNGBLOOD. "...we were all below the window level
of the car."
```

By "below the window level," he clearly means "below where the windows begin." Like an ostrich, he thought because his head was down, they were "all" down... but his body would have been protruding upward atop the Vice-President (who was a large man), and of course the driver's head stayed up. He was mainly referring to the Johnsons' positions, in answer to Specter's question. This proves the Altgens photo was taken before Youngblood moved, because in the photo, a smiling Ladybird has not moved and is upright, well above the top of the doors—the "window level." We also see the *sequence* of events is not at all what LBJ claims, but rather is consistent with what Youngblood and a motorcycle escort (see below) describes... LBJ moved first!

```
YOUNGBLOOD: "He moved towards the center, or towards
his left, yes, sir, and down. And then I sat on this
portion of his arm...."
```
*[in all cases herein, the "**bold**" emphasis is added by the author]*

Notice the chronology: 1. First shot (like a "firecracker") rings out. Agent Youngblood looks around, puzzled. LBJ has already leaned in toward the center of seat and bends down. 2. Second shot strikes JFK, he instantly brings his hand to his throat; Altgens snaps photo. LBJ has now bent over **out of sight** of Altgens' lens. 3. *Then* Agent Youngblood reacts and could reach LBJ's right shoulder and push him down further. 4. Next the Agent yells 'Get down!' as he looks around again 4. Finally, Youngblood climbed over into to the back seat and used his body to shield the Vice-President—just as Clint Hill would do for the President and Jackie—albeit too late.

Secret Service Agent Youngblood was under pressure (and implies as much) to have his account not drastically contradict that of his boss. As the *WCR* reports, "Youngblood was not positive that he was in the rear before the second shot, but thought it probable **because of President Johnson's statement** to that effect."[34]

All the camera evidence and testimony from others contradicts Johnson's version of events. The lone exception was LBJ's buddy, Clifton Carter, who (according to his associate, Attorney Barr McClellan) was also involved in the plot and cover-up. The fact that Cliff Carter sided with Johnson, in direct contradiction to photographic evidence, indicts them both.

Our case here does not rest on the photo or upon Youngblood's testimony alone. Dallas Police Officer Billy Joe "B. J." Martin said that according to his fellow motorcycle cops "who were escorting [the Vice-Presidential car,] he started ducking down in the car a good 30 or 40 seconds before the first shots were fired...." He said, in reflection upon the moments before the shooting, "our new president is either one jumpy son of a bitch or he knows something he's not telling about the Kennedy thing."[35]

No surprise, then, that the press and the Commission printed the Altgens photo (Exhibit CE203) cropped in such a way as to leave out the Vice-Presidential car. Proof of LBJ's fore-knowledge of the shooting is also tied to a cover-up: LBJ's lies about the events, Specter's failure to ask the right questions of Youngblood, and the WC's failure to include a full Altgens photo or the testimony of Officer Martin.

Within hours of Oswald's arrest, Captain Will Fritz, head of the police investigation (and the only law enforcement agency to have immediate jurisdiction in the case), received a call from the White House. The new President instructed him to stop the investigation and turn the evidence over to the FBI. He did... and we have photos showing the files being trucked from the police station to the hands of Hoover's agents. The cover-up had begun in full, and LBJ (as we shall further prove at the end of our report) was the man directly responsible... with the conclusion already decided: a lone gunman.

Lie Number 8: Just Three Shots: "[T]he preponderance of the evidence...led the Commission to conclude that there were [just] three shots fired." ~WC Report, p. 111

Before the sun set on November 22nd, the ink was already dry on the official story: Hoover's FBI, the Dallas Police, *CBS*' Dan Rather and others declared Oswald to be the lone shooter of three shots—the only three shots. Contrary to that lie, overwhelming evidence indicates **more than three shots**. And much of the proof is found in the WC Report itself... buried in the avalanche of verbiage from 26 volumes. The Commission was determined to downplay all the contrarian eyewitnesses, and to ignore the fact that so many eyewitnesses, including trained officers, believed shots had come from places in addition to the Texas School Book Depository. The *earliest* news reports also indicated a different "story." **The day of the shooting, the *Dallas Times Herald* reported "six or seven shots were fired."** The first UPI release stated that President Kennedy had been "cut down by assassins' bullets" in downtown Dallas," using a **plural** *assassins.* Other reports spoke of "three bursts" (*Dallas Times Herald*) of "automatic" weapon fire (Jean Hill), "a flurry of shots," (Roy Kellerman) and "a fusillade" of shots (Walter Cronkite). The evidence for three shots from the Sixth Floor is strong, but even stronger evidence proves there were additional shots from another location(s).

- Read pages 110-117 of the *WCR*, where the Commission shares only a portion of the evidence regarding the number and order of the shots: which shot(s) missed, which hit Kennedy's head, which hit his back, which hit Connally. It is almost comical to see the WC strain to explain the unexplainable, limited by their lone-gunman and three-shots-only claim, like players in a game of dodgeball who have drawn the boundary circle too tightly around themselves. The only way to make sense of all the facts is to accept broader parameters: that four or five shots were fired and at such a speed and spacing, they could not have all come from Oswald's rifle on the sixth floor.

- Only a **small minority of witnesses** claimed with certainty they heard *exactly* three shots (some heard only two, some heard four, some heard five or even more). An oft-overlooked point is that usually witnesses heard only the shots nearest them—thus undercounting. Noise from motorcycles, cars and crowd noise hindered an exact count. Many heard four or more. Young Amos Euins stated, "I believe there was four, to be exact."[36] Like many others, he said the last two came together. We could cite many other witnesses who heard four or more shots, but such an exercise is futile —skeptics just dismiss audible shots as echoes.

- **Over 50 witnesses** described a firing pattern to the shots that simply does not fit an evenly-spaced triad of shots, the latter being necessary to make the limited timing of the Zapruder film fit with the time it would take Oswald to fire and re-load. Several testified to a cluster of shots **so close together to almost**

sound as one. This is why it was hard for people to ascertain an exact number of shots, and why some people heard only three (out of the four or five). Take the 50 various witnesses who assert that the last two shots were clumped together, assemble them into a timeline, and it points to four to five shots, not three. A consensus of the typical testimony we read again and again (including several Secret Service agents whose car was a stone's throw from the Grassy Knoll at the time) goes something like this: *I heard one shot, then a pause... then two shots right together "in rapid succession." Bang. Pause. "Bang-bang."* Over a dozen described the final two shots as an "almost simultaneous" "flurry of shots," as if from an "automatic weapon." Agent Clint Hill described it as "almost a double sound."[37] Oswald, if he had a gun at all, certainly did not have an automatic.[38] In fact, no sniper would use an automatic weapon at the distances involved, so the obvious answer is that four or more shots were fired from two or more locations. But again, this does not depend on auditory evidence alone, as we now detail (also see Lie Number 17).

• Dallas policeman J.W. Foster testified that he **saw** a missed shot hit the grass near the underpass. The *WCR* dismissed the report from this credible witness simply because the bullet could not be found.[39]

• Eyewitness Virgie Rachley reported she **saw** sparks as a missed bullet struck the pavement behind the limousine, at about the same time as the first shot.

• The *WCR* was forced to admit that one shot missed, yet refused to state *which* shot missed, so that any objection raised about the number and timing of any particular shots could be addressed with a vague and variable answer. That's because every answer offered within the rubric of a single-shooter-**only-3-shots** raises problematical questions: **1.** It could not be the first shot that missed, because based on films and photos of the event, position and timing, Oswald would have been firing with horrible visibility through tree leaves. Why would he waste time on an obstructed shot and risk the motorcade speeding away from him? **2.** It could not be the middle shot, because that would crowd the 2.3 second timing limitations regarding the two shots that hit Kennedy. **3.** But it could not be the last shot that missed, because why would Oswald have continued to shoot after he had seen Kennedy's head explode as the car was moving out of range? So the WC concludes, "We don't know." The more logical answer is that this, among other facts—indicates at least four shots. There were two or more shooters firing more or less simultaneously, and *two* shots missed out of a total of five or six.

• We have "blood" evidence and "metal-to-concrete" evidence: the one missed shot that the WC reluctantly accepted, which grazed James Tague's face, presents two real problems for them: a *ballistic* problem (its metal trace did not match a Carcano full metal jacket spectroscopy), and a *timing* problem, as mentioned above. It also gives a glimpse of the "cover-up agenda" of the WC, as they answered the Tague bullet with a fuzzy ambiguation. Initially, the WC Report would not even call it a bullet, merely stating that "an object" hit his cheek.[40] Then, in desperation, they suggest that Tague was hit by a "fragment" from one of the same shots that hit Kennedy, bouncing off the limo's windshield. They make no effort to explain how a bullet coming from behind could ricochet off the limo, fly upward (over the windshield, because the Warren Commissioners claim the windshield was cracked, not pierced), travel another 250 feet, then curve downward, strike a concrete curb, and bounce up to draw blood on Tague's cheek. The WC imagined a lot of magic bullets that day.

• The *WCR* never entertained the possibility that additional shots might have come from a weapon equipped with a silencer, and thus not heard. If a third gunman had fired from a lower floor of

the Dal-Tex building, he would have had a straight shot at the back of the President's head, without the interference of the oak tree. From the curb where a bullet struck near James Tague, if we draw a line back to a point near the President's head, and then extend that line farther back, it points to the DalTex building, *not* to the sixth floor of the TSBD. See this website— www.jfkresearch.freehomepage.com/MissedShot.htm
—for a compelling argument that a gunman, using a silencer, may have been arrested (but released) as he emerged from the Dal-Tex elevator. All this evidence utterly destroys the one-gunman, three shot canard.

Lie Number 9: No Second Shooter: "There is no evidence of a second man... [or] of other guns."
~Congressman Gerald Ford (*Life* magazine, Oct. 2, 1964)

Mountains of evidence point to a second location source for some of the shots. This is related to the point above, which focused on the *number* of shots, but here we add another layer: multiple *sources* of shots. Because there was only time for Oswald to have fired three shots, and there were four or more, we've already proved the presence of a second gunman. Now we add a convincing dose of testimony (and later medical/ballistic forensics) indicating a second location for a shooter... proving Ford dissembled about "no evidence" of other gunmen.

But first, let's consider what sorts of evidence and testimonies are admissible. Conspiracy de-bunkers such as McAdams and Posner try to reject eyewitness testimony (especially when it refutes their version of events) as invalid. JFK researchers are not stupid; we know that eyewitness testimony and early media reports do not constitute, in isolation, ironclad proof. But as stated previously, careful eye-testimony is a useful and court-admissible form of evidence, and can even be a very *strong* form of evidence in two particular scenarios: when there are clear signs that the physical evidence has been tainted/altered (clearly the case here), and when the eyewitness testimony meets a **high standard of credibility**. That standard was met in Dealey Plaza: 1. It was **broad daylight** and every eye was **focused** on the crime victim (JFK); 2. Over a **hundred** witnesses were present and their collective eyes, ears and even noses, as a whole, point to shots coming from two locations. 3. Over **fifty** of the witnesses were **expert witnesses**. Law enforcement/police, Secret Service, military vets, and hunters (all experts in their knowledge of guns and gunshots); news reporters (experts at observation and recording detail); the staff at Parkland hospital, who closely observed the wounds (expert medical witnesses).

    The earliest press releases (via teletype), and the announcer on Dallas WFAA-TV, first stated that "assassins" had shot the President... plural. These reports came from a multitude of news reporters in and around the motorcade (most were riding further back in the motorcade). Five reporters on the ground in Dealey Plaza said shots came from the Knoll or Triple Overpass area. Mary Woodward, reporter for the *Dallas Morning News*, was standing on Elm, fifty feet from the Triple Underpass. She said she heard a "horrible, ear-shattering noise coming from behind us," referring to the Underpass area. Compare Mary's observations to that of the people near the sixth floor window, who were closer to the TSBD sniper than Mary was to the Underpass and Knoll. They were not even sure if the noise was a gunshot. But Mary Woodward obviously was not hearing a mere "echo."

    When the "amateur" witnesses are saying things consistent with the "expert" witnesses, we see how disingenuous it was for Ford or Posner or Bugliosi to make emphatic statements about their being "no evidence" for a second shooter. If Gerald Ford had said he believed Oswald fired the fatal shot, perhaps we could believe he was sincere but mistaken. However, for Ford to say there is "no evidence" at all is an outright lie. Even if someone stubbornly believes Oswald did it, it remains undeniable that *evidence* of a second shooter exists. Over fifty witnesses went on record saying at least one or more shots came from west of the Depository, in the vicinity of the Grassy Knoll. The proof does not rest on "ears," but we also cannot ignore such a large number. Add "eyes" to the count, as we've shown. And as this book documents, hard evidence abound... medical, ballistical, acoustical (police recording), all pointing to a second gunman. We will discuss the famous Magic Bullet, demonstrating how ballistic science proves an extra shooter; we will re-examine the autopsy records which prove a frontal shot; we will hear more eye-witness testimony about suspects behind the fence. Perhaps the strongest proof is photographic: several policemen, followed by an eager mob, are seen running up the Grassy Knoll to the fenced area in pursuit of a second shooter.

The testimony of Amos Euins is also damning to the WC claims (and thus they dismiss his credibility). Not only was Euins' description of the TSBD shooter incongruent with Oswald, but also we find in Euins' testimony an indication that the police initially looked elsewhere. The boy's words confirm what the photos demonstrate: more police were pursuing a sniper in the area of the Grassy Knoll, rail-yard and underpass than in Oswald's direction. Young Euins stated that when he first spoke to a police office, the officers had been headed to the Grassy Knoll area:

```
Amos Euins: "[I] told the policeman I had seen the
shot, because they were looking at the railroad
tracks.... then he called some more cars.... And then
the policemen came from the tracks...."
Arlen Specter inquired, "Did you see the policemen
come from the tracks to go around the building?"
Euins: "Yes, sir... about 14 or something like that.
```

They were coming from the tracks here."[41]

Here Euins pointed to the WC's map display, to the area atop the Grassy Knoll.

Later we'll return to the two gunmen issue. But let us digress a moment to a bigger concept about the very nature of this case.

Lie Number 10: We're Obeying Occam's Razor:
"Lee Harvey Oswald, a 24-year-old nuthatch, was lucky enough to have... things all align themselves into perfect harmony on November 22, 1963."
~David Von Pein
"The conspiracy theorists shun simple plots in favor of more convoluted and improbable ones."
~Robert Platt Bell

No, Mr. Bell, the opposite is true. Conspiracists favor the simplest explanation: **more** than one person fired at Kennedy. At first glance, it may sound "simpler" to say the bullets all came from a lone crazed gunman... but any explanation that doesn't account for a hundred inconsistencies is actually no explanation at all. Occam's Razor is a helpful scientific tool in many fields but especially in crime forensics. It asserts: "Simpler explanations are generally closer to the truth than more complex ones." But it assumes the researcher is picking the simplest from a list of several *possible* explanations. It is not possible for Oswald alone to have been responsible for all the particulars in this case. It takes a convoluted effort to squeeze the forensics of two shooting angles and four or five bullets into a one lone-nut scenario. In attempting to do the impossible, Warren Commission devotees have painted themselves into a corner. To get out of their quandary of one gun, three shots, they were forced to ***create complexity***. They create complicated ballistic explanations (a serpentine "Magic Bullet"...see below), they offer strained speculations about the motives of Oswald and Jack Ruby, they dig up trivial reasons to dismiss over fifty contrarian witnesses, *etcetera, etcetera*. Trying to wedge a square peg into a round hole, the WC version of events spawns a hundred complications filling up 26 volumes.

Again, if you are not familiar with the ancient principle of Occam's Razor, please re-read it, let it sink in: **"Simpler explanations are generally closer to the truth than more complex ones."** If a stage magician pulls a rabbit out of a hat, Occam would say it is far more likely that it was a simple trick of a hidden rabbit, not a supernatural creation of a furry animal out of thin air, violating the laws of physics and biology.

In the previous section, I admitted the JFK case is very complex, and I concede that Oswald was a "complicated" young man. But overall, the **original shooting** itself was *not* that complicated: an open-air car was driven slowly past tall buildings, open windows and a shaded fence, and two leaders received at least six wounds, so... you guessed it... all the evidence points to the fact that the shots came from an open window *and* a shaded fence. The ambush was pulled off flawlessly by professional assassins who blamed it on a "fall guy"—and then they silenced him. The case only becomes magically complicated *if* you try to reduce the evidence to one shooter, whereupon you must eliminate the shaded fence and the man behind it (whose head can be seen there in film and photographs), hide the difference in bullet behaviors, ignore the eyewitnesses, explain away conflicting medical reports, fit all the wounds to match just two bullets, explain why various parties (CIA, FBI, Dallas Police) lied, explain Ruby's role in silencing the patsy... and then do back-flips to cover-up, change, deny or explain *why you just did all those gymnastic twists in the first place.*

A surgeon uses a razor-sharp scalpel for a reason: the razor cuts so efficiently, cleanly, quickly and accurately because it is so sharp—the metal is "focused" to a critical, incisive point. An intelligently-wielded razor can save a patient; using a thousand dull butter knifes would kill the patient. More is not often better. The encyclopedic 26 volumes of the Warren Commission are not thorough, they are obfuscatory. The pages of the WC are not sharp or focused, they are a thousand dull butter knives designed to kill the patient—a patient named Truth.

After it occurred to me to apply *Occam's Razor* to this case, I discovered David Von Pein had beaten me to the idea—but he has applied Occam's logic in a blatantly- dishonest manner, pretending that conspiracy theorists claim Oswald was a completely-uninvolved, clueless patsy. What we claim is, ironically, much more complex—Oswald *was* entangled in the conspiracy but as **a double-agent who was double-crossed**. While this answer is complex, it still fits the rubric of an Occam-like solution because it is *less complex* than the labyrinth of lies otherwise required to answer all the enigmas. Like most debunkers and lone-gunman advocates, Von Pein points to the contradictions in Oswald's behavior, and to his ownership of the rifle found on the sixth floor, as proof LHO was the crazy assassin.[42] But these facts do not stand in isolation. Placed in the context of facts discovered by Mary La Fontaine and other researchers, we see that Oswald was very sane and deliberate in a long series of choices and actions leading up to D-Day in Dallas. Thus a "crazy assassin" looking for fame is not a satisfactory "razor-sharp" answer at all. (Also see Lie Number 23, regarding Oswald's motivations.) The conspirators had manipulated the young man and planted evidence to indict him. Of course, it was impossible for the plotters to fully control every detail and anticipate every problem, and so as they answered each new "problem," the convolutions surrounding

Lee Harvey Oswald grew more unbelievable.

Like Bell and Von Pein, Gerald Posner also had the audacity to claim that conspiracy "nuts" are the ones ignoring a simple explanation. In his Preface to *Case Closed*, he blames the "nuts" for "ever-expanding conspiracy theories." But the expansion on this topic would not be necessary if Posner and his ilk had not **continued to fight discomfiting facts with contrivances**. Explaining away all the inconsistencies swirling around the case is a full-time job. Two thousand books have been written on the subject, and here it is 50 years later and we are still pondering the complexity brought about by 26 volumes of the WC's labyrinthine work-arounds to a hundred different questions and problems. Posner added 600 pages of excuses, but that was still not enough. So author and prosecutor Vincent Bugliosi published his *1,600* page rant against conspiracy "nuts." With great irony, Bulgiosi makes the same inverted claim: "Conspiracy theorists have succeeded in transforming a case very simple and obvious at its core—Oswald killed Kennedy and acted alone—into its present form of the most complex murder case... in world history."[43] Bugliosi's assertion is self-evidently absurd: if the case was so simple, why does he need 1,600 pages? And don't tell me, Vincent, that it's because of a complexity created out of thin air by the conspiracy community. Before we ever said a word, the WC discovered that not a single piece of evidence was open and shut. To their chagrin, around every corner, more questions and discrepancies abound. **Name any *one* aspect of this case, and I'll show you *two* things problematical about it.**

The most troubling example of "creating complexity" regards the timing and number of shots. Film evidence showed that Oswald's old, manual bolt-action rifle could not have been fired quickly enough to get off more than three shots in his window of motorcade visibility (both his literal half-closed window and his limited *time* window). Add one extra shot, or one bullet whose ballistics don't match Oswald's rifle, and the entire WC house of cards falls. So how does Posner explain away all the evidence for extra shots that did not come from the Book Depository? He endorses the tall-tale of the Magic Bullet theory ((discussed at length in the next section), *and* he tries to explain why the "Tague bullet" has a different metal spectroscopy than the bullets from Oswald's gun. Here Posner's rationale again insults our intelligence: he suggests that Oswald's first shot travelled through the foliage of an oak tree, hit a tree limb that neatly peeled off the full metal jacket but left the lead core of the bullet unimpeded, which then ricocheted some 300 feet to hit the curb near Tague. (*National Geographic* tried to claim it was the traffic light, even though it was not within the trajectory.) Furthermore, Posner suggests that the stripped copper jacket was deflected downward and hit the pavement behind JFK's limo, where witness Virgie Rachley saw sparks. This overly-complex "logic" stretches the imagination. There is not a shred of physical evidence to support it: no mark in the oak tree, no copper jacket found in the street, no logical reason why Oswald would fire with an obstructed view, no real-life test that the particular oak limbs (or a traffic light) could possibly strip a copper jacket so cleanly. Posner, *Geographic* and the WC expect us to believe that *at the greatest distance*, Oswald hit a six-inch wide target dead-on, but on the much-closer shot, he had missed by ten feet.

Occam's Razor, however, can be satisfied with a simpler explanation: two or three professional assassins ambushed the President in a cross-fire. **A likely scenario:** An early shot, possibly from the Dal-Tex building with a silencer (silencers cause a less-accurate shot), missed and sailed over Kennedy's head. This bullet travelled a straight line from the Dal-Tex, free of oak tree interference, to Tague's location. A near-simultaneous first shot from the sixth floor also missed, causing sparks on the pavement in front of the building. Overcorrecting for too high of a shot, a second shot from the Dal-Tex building hit JFK in the back. A moment later, the sixth floor sniper's second shot hit Connally. Finally, a very short (just thirty yards from the Grassy Knoll fence —see HSCA Vol. 6, Figure II-27) and easy shot found its mark, entering Kennedy's head from the front and exploding out the rear. Thus two or three shooters are a simpler scenario than a lone gunman with a freakish ricochet off a tree limb. The presence of triangulated shooters best explains the extra shots and extra lead fragments (detailed in the next section), the multitude of wounds on Kennedy and Connally, and the bullet damage to the limo. A "multiple shooter scenario" perfectly matches the film, ballistics and eyewitness evidence, and explains why the Tague bullet was of a different metal. The conspirators' need to cover-up the additional shots explains other curiosities in the case as well.

To recap: IF the WC's scenario were true, it would be a very simple case. A psychologically-troubled young man buys a rifle, carries it to his work-site that happens to overlook the Presidential motorcade, and shoots the President, and two of his three shots hit the target. Ask yourself: "If this is so, then why did the Warren Commission need 26 VOLUMES to make their *simple case*?" President Clinton appointed the Assassinations Record Review Board (ARRB) to attempt to release more of the secret files. In 1998, the AARB published its final report along with over **500,000 pages** of previously classified documents. **A simple case does not produce a half-million pages!** A simple case is not one in which the assassin has no motive and is killed before he can testify, nor in which **every single aspect of the case raises additional suspicions**. Applying Occam's Razor to the mysterious profile of Oswald yields only one "simple" *correct* answer: he was the fall guy, a manipulated scapegoat. He does *not* fit the profile of a crazy-yet-effective assassin, nor of a left-wing communist willing to waste his life to kill the most left-leaning President of his time.

Lie Number 11: Obeying Occam's Razor, Part 2:
"Posner looks at all the evidence... and his logic is breathtaking." ~Fredric Dannen

Another lie. Throughout this tome we expose weaknesses in the "lone gunman" argument. This section focuses on Gerald Posner's failure of "logic" and his failure to look at the big picture. But first, we must say a few harsh words about the integrity of the "conspiracy-theory" critics and so-called debunkers. Posner, the man most famous for attacking the veracity and character of witnesses and conspiracy researchers, has had his own character and credibility seriously questioned in recent years, beginning with his being fired from a major online media company for plagiarism (see Lie Number 49). Worse, just as this book was in the final stage of editing, I learned that Gerald Posner was being sued for taking advantage of my friend, Harper Lee. (I was her pastor for six years and can assure you that the Pulitzer Prize-winning author of *To Kill a Mockingbird* has impeccable integrity.) Ms. Lee, at 87, is suing her literary agent, Samuel Pinkus, who was in partnership with Posner, for trying to steal the copyright (and royalties) for Lee's 30-million-copy bestseller. Her lawsuit asserts that Pinkus and Posner created a company in 2011 called Philologus Procurator Inc., headquartered at Posner's Florida home.[44] As proud as I am of my association with Nelle Harper Lee, and as incensed as it makes me to think anyone would try to swindle my aging friend, the reader must know that everything else I wrote herein challenging Posner's credibility was written well before he was named in Lee's lawsuit.

I do not need to attack Posner with insults. I challenge him with facts. Contrary to the Lie above about the "brilliant," thorough logic of Gerald Posner, he doesn't look at "all the evidence," as Dannen claims... by that, I mean he fails to look at the evidence as a whole, all at once, as a big picture. He fails to understand *gestalt*. Or, I suspect, **chooses** to hide his eyes from the full landscape.

Posner's trick is to take a hundred oddities and, one by one, point to a flaw (real or invented) in each. His work is the disassembly of a jigsaw puzzle... not a work of brilliance. As a child, I loved to see the image form as I painstakingly, over days, put a 1,000 piece puzzle together. Taking it apart to put the scrambled pieces back in the box took just a moment. Posner's work is not "brilliant," it is child's play deconstruction.

Solving the JFK case is a puzzle assembly, and each piece must be taken seriously before either discarding it as a misfit or finding its place in the bigger picture. Solving a puzzle begins with putting together pieces that form patterns, and then assembling the patterns to form a big picture.

When it comes to evaluating the truth of a scientific hypothesis, statisticians consider—and then dismiss as non-evidentiary—a *small* percentage of coincidences because there are not enough pieces to form a pattern. But a *high*-percentage of anomalies may begin to indicate a meaningful pattern, and further investigation may yield proof of a new theory, a new paradigm.

Thousands of pages have been written in an effort to explain away the strangeness of the JFK enigma. Certainly some of the freakish coincidences were just that: random coincidences, pieces that don't belong to the puzzle. However, because of the known lies and cover-ups on the record, and the sheer number of coincidences, the statistics point to *order*, not random happenstance. Too many synchronicities.

The JFK crime is not a pretty picture... it is a rotten mess. So let's change metaphors a moment. Lay people may not know the details of statistical science, but we have an innate "bullshit meter" based on the same premise: when we see two or three odd occurrences around an event, we dismiss it, but when we see a *dozen* or more synchronicities associated with the same mystery, we know something stinks! Here are more examples of the improbabilities that Posner and the WC ask us to hold our nose and ignore:

•**Left Equals Right:** Oswald coincidentally put the address of former FBI-agent and intelligence-operative Guy Bannister, a virulent *anti*-Communist, on his *pro*-Castro propaganda brochures. No debunker has ever given a satisfactory answer to this paradox. Several witnesses linked the ultra-conservative Bannister and the communist Oswald— unlikely bedfellows.

•**Right Place at Right Time:** We are asked to believe that a mere month before the shooting, a lone nut with a sniper's rifle just happened to gain employment at the Texas School Book Depository (TSBD) overlooking the only double turn on the Presidential motorcade route. Oswald got his job at the TSBD on October 15; the newspaper did not print the parade route until November 19. Had the route been publicized before Oswald took the job, we would not view this as a grand coincidence, but as evidence of pre-meditation by the "lone nut." But that was not the case, according to the *WCR*. Someone else arranged the job for him, and someone else planned the motorcade route. An unexplained coincidence that was essential to the claim that Oswald fired on the motorcade.

•**Specificity of Sound:** We are told to believe that despite widely-various locations, 50 eye-witnesses interpreted coincidental echoes in such a way as to think shots came from the Grassy Knoll—not from the concrete overpass.

•**7 Second Miracle:** We are asked to believe that Oswald, a fair marksman at best, with a 1938, $13 rifle and a mis-aligned $8 scope, hit a moving target with two out of three shots through tree leaves, using a cardboard box for a "tripod." This feat required a fast and flawless series of action: aiming, firing and missing; bolt loading a second bullet; aiming, firing, and hitting the moving target (JFK); bolt loading a third bullet; aiming, firing, and hitting the target again but at a distance of 90 yards. All within a time frame of about 7 seconds, looking down from six floors up. Re-creations of the feat were accomplished calmly, after rehearsals, on a shooting range with straight-moving targets and after the misaligned scope had been adjusted. Oswald's feat was fear-filled and unrehearsed, hitting a human target that was moving *within* the car, a car that was moving in three directions at once: forward, downward, and on a gently curving street that slopes down as it heads into the tunnel of the triple-overpass. Skilled marksmen have never re-created *every* aspect of this shooting feat (see Lie Number 46).

•**FBI Oops:** The FBI just coincidentally destroyed a note from Oswald and lied about Oswald's cellmate (more on that later). They failed to report a Russian defector... with the President coming.

•**Investigatory Oops:** all the many lost pieces of evidence, botched tests and destroyed documents happened to things that might have exonerated Oswald.

•**Investigatory Genius:** Thanks to an anonymous tip, they arrested the assassin within an hour of the shooting, without a name of a suspect, without a vague description, in a city the size of Dallas... even though he had escaped the scene of the crime.

•**Fifty+ Deaths:** Dismiss the odd deaths in the case, they say. It's an insignificant coincidence that over fifty people—key witnesses or persons significantly connected to the events of November 22nd—died mysteriously and/or violently. Some researchers count over a hundred total now. That's about the number of U.S. soldiers killed by enemy fire during all of the Persian Gulf *War*.[45]

- **Fast But Not in a Hurry:** Oswald supposedly sped down from the sixth to the second floor... but all indications are the sniper dawdled after the shots. According to witnesses, he paused to examine his "kill," paused to line up the three empty shells neatly on the floor, paused to wipe the rifle free of prints, paused to hide the rifle, and crept quietly down four flights of stairs. In less than 90 seconds. He took time to buy a Coca-Cola before leaving, and Mrs. Robert Reid saw him and informed him the President had been assassinated and he took time to speak to her before heading to the front door. Oswald, soda bottle in hand, still not out the door, next took time to assist two reporters who asked to use a phone, one of them being NBC newsman Robert MacNeil. The phone company billing registered the call from MacNeil at the TSBD (that call, by the way, included MacNeil reporting that "Police chased an unknown gunman up a grassy hill.") A few minutes later, the non-hurried Oswald took a city bus, then changed to a taxi when the bus was stalled in a traffic jam. Next he was in such a non-hurry, he offered to give up his taxi to an older woman. The slowest fast getaway in history.

- **Got 'Em But Reload Anyway:** If Oswald was a lone shooter, **why did he take time to eject his third shell to load a fourth bullet** if he had just seen that the President's head had exploded from his third shot? It makes zero sense. He was in a hurry to discard the rifle and run downstairs to pose calmly by the Coke machine. Why waste even a precious second to go through the multi-stage operation of ejecting a spent round and loading a live round? The WC itself admits that the rifle was found with a live round in it, and that three empty shells were found in the sniper's nest. And according to the WC's own words, Kennedy's head would have "filled his scope." So Oswald would have instantly seen the President's catastrophically-destructive head wound.

Why waste another moment fiddling with the rifle? Any answer you may offer is pure imagination. The only logical answer is that the third shot from the sniper on the sixth floor of the TSBD missed (or hit Connally), it did *not* explode Kennedy's head. The sixth-floor sniper ejected his third shell because **the President was *not* yet dead**... so he loaded his fourth... but then, through the scope, he saw that his accomplice on the Grassy Knoll had hit his target, thus rendering a fourth shot from the sixth-floor sniper unnecessary. **The re-loading of a fourth round—according to Occam's Razor—indicates the fatal shot came from elsewhere.**

Speaking of three shots vs. four, our next set of Lies constitute the most famous example of an "anti-Occam's Razor" claim: *The Magic Bullet Theory.*

Lie Number 12: The Magic Bullet—Intro:

"Try as the conspiracy kooks might, the Single-Bullet Theory has still not been proven to be an impossibility." ~David Von Pein

"All evidence indicated that the bullet found on the governor's stretcher could have caused all his wounds." ~*Warren Commission Report*, p. 95

Necessity is the mother of invention. Once it became known that one or two bullets had completely missed, WC Counsel Arlen Specter *had* to invent the "Single Bullet Theory" (SBT) in order to explain how, **supposedly, only two shots made three separate, major wounds in Kennedy, four more wounds in Connally, dented the limo windshield frame, put a hole/crack in the windshield at another spot, and caused sparks on the pavement** near the limo. So all that damage came from two bullets, one of which survived completely intact? (The "third" bullet that had completely missed hit a curb at the distant opposite end of the Plaza—on a completely different trajectory than the bullet that hit the pavement near the TSBD. That so-called "Tague bullet" went nowhere near the limo, so it cannot explain the multiple impacts on the limo.)

The first reports that leaked out from the autopsy reveal an that the Single Bullet Theory had not been deemed necessary by the conspirators at the outset. In mid-December 1963, less than a month after the shooting, the *New York Times* and *Washington Post* reported that the pathologists found the first bullet had hit the President in the back of the right shoulder, five inches below the collar-line and "the bullet had lodged in the body," where it caused a hematoma. Based on leaks from the initial autopsy, the newspapers reported that the second shot "hit the right rear of Mr. Kennedy's head" and a *fragment* of this bullet passed out the front of his throat, and another bullet hit higher on his skull, exploding it.

Hoover's initial report to LBJ also spoke of bullets coming from the front of Kennedy and of a bullet that had lodged in his back. Later, for reasons we shall see, **all of these early reports were ignored or changed**, and Specter would soon spin a completely different tale: he claimed the neck wound came not from a fragment from the head shot, but via a whole bullet from the *back* of JFK's lower neck. That "magic bullet" supposedly entered the President's back, passed through his muscles missing bone, exited at his necktie knot, and then entered Governor Connally's right back. This same bullet next passed through the Governor's chest, shattering bone, then came out and shattered his right wrist, and finally landed in his left thigh— wholly intact. Finally, it just fell out on a stretcher (despite a Parkland doctor stating to the press on November 22nd that the bullet would have to be surgically removed). This amazing bullet left behind a multitude of lead-particles but was magically undamaged on its nose-tip, and most of the lead missing from its base is what the FBI extracted for their ballistics tests.

So what unfolded was **not a consistent set of facts that merely needed to be connected** like dots as the investigation moved forward. No, what we hear instead is **a constantly-evolving serpentine story** that makes sense only after a hundred explanatory "ifs" and "maybes" were applied retroactively. In sum, the solution spun a new set of lies.

The conspirators were not initially worried, because they controlled most of the hard evidence. The investigatory files and material evidence came into the hands and control of agencies which LBJ, Hoover, Dulles and others could manipulate. But to the horror of the conspirators, there was a film made of the event by citizen Abe Zapruder. Texas newsman Dan Rather had already seen it and, unfortunately for the conspirators, said some things that made it clear the film would likely reveal timing issues and separate shots on JFK and Connally. If conspirators could get their hands on the film, they could alter some of this—even with 1964 manual technology. This is the point at which many people balk at accepting a conspiracy, because it requires admitting that multiple agencies within our own government collaborated to deceive the American people. I understand, it seems crazy. But it would only take a few agents in each agency to work out the subterfuge, not an entire department.

The expert technical examinations of the film, and the on-site witnesses, point to no other conclusion—**the Zapruder film was altered.** You must either believe the film was altered (to hide the gaping rear head wound), *or* you must ignore specific, clear, compelling testimony of Officer Hargis, the Secret Service agents, and a multitude of doctors who saw up-close the "massive" wounds on the "back of the head" (their words). There is no honest middle ground.

The conspirators did both: they *ignored* witnesses *and* they *altered* evidence. They doctored the film and altered the autopsy reports/photos/drawings, *and* they twisted eyewitness testimony, *and* they persuaded Arlen Specter to invent the Single Bullet Theory. This solved their problem of being self-limited to just three shots, but the SBT created a whole new set of problems for them.... like handling the proverbial Tar Baby of the *Uncle Remus'* fable, the more the conspirators juggled their far-fetched explanations, the dirtier they got. To make the just-two-bullets in JFK and Connally fairy-tale believable, they had to ignore or alter testimony from doctors and police, they had to change the autopsy report and hide the photos, bury 50 witnesses' testimony to the Grassy Knoll shooter, and create a score of other lies, as we shall see. (But they had no choice. Likely, the original plan had hoped that no frontal shots would have been necessary; the Grassy Knoll shooter was the "last resort" back-up plan.) So before we dig deep into the question of the film alteration (see Lie Number 21) and the fake autopsy report (see Lie Number 20), let's first look closer at the Magic Bullet problems, detailed in a set of Lies I call "the ABC's of the Magic Bullet." The WC flunked all of their ABC's! Here's an outline of this section:

THE ABC's OF THE MAGIC BULLET

The magic simultaneity of JFK and the Governor's wounds is disproved by:

Angles/Alignment (Lies 13, 14, & 15 Parts AI & AII)

Ballistics (Lies numbered 16 & 17, Parts BI & BII)

Chronology/Timing (Lie number 18, Part C)

Lie 13: Magic Bullet, Part AI: *Angles/Alignment:* "[The alignments of] the bullet wounds... were consistent with the Single-Bullet Conclusion."
~Arlen Specter

Indulge me in some introductory ramblings for this complex *Magic Bullet Angles* topic: **We have two means to assess bullet angles:** the first is the **medical evidence** (that is, the actual wounds on JFK and Connally... and there is a separate debate about how trustworthy the written reports are). The second is the **photographic evidence.**

The first: Parkland doctors, a Parkland nurse, and at least two Secret Service agents, who viewed the shooting firsthand and/or saw Kennedy's head-wound close-up **within the hour**, all gave testimony that directly contradicts the official story. They stated that one bullet entered JFK's neck at the Adam's apple and likely did not exit, another bullet entered his temple and blew out the back of his head, and another bullet entered at least four to five inches down JFK's back... **not** in the back of his *neck*, as some claimed. In helping draft the *WC Report*, Gerald Ford falsely wrote that the back shot was near JFK's neckline, a lie repeated in 2012 by *Fox News* commentator Bill O'Reilly. The true location of the back shot is confirmed by an autopsy photo released in the nineties, and is consistent with autopsist Humes' drawing, and with the holes in JFK's shirt and coat that are closer to the shoulder blade than to his "neck." Yet another confirmation comes from FBI agent James Sibert, a witness to the autopsy. He went on record saying:

"I'm not an advocate of the single-bullet theory... I don't believe it because I stood there two foot from where that bullet wound was in [JFK's] back, the one that they [Gerald Ford and the WC] eventually moved up to the base of the neck. I was there when Boswell made his face sheet and located that wound exactly as we described it.... Furthermore, when they examined the clothing after it got into the Bureau, those bullet holes in the shirt and the coat were down 5 inches there. So there is no way that bullet could have [entered] that low then rise up and come out the front of the neck, zigzag and hit Connally and then end up pristine on a stretcher over there in Dallas.... There is no way I will swallow that. They can't put enough sugar on it for me to bite it. That bullet was too low in the back."[46]

Agent Sibert is dead right: the Magic Bullet theory is disproved by this clear evidence: the hole in the back of JFK's shirt is lower than his neck wound, thus showing that one bullet angling downward from six floors up could **not** have caused both wounds. We find in most online and media "debates" about the Magic Bullet, the critics point to the fact that JFK's car seat was higher than Connally's removable "jump seat," a truth that has nothing to do with the impossible angle between JFK's two body wounds.

The key to understanding the problem with angles is found in the Dealey Plaza photos. Ignore worthless computer "re-creations" and drawings that claim to be based on photos of the limo, but are not. Let's take a moment to consider the real photographic evidence relative to JFK's posture *at the time of* the shots (not in the moments *after* the fatal one, as some documentaries have done). Several experts see signs the Zapruder film has been altered: the timing was shifted (via skipped frames), a road sign enlarged, and the back of JFK's head blacked out to hide the gaping occipital wound. Even without alteration, the Zapruder film would have been imprecise. Mr. Zapruder's camera had no electronics, no digital precision—it did not even have an electric motor to steadily drive the film, relying instead on a mechanical spring. A shaky handheld camera with a distorted lens that used a wind-up mechanism, it produced an imperfect and fuzzy piece of chemical-film. It has no sound-track. The original was "enhanced" by the government labs, and the copies differ. Therefore, no one (on either side of this debate) should make a case based solely on the Z film. Use the film for approximations, but not for exact measurements of angles and distances, or for establishing timing of shots with any precision beyond half a second.

Other still camera photos in Dealey Plaza are somewhat better, but still surprisingly blurred. Conspiracy theorists have reason to suspect that any *clear* films or photos were confiscated and destroyed. It is hard to pin-point the exact spot where each photographer was standing, thus hard to ascertain exact angles, distances and proportions. But there are objects in the background that provide definitive basis for angles, and I certainly trust film evidence more than computer animations and artist's sketches. Duh.

Some of the helpful photos include ones taken by Robert Croft (see below), and slides taken by Phil Willis as he stood just west of the corner of Elm and Houston, across the street from the Depository, facing the Grassy Knoll. Willis' 35mm color slide taken of Kennedy (commonly known as "Willis 5" and also called "Slide #7) corresponds to frame Z202, a moment before the third shot (out of four shots... the first shot missed, the second hit JFK, the third hit Connally, and the fourth killed Kennedy... and that's ignoring the frontal neck wound). Willis 5 shows the immediate reaction of JFK from the second shot and his upright posture just before the fatal shot. [view Willis 5 here: www.jfk.org/go/collections/item-detail?fedoraid=sfm:2002.040.0007]

The President's nearly-upright posture is confirmed with the Moorman photo, taken at the exact instant of the fatal bullet. (Read more in the next section.) View the Moorman shot here: www.geocities.ws/jfktruth/MOORMANPIX.jpg

The best reference point for angles is the Croft photo, which has a concrete structure in the background that will be essential for establishing an inarguable plumb line for angle measurements (see AII).

So what we have is **medical testimony** from Parkland, plus testimony and drawings from the Bethesda autopsy, all indicating wounds on JFK that don't line up with the sixth floor (i.e. with the "lone sniper"), AND photo evidence that will show the same problem (that JFK's posture in the photos, the holes in his shirt, etc. don't align).

How does the WC answer this dual problem? In desperation, they ignored Sibert's testimony and claimed JFK's jacket and shirt were "bunched up" and/or that he was "hunched over." These are two more lies (we examine next) that I call the "bunched and hunched" nonsense.

Lies 14 & 15: Magic Bullet, Part AII—*Angles,* cont.: Lie Number 14 (Hunched) & Number 15 (Bunched):
•JFK was hunched over when first struck.
~Warren Commission claim
•His Jacket was "severely bunched up" so the bullet hole in it does not indicate a lower back wound.
~John Hunt, Jr., at McAdams' "debunking" website.

Bunched and hunched is how the Warren Commission—and even the Failure Analysis computer animation—tried to make the angles work. When the first bullet struck, the photographic evidence (see photos by Croft and Willis, as mentioned above) and all eyewitness testimonies indicate that Kennedy had lowered his hand from a wave or a brush of his hair, and his coat is a bit bunched at the center near the collar, but elsewhere sits smooth and flat on his shoulders. More importantly, the President was clearly seated upright, not the least bit bent over, and his shirt was tucked in and clinging to his perspiring body, unlikely to have moved upward more than an inch. Indeed, the hole in the shirt matches perfectly with the best eye-witness testimony about this wound. Admiral George Burkley, present at the autopsy, stated on the death certificate that the back wound was "about the level of the third thoracic vertebra," which matches the testimony of Agent Clint Hill, who described the back wound as "about 6 inches below the neckline..." and the reports from FBI Agent James Sibert (see above). Their reports are consistent with other medical personnel at Parkland and Bethesda Naval hospitals (though most at Parkland never saw the small back wound). Dr. J. Thornton Boswell's diagram on the autopsy cover sheet also places the back wound nearly six inches down from where the neck joins the shoulder... and all of this is confirmed by the hole in the President's shirt.

Two months after the shooting, the Commission had no idea of the complications that would arise by having to turn two bullets into one, and how critical the angles would thus become. Unguarded, they had already allowed word to get out about the rear-entry bullet. On January 27, 1964, General Counsel Lee Rankin in a WC Executive Session said: "[T]he bullet entered below the shoulder blade to the right of the backbone." *Below* the shoulder blade. Soon they realized that such a wound placement was too low for their magical theory to work—so they had to begin changing the wound descriptions. Despite all the proof of a lower back wound, the faked WC drawings and Gerald Ford's re-write (mentioned previously) changed the location from the "back" to the "neck." The obvious falsification of the record—by Dr. Humes, Gerald Ford, Arlen Specter and others—is yet more proof of a cover-up. (It would take another book to ponder the fact that the two men most responsible for fabricating the Single Bullet Theory, Ford and Specter, became President and Senator.)

When we place the wound where ALL the trustworthy evidence places it, it destroys the Single Bullet Theory—including the so-called "scientific" computer re-enactments aired by *Discovery Channel* television (which reported graphics from the *Failure Analysis* group). A bullet that angled downward from the sixth floor would have hit JFK at an angle of at least 18 degrees. Entering five or six inches down JFK's back, this Magic Bullet would then have to ricochet (even though it did not hit bone) and reverse its trajectory-angle, turning upward in order to exit out at the top of his necktie knot. Then after exiting Kennedy, now headed in an *upward* direction, it would need to turn downward again in midair, turn slightly right, and hit Connally in the right side of his back, then head downward, exit out near his right nipple, turn right again *and* angle upward to hit his wrist that rested on the car door, ricochet out, down and to the left, to land in his lower leg. (Posner's drawing portrays Connally's wrist lower than it is seen in the Zapruder film.) I believe in God, but I don't believe in magic. Which shows more acrobatic contortion: the twists and turns of the Magic Bullet, or the convoluted logic of Specter, Posner, and the *Failure Analysis* group, as they try to align trajectories that do not align? And they had an advantage because of alterations to the Zapruder film and to the autopsy photos.[47] Examine the close-up, digitally-enhanced, slowed version of the film here: www.youtube.com/watch?v=iU83R7rpXQYk

For a better look at the position of Kennedy and Connally just before impact, examine Phil Willis' slide, which shows the President sitting up straight in the seat—not head down or hunched over, as the WC, and later the computer graphics analysis, had to falsely position him. Look at the photograph by Robert Croft (with Jackie looking straight at his lens), which correlates to Zapruder Frame 161, less than 2 seconds before the "Magic" back-to-throat shot. On the far side of the President, we see a concrete structure with a straight, plumb line that matches the plumb line of the Texas School Book Depository building. Forget shaky Zapruder frames... this is *the* best picture of the geometric angle of the limo and of JFK's head/body. We find that his head is erect, his ear lined up with his shoulder, his head and body only slightly curved forward (nothing like the cartoon sketch shown in the *WCR*). If you line up the wound in his back (*at least* four inches down) with his "necktie" wound, using a protractor (not based on the sloping street, but using the plumb line established by the pergola and the TSBD building's walls, thus comparing "apples to apples"), it would have required a shot angled at about **2 or 3 degrees**. But everyone agrees this shot, if it came from the sixth floor, had to be at an angle of about **18 degrees** (after factoring in the street slope). In order to make the "Magic Bullet" line up, Gerald Ford and others had to misrepresent JFK's body position and drastically "move" the back wound in the final report.

Let's look more closely at the evidence. Other than medical personnel, Agent Clint Hill had the closest view of the back wound, and placed it, quote, "about six inches below the neckline." In the Seventies, the House Committee carefully examined the evidence (photos, shirt, etc.) and ascertained that the back wound was over 14 centimeters down from the shoulder-line (4.5+ inches). The hole in the shirt places the wound 5.75 inches below the top of the collar, or about 4.5 inches below the bottom of the collar. Comparing this to the so-called "exit wound" at the necktie knot, and using the posture shown clearly in the Croft photo, we find the angle of the shot through JFK's body is 4 degrees or less—nowhere near the 18 degrees required for alignment with "Oswald's" rifle. Ask yourself: *Why do CBS, NBC, ABC and Fox (Bill O'Reilly) not report this fact to the American people?*

JFK's jacket was a bit bunched, but not "severely" and not enough to change the location of the entry wound by more than two inches... still not enough to allow an 18 degree angle. The photograph by Robert Croft (correlating to Z161, as mentioned) does indeed show a bunched jacket. But look closely: most of the bunching is headed backwards (parallel to the street), more than upwards. Upwards would change the wound location;

backwards would not. The bunching is in the center at the collar, but the coat looks fairly-snug and level on his shoulders. Nevertheless, naysayers Hunt and McAdams say otherwise and use very blurry photos of the President's coat. The coat bunching they claim is subjective and mostly irrelevant. Therefore, we should forget the jacket and instead **look to JFK's shirt** to get a more accurate location for the back wound. JFK's shirt was: a) closer to the wound b) tucked in and stuck to his body by sweat and thus unlikely to have slid upward, and c) the shirt collar does not look abnormally high. A quality, well-fitted dress shirt has a collar that sits somewhat high, touching the back hairline... that's the way they are designed. The shirt collar changes little whether sitting or standing. Wearing a men's dress shirt, do this experiment: reach your left around your back and stretch to point your index finger to the approximate location of where the best evidence shows the back wound (just to the right of the spinal column, as far down as you can reach). Now lift your collar an inch higher than it normally sits: you will feel that the shirt does not even move where your index finger rests. Now lift your right arm to brush your hair, as Kennedy did before the shot. This time you will feel the shirt rise at the wound point—by less than an inch! The *most* that we can see, based on the photos and on the behavior of a dress shirt on a sweaty body, is a one inch rise. So let's concede that and place the shot only 3.5 inches down JFK's back. This would shift the angle to approximately 9 degrees. But again, we *know* the angle of the final shot—if it came from the sixth floor—had to be 18 to 19 degrees (again: this is an angle based on the building plumb line, just as I used the concrete "plumb line" measure on JFK, thus eliminating the need to factor in the street angle). We derived the 9 degree angle by utilizing a plumb line in the Croft photo and the actual bullet holes in JFK's shirt and tie—and the descriptions provided by Parkland doctors and

Agent Clint Hill, the testimony by the autopsist, Dr. Humes—all which are consistent in placing the back wound much lower than later autopsy drawings—and Gerald Ford—would place it. The publicly-released drawings were not made by direct observation. The sketch artist was instructed *verbally* where and how to place/draw the wound —the equivalent of hearsay evidence! Anytime you see the WC, Posner or a TV documentary using drawings instead of photos, you should smell a rat.

As mentioned, debunkers add in a red herring here, an irrelevant distraction: they point out that Governor Connally (a tall man) was seated in the limo's "jump seat," which put him lower in the car than the President. They then draw a line back from Connally at an angle through JFK and then back to the sixth floor. Connally's position to Kennedy is irrelevant: the angles fail on the basis of Kennedy's wounds and position, not Connally's. Failing at that distraction, they also claim that any skewed angles are the result of the bullet hitting bone and ricocheting. But if the bullet hit bone in Kennedy at high speed, it would surely have been deformed on its tip; it was not. And in Lie Number 21, we see that Governor Connally was absolutely certain he was hit by a separate bullet (see Lie Number 18).

To recap and seal my argument: A back wound even 3.5 inches down JFK's back rules out the angle of sixth floor shot. The autopsy cover sheet placed the back wound even lower, at six inches down. JFK's death certificate located the bullet at the third thoracic vertebra, also lower than my calculations here. I'm using the most conservative (highest) placement of the wound at 3.5 inches (after allowing a very generous one-inch "bunching up" rise in the shirt). This places the body-wound transit angle at less than 10 degrees; and we are being equally generous to the opponent's claims by calling the sixth-floor gun angle just 18% (most say it was 19%). So anyway one measures it, based on the clearest photo (Croft's), **nothing lines up**. Moreover, Dr. Humes briefly explored the back wound with his finger, said he could feel no exit route, and described the trajectory of the missile "at a downward position of 45 to 60 degrees."[48] The initial FBI report also stated the back wound angled at "45 to 60 degrees downward." So 9 degrees on the body does not match 18 degrees of the building-to-limo angle and *neither* is compatible with the "45 to 60 degree" angle described by the autopsist.

This proves two things: one, if it was a single bullet transiting from JFK's back out his throat, the angles rule out a shot from Oswald in the TSBD; two, the autopsy photos of the back-wound are bogus (as are the crude, inaccurate drawings the WC used). This leaves only the possibility of a major bullet turn, a ricochet off of bone inside JFK's body… but everyone agrees that the bullet entered JFK's back to the right of the spinal column. Ballistics experts agree: if the bullet, traveling at high speed, had immediately hit bone, it would have been grossly deformed. *If* it had exited the throat, as claimed, it may have struck bone there, but if anything, this would have deflected the bullet sideways, not upward. The pro-Single Bullet folks are *damned if they do, damned if they don't*: they claim the near-pristine bullet is undamaged because it initially went through soft-flesh in JFK and slowed… but if it didn't hit bone, it couldn't have been deflected enough to explain the odd upward turn.

Initially, Humes did not believe the bullet even exited (until someone persuaded him differently), and he proposed that the bullet had fallen out on the stretcher at Parkland. The FBI report states "Medical examination of the President's body had revealed the bullet which entered his back had penetrated to a distance of less than a finger length," and "there was no point of exit."[49] But of course, if that were true, we would need another bullet to explain the wounds in Connally… something the WC's scenario cannot allow.

Whether this bullet came from the second story of the Dal-Tex building, or from the sixth floor of the TSBD, it most certainly did not exit the throat in a wound the Parkland doctors described as a separate "wound of entrance" (a frontal wound). Therefore, we have one or two extra bullets to contend with—and a conspiracy.

Lie No. 16: The Magic Bullet, Part BI: *Ballistics*: "Neutron activation... determine[d] ...that different fragments were part of one bullet."
~Gerald Posner, in *Case Closed*

This magic bullet is the same one they claim to be so powerful it went through JFK's suitcoat, shirt, and back-strap muscles, out JFK's neck, through his shirt and tie, through Connally's suit, shirt, and back muscles, then penetrated and shattered his rib bone, tore through the front of his shirt, then into his wrist bone, shattering it and leaving behind lead fragments... *wait, there's more*... it then came back out through his wrist flesh, next through his pants, and finally into his leg—where it also left behind yet more lead fragments (seen in X-rays). Then it fell out, essentially whole, onto a hospital stretcher where it was discovered hours later. Quite impressive for a 19-year-old bullet from a rusty war surplus rifle, considering the bullet remained completely intact and only slightly flattened (longitudinally... **the nose was not damaged at all**). And most of the slight visible damage to CE399 is a divot of missing lead from its base, a *divot caused by the FBI as it removed a lead sample for its tests*.

Those who try to explain the near-pristine condition of the Magic Bullet CE399 claim that after penetrating Kennedy, the bullet was *slowed* enough that striking Connally's wrist bone did not cause much bullet deformation (the "diminishing velocity" theory). But to thoroughly demolish a rib bone and still have enough velocity to splinter a dense wrist bone, as CE399 did, the bullet would have been deformed more than it is. **No real-life dual-human cadaver test has shown otherwise.** Arlen Specter and the WC were told in 1964 by government ballistics experts Joseph Dolce, M.D. and Dr. F. L. Light of the Wound Assessment Branch at Edgewood Arsenal that CE399 could not have caused the injuries it did and remained undamaged: "This is impossible. It doesn't work that way." Specter's response? He ignored them and hired a veterinarian to fire bullets into a goat! Seriously, **a veterinarian and a goat.**

Beyond the silliness of a goat, there are major problems with the ballistics tests used to assert that all the bullets came from Oswald's gun. The scientific test of trace metals, called the nuclear or Neutron Activation Test (NAA), only gives probabilities, and is only relevant if all the real bullet fragments had been submitted for testing (they were not) and if the fragments/bullets had proper handling and secure provenance (they did not). Even if we accept the shaky proposition that the FBI testing was never fudged or altered, nor the bullets swapped or contaminated, a variety of problems prevent us from accepting the NAA or CBLA (Comparative Bullet Lead Analysis) ballistics tests as having any probative value in this case:

•Even if the bullets could be absolutely tied to the Mannlicher-Carcano (as Posner and Dr. Guinn claim), that does not prove that Oswald *fired* the Carcano. We have already established that the only eyewitness who thinks he may have seen Oswald fire the rifle is unreliable. Considering the strong evidence that Oswald was hired by the FBI to investigate illegal gun sales, even if he owned the Carcano, it means nothing. He likely had been instructed to order the gun for a gunrunning investigation, for the higher purpose of framing him. Both firms he ordered guns from were being investigated by a Senate sub-committee on mail-order guns.

• Even *if* Oswald was the one firing the Carcano rifle and even *if* the ballistics had matched, that does not preclude a fourth shot (coming from the Grassy Knoll). That fourth fatal shot exploded JFK's head and apparently exited the back of his skull, and if it was found, its existence was suppressed. That bullet seems to have fragmented. Initially, there was no NAA testing of lead fragments actually found *in* JFK's brain/body—and later testing is predicated on the false belief that the correct fragments (from the head shot) were presented for testing.

• We know someone tinkered with autopsy evidence, so the provenance of that lead is uncertain. The NAA tests depend upon one's faith in the provenance of evidence, which in turn requires we trust fully every single FBI agent, autopsy official, and Secret Service agent who ever touched the bullet fragments. So for Rahn and others to claim ballistic science proves the bullets were fired by Oswald is a blatant disregard of the full package of evidence.

• Dr. James Beyer was a pathologist at an Arlington hospital, previously with the Army Surgeon General's office, who had written the section on wound ballistics in the Army's official medical history of World War II. Soon after hearing the report of JFK's attending physicians, he said: "I'm still surprised at the reported size of the head wound if a normal, completely jacketed, military type bullet was used—and if it did not strike some object, such as a portion of the President's limousine, before hitting the President's head." Ordinarily, Beyer said, a military-type bullet, if fired from a range of nearly 100 yards, would cause only a relatively small wound at the point of entry, and would not necessarily cause extensive damage inside the skull. In contrast, he said, a soft-nosed hunting-type bullet tends to "mushroom out" after striking a target, causing a devastating head wound—as we saw with JFK. Since we know the fatal bullet did not first hit the limo, and since the Carcano's fully-jacketed bullet would not have mushroomed, Dr. Beyer was highly skeptical that this shot came from Oswald's rifle.

•Scrapings of lead from the curbstone hit by the bullet that caused James Tague's wound were not initially linked to Oswald's rifle at all. FBI Agent Shaneyfelt testified to the Warren Commission that he couldn't even state conclusively that it came from *any* Manlicher-Carcano rifle or even from a 6.5 mm bullet.[50]

•In the July 2006 issue of the *Journal of Forensic Science* by Dr. Erik Randich and Dr. Patrick M. Grant, the authors challenged the original NAA data and the metallurgical profile of the Mannlicher-Carcano ammunition.[51] Dr. Randich is a metallurgist with the Lawrence Livermore National Laboratory. Dr. Grant, a chemist, is the director of the Lawrence Livermore Forensic Science Center and is a former colleague of Dr. Vincent Guinn's at the University of California. The authors concluded that **the material composition of the lead specimens from the assassination could be consistent with *any* number of bullet-types** —not just the type used by Oswald's Carcano. The antimony concentrations measured by Guinn show that the bullet fragments in evidence are not unique. Their methodology is consistent with work by Dr. Arthur Snyder of the Stanford Linear Accelerator Laboratory. No peer-reviewed scientific journal has challenged it. So s science/forensics does NOT rule out a conspiracy; in other aspects of the case, forensic science is only as good as the evidence in hand—and planted, faked or altered evidence obviously results in skewed conclusions.

•A 2002 paper entitled, "A Metallurgical Review of the Interpretation of Compositional Bullet Lead Analysis" co-authored by Randich and former FBI Chief Metallurgist William

Tobin analyzed several years of records kept by two ammunition lead suppliers (smelters). They measured the levels of 15 trace metals from samples taken from various batches of poured lead poured by smelters in Alabama and Minnesota, and found it was impossible, using the FBI's chemical profile standards, to distinguish between batches poured months apart.[52] This finding recently (2005) **prompted the FBI to cease using bullet lead analysis** (CBLA) for forensic purposes.[53] And in 2013, the Justice Department found FBI crime lab results unreliable in scores of cases.[54]

Lie 17: The Magic Bullet, Part BII: *Ballistics* cont.:
"Not one speck of any bullets/fragments other than those coming from Oswald's... rifle were discovered...." ~David Von Pein
The bullet fragments add up to just three bullets.
~Gerald Posner

The truth: there is too much lead floating around to have come from only three bullets, and the Tague bullet (the lead and antimony "smeared" on the curb) does not ballistically (metallurgically) match the other bullets.
• A stray/missed bullet or fragment drew blood on a third bystander, James Tague, some distance away from the limo. The stray shot left a significant lead mark on a curb near Tague, but the bullet never showed up in evidence. But spectroscopic/metallurgical analysis on this remnant did not match "Oswald's" bullet. As stated above, another witness, Virgie Rachley, had reported a stray shot hitting the pavement, causing sparks, near the Book Depository... not the same shot that hit Tague's curb, on different trajectories. Yet another witness, standing on the Triple Overpass, saw a bullet hit the turf (substantiated by a newspaper reporter who said that a whole

bullet had been found in the grass, and by photos showing an officer examining the ground, picking something up and putting it in his pocket). This unaccounted-for bullet never showed up in evidence.

To believe the official story, all the lead listed below must be explained by only the TWO bullets that hit JFK and Connally:

•As mentioned above, an entire, almost-whole bullet was found on a hospital stretcher. Bullet CE399 and was missing only 2 grains out of 160—at least one grain had been removed by the FBI for ballistic tests. The Commission claims that "all these fragments [found in Connally] were sufficiently small and light so that the nearly whole bullet found on the stretcher could have deposited those pieces of metal...." (p. 95). Another lie.

•Dr. Robert R. Shaw, Governor Connally's attending physician at Parkland, first said to the press: "He seems to have been struck by just one bullet, which entered the back of his chest and moved outward, taking out and fragmenting a portion of a rib. The bullet emerged from his chest and struck his wrist and thigh… The bullet is still in the leg. It hasn't been removed." Yet that is the bullet (the Magic Bullet) supposedly found on Connally's stretcher *before* Shaw made this statement Perhaps Dr. Shaw meant to say a "bullet fragment," as later two fragments were reported associated with Connally's leg, and smaller fragments of lead remained in his wrist and leg for years... but he said "*the* bullet," not *a* bullet fragment, and either way, it doesn't compute.[55]

•In 1988, Dr. Shaw was interviewed in the documentary, *Reasonable Doubt*, and said, "I am sure that the bullet that inflicted these wounds on Governor Connally was fragmented much more than this bullet [CE399] shows." Years before, he had told Arlen Specter something similar, that his study "of the wrist both by X-ray and at the time of surgery showed some fragments of metal that make it difficult to believe that [CE399] could have caused these two wounds."

- Contrary to how Gerald Posner describes fragments as "flakes" of near microscopic size, Nurse Audrey Bell, the Parkland Hospital operating-room nurse who handled the fragments removed from Governor Connally's wrist, insists they were not merely flakes but were identifiable pieces of metal *at least* 3 millimeters in length by 2 millimeters wide. While some fragments were removed from Connally, some lead was left in his body (and remains there to this day), so Posner has no factual basis to speak of near-weightless "tiny flakes of lead" when he cannot know their weight based on blurry 2-D X-rays.
- The FBI report stated that the Magic Bullet came from Kennedy's stretcher; to preserve the Single Bullet Theory, the WC changed this FBI-reported *fact* to a "rumor," and concluded that the bullet came from Connally's stretcher. Tape recordings released in 1996 from the Lyndon Johnson library indicate that FBI Director Hoover told LBJ that this bullet was found on President *Kennedy's* stretcher, not Connally's, probably "dislodged from his back during emergency procedures." This would be consistent with autopsist Humes' notes that reported the back bullet only went in an inch or so. A separate bullet which caused the frontal neck wound may still be lodged in the cadaver or may have "disappeared" in the autopsy room.
- Of the limo fragments, the Commission reported that the Secret Service found "one fragment...that weighed 44.6 grains and consisted of the nose portion of a bullet.[56] The other fragment...weighed 21 grains and consisted of the base portion of a bullet." These were large enough that on both, according to the FBI, markings could be seen that matched them to Oswald's rifle. And the FBI found "three small lead particles, weighing between seven-tenths and nine-tenths of a grain each, on the rug..." and "a small residue of lead on the inside surface of the

laminated windshield." Together, at least 68 grains of lead were reported in the back of the limo, which makes up nearly half of the weight of a bullet!

•Before the limo left Dallas, Special Agent Paul Landis picked up a relatively-large "bullet fragment" from the back of the limo and placed it on the rear seat—but some believe this was lost in the confusion, and the fragments in the limo listed in the WC Report were not from the rear seat, but from the floorboards.

•The amount still in the President's corpse is unknown, but significant—the FBI report states that 40 small fragments were left in Kennedy.[57] Fragments are seen in JFK's autopsy X-rays, including (and this is the WC's own wording) "a sizable metal fragment lying just above the right eye." The autopsy surgeons observed in X-rays "30 or 40 tiny dust-like fragments of metal running in a line from the wound in the rear of the President's head toward the front part of the skull, with a sizable metal fragment lying just above the right eye."[58] The X-ray also shows a 6.5 mm circle—indicating a large fragment toward the *back* of his skull.

•Other larger fragments were *removed* from his body and kept as evidence. "Two small irregularly shaped fragments of metal were recovered and turned over to the FBI."[59]

•A nurse at Parkland picked up several fragments and turned them into the authorities (they disappeared).

•Another large fragment (possibly part of the bullet that caused the front neck wound) found at the autopsy was lost.

Here's a list of the larger fragments that were removed, retained and catalogued in the WC Report (remember, this does not include all the many fragments listed above, some still remaining in the flesh of JFK and Connally, nor does it include the whole bullet lost after striking Tague):

•CE 567 (found on driver's side front seat of limo)

- CE 569 (found beside front seat of limo)
- CE 840 (3 fragments found on floorboard underneath the left jump seat... one of these is now missing from National Archives.)
- CE 842 (Connally's wrist fragments removed at Parkland)
- CE 843 (two fragments removed from President Kennedy's brain at Bethesda)

All total, that's a bucket-load of lead and copper! Nevertheless, the WC somehow convinced the American people that Oswald fired just three bullets. The two recovered bullets "magically" carried the lead equivalent, and wounding impact, of five bullets. In an age of skepticism toward the supernatural, they convinced the media of the reality of magic. Wizardry trumps wisdom.

Lie No. 18: The Magic Bullet, Part C: *Chronology*
"It is possible to pinpoint the precise time of the second shot." ~Gerald Posner, in *Case Closed*, p. 328.

The magic simultaneity of JFK and the Governor's wounds—supposedly caused by one magic bullet—is disproved by **angles**, **ballistics**, and **chronology (timing)**. Timing issues are harder to pinpoint than angle issues, in part because of problems in the Zapruder film: a shaky hand holding the camera, a shift Mr. Zapruder made to try to keep Kennedy in focus despite obstructions, the distance and blurriness, missing frames, and the fact that it is a mechanical camera which ran from a hand-wound spring and its speed changes as the reel sizes change. So it is absurd for Posner to claim he knows precisely when JFK was first struck, especially when the President was hidden behind the large freeway sign!

But the film does enable us to discover *enough* about the

timing to know the sequence of events, and to raise serious doubts about the magic bullet.

The first shot probably came before Z180... immediately after the limo made the turn onto Elm. But the timing of it is not so crucial, especially considering there were likely *two* shots fired before the President was struck, one coming from the Dal-Tex building. During a first (missed) shot, the oak tree at Elm, between the sixth floor sniper and the limo, blocked visibility from frames Z166 until Z206—except for one small opening in the foliage that provides a split-second opportunity at Z183. Thus it is more likely that the first missed shot came earlier, at around Z160. The shot that first *struck* JFK had to be between Z206 to Z220. The FBI, CBS News, and the WC all place that shot at around Z220-Z222, in order to make it closer in timing to Connally's "hit." Based on JFK's reaction time, the first hit on JFK happened slightly *before* Z220, and changes in JFK's (blurry but still definite) facial expression at 206 indicate a possible strike even then. **So Z206-Z217 is a very solid estimate of the first bullet *strike*.**[60]

Next as the film rolls, it is obvious that Governor Connally is not yet hit when he emerges from behind the road sign at Z222—and at Z224, JFK has clearly gone into a full arm-movement reaction to his first hit. By contrast, Connally has a calm expression, still holds his hat in hand (the same hand that would be hit with a bullet), and his energetic (but not panicked) movements after this point are not those of a man yet hit in his back, lung, wrist and leg... not until at least Z235. The *earliest* possible frame in which Governor Connally could have been hit, based on his movements and other facts, is around frame Z235. This is based on careful scrutiny of the film by Connally and his wife and the opinion of many experts, critics and witnesses. Connally was emphatic, and though years later he was cajoled into crawfishin'[61] because his testimony was ruining the Magic

Bullet Theory, **one cannot go back in time and erase his original, unwavering testimony already on record.** Connally was dead-sure in 1963 that separate bullets hit him and JFK, and he was still confident in this TIME magazine interview in 1967: "I know every single second of what happened in that car.... My recollection of that time gap, the distinct separation between the shot that hit the President and the impact of the one that hit me, is as clear today as it was then. It's a certainty." They asked his opinion of the Single Bullet Theory, he refused to comment except to add: "There is no *theory*, there is my absolute knowledge, and Nellie's too, that one bullet caused the President's first wound, and that an entirely separate shot struck me. It's a certainty; I'll never change my mind."[62] Indeed, the Governor's wife, Nellie, likewise testified to the WC, "I heard a noise... I turned over my right shoulder and looked back, and saw the President as he had both hands at his neck... Then, very soon, there was the second shot that hit John."

Every single piece of testimony and evidence confirms the Connally's insistence that refutes the Single Bullet Theory (the ballistic angles, the lack of damage to the bullet, the photos, the testimony of every witness with an opinion on it). Z235 is the only frame that satisfies the vivid recollections of *both* the Governor and his wife, when they viewed the film, and Z235 is consistent with medical experts who say the shot into the back of Connally's lung (which the Governor described as being "hit with a fist") caused air to expel instantly and rapidly, which in turn caused his cheeks to puff out, as seen in frames Z236-238. Again, because of the obstruction of the freeway sign, it is harder to ascertain the exact frame JFK was first hit, but the latest he could have been struck in the neck is Z220, since at Z224, when Kennedy begins to emerge from behind the sign, he has already ceased waving and has brought his arm/hand to his injured neck. The best consensus of fair-minded eyewitnesses and a study of the Zapruder film and other photos shows that JFK was shot in the throat at about Z217, while Connally was hit at Z235: an 18 frame difference, a full second *after* JFK. This means another bullet was required, which spells the end of Magic Bullet fairy tale.

How did the WC attempt to explain this discrepancy? A "delayed reaction" in Connally and a blind eye to all the hard evidence. To accept this delayed reaction, we would have to believe that JFK reacted *immediately* to his wounds with his arms, but that Connally's puffed cheek is a *delayed* reaction — even though the wind in his cheeks was a product of lung impact, an instantly mechanical and involuntary air expulsion, not something as slow as an arm movement (via nerve to muscle). We've already allowed for a three frame delay between when the bullet hit Connally and the air puffing his cheeks. Comparing Kennedy's visible reaction to Connally's visible reaction, we have at least a second (18 frames per second) differential: two bullets required. **The bolt-action Carcano could not fire two bullets that fast.**

It's All in the Wrist!

From frames Z225 until Z245, Connally's right hand is higher than his nipple (the exact location of the bullet). This means a magic bullet had to have struck a rib bone with enough impact to completely change its direction in an upward ricochet into his wrist, and then completely change direction again to hit his leg. So even if we denied all contrary evidence and claim just a single bullet, the WC still has a major problem: the magic bullet in evidence is only slightly deformed and missing only a few near-microscopic pieces of lead (since some of the missing lead is accounted for, having been extracted for ballistics tests by the FBI). While the critics are right to say the bullet was not perfectly "pristine," the *nose* of the bullet is indeed "pristine," which is impossible, because to make the angles and multiple wounds work, it would have had to hit three or more bones in its crooked ricocheting path through JFK and Connally. The best explanation for the wrist injury is bullet *fragments* (possibly bouncing from the windshield frame of the limo). The magic bullet (CE399) did not fragment.

The WC did not investigate the missed Tague bullet until much later... so they needed a time machine to go back and try to change the testimonies of Connally and other witnesses. Reading the reports of the news media in the weeks and months following the shooting, we can see that as more facts came out proving a second (or third) shooter and a Grassy Knoll location, the more the WC tried to retroactively adjust the party line. Look at the unfolding reports (from print, radio, and TV), and find that they initially stated "facts" that completely contradict the later-created Single Bullet Theory:

Reporter John Berbers wrote in the *New York Times* on November 26, 1963, that Parkland doctor Kemp Clark said of the bullets, "one struck [Kennedy] at about the necktie knot. It ranged downward and did not exit." Oops, have to get rid of that one, as it mentions a separate frontal shot. Reporter Berbers quoted Kemp further, saying the second shot struck the "right back of his head." The *New York Times* concluded: "Since one bullet did not exit it is presumed that the bullet that struck the President's head was the one recovered from the stretcher that bore the President into the hospital. A third bullet was found in fragments in the car and is presumed by official sources to be the one that coursed through the body of Governor Connally." Oops.

Why did the early reports all point to more than three shots, more than one gunman, more than one sniper location, and major damage to Kennedy's rear cranium? A contrary scenario begin to emerge only *after* the government grabbed full control of all the evidence and began to spin reports and "adjust" witness testimony. Within weeks, the official only-three-bullets story—the Big Lie—started taking shape. *Life* magazine reported in December 1963: "Three shots were fired. Two struck the President, one Governor Connally. All three bullets have been recovered—one, deformed, from the floor of the limousine... one from [a] stretcher... one that entered the President. All were fired from the 6.5 mm Carcano carbine which Lee Oswald bought." Oops, the Big Lie, at that point, failed to account for a **fourth** bullet—the Tague/curb bullet. So the Big Lie had to evolve further. Enter Arlen Specter and his magic bullet.

To summarize this "Magic ABC" section: knowing the angles are wrong, the ballistics are flawed, and the timing off, we have a triple-strong case that the Single Bullet Theory is bunk. It should be added here that, despite the attention and energy many of us expend on the Single Bullet controversy, it is just one part of our extensive case proving a conspiracy.

Lie Number 19: A Tiny, Rear-of-Skull Entrance Wound: "The smaller hole... in the rear of the President's skull was the point of entry."
~*Warren Commission Report*, p. 86

The head injury is a bigger key to the case than the back/throat wounds and even more important than the "Magic Bullet." Exposing this Lie Number 19 not only proves a second gunman shot from the front, but also proves a government cover-up and conspiracy. And ironically, it is the lie easiest to expose.

Beverly Oliver, one of the nearest of street-side bystanders, within a few feet of the fatal shot, states unequivocally: "I know beyond a shadow of a doubt that he was shot from the front and the back of his head blew off."[63] She is actually *the least credible* witness to assert that the gaping rear wound did not come from Oswald's rifle (because her story had inconsistencies across the years). But *scores* of more reliable witnesses saw the same thing: a large, gaping, brain-opening exit wound in the back the President's head, in complete contradiction to the WC's claim of a tiny bullet-sized entrance-hole.

And yet, strangely enough, the proof of a massive rear head wound is found right in the pages of the *WCR* itself. Read pages 140-142 of Volume 2 of the full WC report, excerpted below: Secret Service agent Clint Hill laid on top of the Kennedys as they sped to the hospital. Since he saw JFK's head wounds as close as any doctor, and in the light of day before any alterations or medical procedures, his testimony must be considered the most accurate of any. Counsel Arlen Specter led the interview:

```
Mr. Specter: "What did you observe as to President
Kennedy's condition on arrival at the hospital?"
Mr. Hill: "The right rear portion of his head was
missing. It was lying in the rear seat of the car....
There was so much blood you could not tell if there
had been any other wound or not, except for the one
large gaping wound in the right rear portion of the
head."⁶⁴
```

What Hill saw—"a gaping wound... in the right rear" —is consistent with the location of the large wound described by the Parkland doctors, specifically the *occipital*, or lower rear of the skull. This should not be confused with the parietal or temporal, terms which apply to another wound on the *side* of JFK's skull. The parietal can also refer, in part, to the rear, but it extends forward toward the side/ temporal, where the WC wants you to think the bullet "exited" on the right side. The WC favored the word "parietal" rather than "occipital" whenever possible, since it was less specific. The separate right-side wound (forward of the occiput: in the parietal and temporal regions) is visible in the Zapruder film, and was also a gruesome wound. But the larger wound that three Secret Service Agents and a flock of doctors described was at the *back* of the head, fully in the rear (though more on the right hemisphere than the left).

A sizable fragment of the right rear occipital bone is what Jackie Kennedy climbed on the trunk of the limo to retrieve. It was described by Clint Hill, and later found on the car-seat. There is one brief glimpse in the Zapruder film of this palm-sized object on the truck lid, and it is on the left back side of the limo—even though Kennedy was seated on the right. Jackie retrieved it and brought it back into the car... you can glimpse her picking it up in the Zapruder film. (The rear-flying fragment can be seen clearly in only one frame of the Zapruder film, either because of the speed of the head explosion, the blurriness of the film, or an alteration to the film, which we discuss in Lie Number 21.) A shot from the TSBD entering the rear of the President's head would have sent bone flying forward and sideways to his right, and **not** to the left and far backside of the trunk-lid... which is why reports often speak vaguely of Jackie "trying to grab something" or even "trying to escape the car." The truth is that in a panicked, irrational effort to put Humpty-Dumpty together again, she was retrieving skullbone, as she and Clint Hill later confirmed.

While spread-eagled on top of the Kennedys, Agent Hill made some incriminating observations at arm's length. Clint Hill's unimpeachable testimony here is damning because it conflicts with the (altered) autopsy report and the WC sketches of the almost-unharmed back of JFK's head. Hill's words irreconcilably conflict with the WC's phrase on page 55 of the summary report that described a supposed rear-entry wound as a "small bullet sized hole on the right rear of the President's head discovered during the subsequent autopsy." Hill's observations, and Jackie's actions, prove **a bullet came from the front right and exited out the back, taking a large piece of skull backwards and to the left four feet.** So they buried Hill's testimony in one of the 26 volumes that most folks would never open.

Secret Service Agent Bill Greer saw the President's wounds at Parkland. His testimony to the WC also indicates huge wounds toward the back of the skull. GREER: "His head was all shot, this whole part [pointing] was all a matter of blood like he had been hit."
Mr. SPECTER. "Indicating the top and **right rear** side of the head?" [Specter, before knowing how important it would be for the conspiracy cover-up to make the rear wound small, actually does a good job of cross-examination here... clarifying for the record that Greer was point to the rear of the head.]
Mr. GREER. "Yes, sir; it looked like that was **all blown off.**"[65]

Greer's testimony was also buried in the Volume Set.

Yet another Secret Service Agent, Roy Kellerman, saw the President's wounds at Parkland. His testimony to the WC likewise includes a huge occipital wound on the back of the President's skull:

KELLERMAN: "He had a large wound this size."
SPECTER: "Indicating a circle with your finger of **the diameter of 5 inches**; would that be approximately correct?"
KELLERMAN: "Yes, circular; yes, on this part of the head."
SPECTER: "Indicating the **rear portion of the head.**"
KELLERMAN: "Yes."
SPECTER. "More to the right side of the head?"
KELLERMAN: "Right. This was removed...the skull part was removed."[66]

Kellerman, like almost everyone else who saw the back of the President's head up close, described a 5-inch gaping hole in the right rear portion of the skull. The vivid descriptions of three Secret Service agents and a dozen medical personnel (see below) are irreconcilable, because the autopsy photos show an-almost undamaged rear head with neatly-cropped hair on a fully-intact scalp. It bears repeating again and again: **that stark,**

irreconcilable clash is the most definitive proof of a government cover-up, because only the government had the opportunity to alter the photos.

Even in the one-volume summary of *The WC Report*, the book more readily accessible to the public, the truth can still be found in the doctors' words. Again, the WC tried to downplay and obscure it by scattering the wound testimony on different pages and by using medical terms like "occipital" and "parietal." The reports of the Parkland doctors and nurses confirm the Secret Service agents' observations, all constituting the earliest, most credible testimony: professionals within an arm's length of the victim while he was still technically alive. [The page numbers below are from the *WCR* one-volume summary... see Endnotes]:

•p. 523: **Dr. Charles Baxter**'s written report cites "wounds [of] the rt. [right] temporal and **occipital [rear]** bones." The wound he cited in the temporal was covered at times by a flap of skin and skull. This can be seen in the autopsy pictures. With the flap closed, and with the bloody, matted mess of hair in the rear, some doctors could see only two wounds (the throat and right rear), while those who knew about the flap and who had seen more of the rear of the head described the rear occipital wound *extending* into the right-side parietal area (thus, not just a tiny bullet hole in the rear skull, as shown in the falsified autopsy pictures). So there is no contradiction in the testimony of most doctors and nurses at Parkland. With JFK laying face up on the trauma table, some doctors did not see the full extent of the rear head wound. The only contradictory medical reports came later, with the autopsy and after the conclusions of the *WCR*.

•page 54: "**Dr. [James] Carrico** noted two wounds: a small wound in the front lower neck, and "an extensive wound in the President's head where **a sizable portion of the skull was missing**." Since not much skull was "missing" on the *side* (with the "flap" attached), this refers to the rear wound.

•page 526: **Dr. Robert McClelland**: "a massive gunshot wound of the head.... The **right posterior [rear] portion of the skull had been extremely blasted**."

•page 530: **Dr. M. T. Jenkins'** written report: "a great laceration on the right side of the head (temporal and **occipital**), causing a **great defect** in the skull plate...." •**Dr. Ronald Coy Jones** described "what appeared to be an **exit wound in the posterior [rear] portion of the skull**."

•**Dr. Gene Akin** said that the "**back of the right occipital-parietal portion of his head was shattered**, with brain substance extruding."

•page 54-55: "**Dr. [Kemp] Clark**, who most closely observed the head wound, described a **large, gaping wound in the right rear** part of the head.... Dr. Clark did not see any other hole or wound on the President's head." He specifically did not see the "small bullet-sized hole on the right rear of the President's head discovered during the subsequent autopsy."

•page 524: Dr. Kemp Clark's written report states JFK was "...bleeding profusely from the back of the head... cerebral tissue present...." Cerebral tissue comes from the lower back of the skull. Clark went on to describe (on p. 525) a "**large wound beginning in the right occiput (rear)** extending into the parietal...."

•page 517, Dr. Clark's typed Summary Report (pulling together information from everyone on the scene) cites two "external wounds, one in the lower third of the anterior [front] neck, the other in the **occipital region**." Debunkers try to claim that Clark waffled on his testimony (after later seeing the faked autopsy pictures/reports and doubting his own memory). But Clark's testimony at the time, with fresh memories, is consistent with the other doctors.

- **Nurse Diana Hamilton Bowron** (more from her, below) saw the huge rear exit wound in the occiput. Several nurses reported that JFK's wounds were frontal entrance wounds.
- **Dr. Charles Crenshaw** agrees that it was an exit wound out the back of the head. Crenshaw was the last doctor at Parkland to view JFK's head-wound before the body was sent to Bethesda. He believes that the bullet wounds and photos were later altered so as to appear to come from the rear. Quote: "Had I been allowed to testify, I would have told [the Commission] that there is absolutely no doubt in my mind that the bullet that killed President John F. Kennedy was shot from the Grassy Knoll area," not from Oswald's location in the TSBD.[67]
- **Dr. Malcolm Perry**, 34, attendant surgeon at Parkland Hospital, said he saw two wounds—one below the Adam's apple [the frontal neck wound], the other at the back of the head... it is possible, he said, that "the neck wound was the entrance and the other the exit of the missile [bullet]."[68] In layman's terms, he was saying that, not really knowing the trajectory, the front neck wound looked like an entrance wound since it was small and neat and the rear head wound had the look of an exit wound: large and jagged. Dr. Perry's written report adds, "**a large wound of the right posterior [rear] cranium**... exposing severely lacerated brain."[69] So Perry's assessment of entrance and exit wounds are the exact opposite of what the WC would claim.
- Everyone who saw JFK's neck wound before it was greatly enlarged by the tracheotomy assessed it as an entrance wound (which would have meant a second or third shooter). The wound was variously estimated at from 2 mm to (max) 5 mm in diameter, and thus a "small caliber weapon," (not the 6.5 mm of the Carcano shell), stated Dr. Charles Baxter in a taped 1979 interview. He said the wound "was no more than a pinpoint.... And it was an entry wound."[70] In 1963, Dr. Baxter said within

hours of treating the President that it was an entry wound, and when interviewed again in 1992, Baxter repeated, "Looking at that hole... my immediate thought was that this was an entry wound because it was so small. The hole was only the size of a pencil eraser, about 2 or 2.5 mm across."[71]

You may ask, *Why did the Warren Commission allow so many medical discrepancies to get into the record early-on?* Several reasons:

1. The WC had more pressing concerns: explaining away the contrarian witnesses who saw a Grassy Knoll shooter, explaining away Oswald's curious connections, explaining away the Ruby shooting.

2. The need to invent a Magic Bullet came late in the investigation, and even later came the realization that the doctors' reports pointed to a frontal wound and rear exit wound that in turn pointed to a frontal shooter.

3. It's hard to directly dispute the expertise of doctors—so the WC had to hope most folks wouldn't know the difference between *occipital* and *parietal*. To lower any red flags, the WC rarely used the word "rear" to describe the large wound. They printed many of the Parkland reports as nearly-illegible photostats of the original hand-scrawling, rather than transcribing it. Readers must know anatomical terms and carefully decipher the doctor's scribbling to see the blatant contradiction in the Parkland report and the official government/military autopsy report.

To summarize: the initial reports (oral reports given to the press immediately, and official written reports within the next few hours) of **doctors and nurses at Parkland Memorial Hospital are, taken as a whole, absolutely the most reliable, neutral and trustworthy descriptions of the body as forensic evidence.** They were the medical experts closest to the scene, the only persons to see the body before it was affected by either their own rescue efforts or conspirators' actions to alter wounds. They had more experience with gunshot wounds than the autopsists, they viewed the body with no pre-conceptions and without knowledge of "lone gunman" theories, and were at that point under no pressure to protect peers or cover-up truth.

Debunkers make a big issue about *when* witnesses give their reports. They are quick to dismiss testimony that emerged years later, calling it faulty memory. But the report of Clint Hill and the medical personnel regarding a large rear wound came out early, within a few hours of the shooting.

A few doctors did later vacillate in their testimony when faced with propaganda (including *drawings*, not actual autopsy pictures) from the autopsists, and pressure from the FBI. Many of these doctors were young and did not want to risk their careers challenging an official autopsy done by respected, older peers. After all, Parkland personnel were not shown genuine autopsy pictures. But when a few autopsy pictures were finally circulated years later, some were brave enough to call them inaccurate.

Without a doubt, President Kennedy was shot from the front, and someone hid this fact by altering the body physically and by altering the autopsy report, photographs and X-rays. As usual, one lie leads to another....

Lie Number 20: Trust the Autopsy: "It remained for the autopsy in Washington... to ascertain the full facts concerning the wounds."
~*The Warren Commission Report*, Appendix 12

Days after the rushed and shoddy Navy autopsy was performed late that night (November 22-23, 1963), the final **autopsy report claimed that all the shots entered from the**

rear... in opposition to almost every other bit of evidence and testimony indicating front entrance wounds and a gaping rear exit wound.

This is where we lose some readers. It is hard to accept that military officers and doctors would have conspired to alter and hide the autopsy facts. But wait: it did not require that *every* person involved in the autopsy lie, nor that even those who shaded the truth were "in on" the full conspiracy. Indications of an autopsy deception, although many and persuasive, were hidden from the public for years. In the Seventies, the irreconcilable contradictions became known to us in full when the autopsy photos began to made public at the time of the HSCA investigation... whereupon the witnesses were baffled as they viewed an "official" autopsy photo that portrayed only a tiny bullet-sized entry wound on the back of the head. **They knew the photo had to be a forgery, which proves a government conspiracy, since the U.S. government made the photos**.

As detailed in the prior sections (the redundancy is for readers who jump ahead), at Parkland Memorial Hospital almost all of the doctors and nurses believed the President had been **shot from the front**: in agreement with all three Secret Service agents in the Presidential limo with Kennedy, they saw a large *rear* exit wound, and a small entrance wound in the front of his neck. None of the doctors had seen either of the small, bullet-sized, rear *entry* wounds as portrayed in the autopsy photos. The rear-skull (occipital) exit wound was also seen by many witnesses present at the autopsy... but they were not asked to report to the WC (some did come forward in the 1970's, to tell the HSCA investigators). Autopsy witnesses viewing the large rear (occipital) wound include General Philip Wehle, mortician Tom Robinson, X-ray technician Jerrol Custer, medical corpsman James Curtis Jenkins, Jan Gail Rudnicki, Dr. Robert

Karnei, and Dr. Ebersole. Ebersole added that "a large fragment of the occipital bone was received from Dallas" around 12:30 pm on November 23rd. But those witnesses did not control the final (faked) report—and in fact, most of them were not even privy to the official report and photos, other than that found in the WC Report, with its vague wording and sketched drawings. Dr. Crenshaw, who treated JFK in the emergency room and the last doctor to see the body before the Bethesda autopsy, was shocked when years later he saw the photos. He insists that the bullet wounds or photos had been altered from what he had seen, altered so as to make all the shots appear to have come from behind. Dr. Crenshaw states confidently: "Had I been allowed to testify, I would have told [the Commission] that there is absolutely no doubt in my mind that the bullet that killed President JFK was shot from the Grassy Knoll area." Frontal entrance wounds.

Paul O'Connor said the autopsy drawings were misrepresentations, "total fabrications." He also said that he and everyone involved in the autopsy had been threatened with General Court-Martial if they divulged any information about what they had seen.[72] This is the harshest level of military punishment, usually reserved for serious felony charges like violent rape, extreme child abuse, and murder, and punishable by life imprisonment or even death.

The autopsy, and the summary by the WC, fuzzily described just one large wound as "chiefly parietal... but extending somewhat into the... occipital regions."[73] The *WCR*'s slanted conclusion is found in their summary on page 86: "The detailed autopsy [concluded that] the smaller hole (one-fourth of an inch by five-eighths of an inch) in the rear of the President's skull was the point of entry and that the large opening on the right side of his head was the wound of exit." Contrast this to the testimony in the full *WCR* (Volume 6, p. 136) of Nurse Diana

Hamilton Bowron: "The back of his head...well, it was very bad...." A 1992 interview with Nurse Bowron confirmed this: "When we were preparing the body for the coffin I had the opportunity to examine [the rear head wound] more closely. It was about **five inches in diameter** and there was no flap of skin covering it, just a fraction of skin along part of the edges of bone. There was, however, some hair hanging down from the top of the head, which was caked with blood, and most of the brain was missing. The wound was so large I could almost put my whole left fist inside... it was an exit hole... in the **occipital** area."[74]

Such a gory, significant, vivid detail is not the sort of thing a witness gets confused about, and certainly not *twenty* highly-credible witnesses with the same observation. To repeat: these were nurses, doctors, Secret Service agents and mortician/autopsy personnel who went on record stating clearly there was a gaping wound in the back of JFK's head. If you refuse to believe those highly-qualified witnesses on such an obvious true-or-false question, then the only way to truly "close the case" would be to exhume President Kennedy's body.

Exhumation: Distasteful? Nothing is more distasteful than the fact the conspirators killed him and were never brought to justice.) As a foolish distraction (or CIA disinformation campaign?), some years ago a petition drive persuaded the State of Texas to exhume Oswald's body—with a silly theory that the person in the grave was a double, a fake Oswald... for what purpose? Oswald's body is irrelevant. But Kennedy's body contains the absolute proof of where the magic bullet entered his back, and of the occipital exit wound... proving an inside government conspiracy.

The House Select Committee on Assassinations (HSCA) made a feeble effort to explain the discrepancies. They determined that, legally, the body should never have left Texas without an autopsy, and admitted that those performing the autopsy had insufficient training and no experience with gunshot wounds. Bullet tracks were not dissected, angles not measured, and clothing was not examined. But the HSCA never carried those concerns to the next step, never asked the hard questions: Why the stark inconsistencies? Why weren't the best forensic scientists in the nation called in? Why weren't all the pictures released sooner?

Body Alterations:

Evidence indicates that JFK's body had been tampered with between the time it left Parkland and was unwrapped at the Bethesda autopsy. FBI agents Francis O'Neill and James Sibert, in their official report about the autopsy, noted that there had been "surgery of the head" prior to the official autopsy. Not being medically-trained, the agents just assumed this was something that had happened as the Parkland doctors tried to save the President... but Parkland personnel did not tamper with or cut upon the skull... only the throat. Did the conspirators alter JFK's body to remove any conflicting ballistic evidence and to change the apparent direction of the shots? Before you call this idea preposterous, see the collection of photographs in *The Killing of a President*, by Robert Groden, 1993, for example, to view the discrepancies among various autopsy sketches and photos, or read the detailed documentation by David Lifton in his book, *Best Evidence*. One leaked autopsy photo—taken at Bethesda just before the autopsy—shows a V-cut near JFK's forehead hairline... exactly where one would have to cut to remove evidence of a frontal entry wound fired from the Knoll.

Conspiracy deniers act as if Lifton *et al.* are kooks—as if body alteration were the equivalent of claiming an alien abduction or a moon-landing hoax. But they offer no plausible explanation as to why there was "surgery to the head" prior to the autopsy just as a pre-autopsy photo showed (the V-cut), nor do they explain why the body was seen in two different caskets.

At least six witnesses have reported that the body arrived at Bethesda in a different wrapping than described by the Parkland staff, who had wrapped it in hospital sheets. When the casket was opened at Bethesda, JFK's body was inexplicably found to be in a plastic body bag, according to Paul O'Connor, Floyd Riebe, Jerrol Custer, Ed Reed, John VanHoesen, and Capt. John Stover, MD.[75] Also floating around Walter Reed hospital and Bethesda hospital were two different caskets: Jerrol Custer saw both of them: one being a plain shipping casket, the other being the ornate, expensive bronze coffin that had been loaded onto Air Force One in Dallas. Witnesses to a cheap shipping-type casket were Dennis David, Paul O'Connor, Floyd Riebe, Ed Reed, James Jenkins, and Capt. John Stover, MD. Most of the individuals at the military hospitals who reported two caskets and/or two different types of body wrapping were consistent over time and also with different interviewers.[76]

The chief autopsist, Commander Humes, had zero experience performing an autopsy on a gun-shot victim. (He also noted the prior surgery to the head but offered no question or answer as to why.) He changed his report between Friday and Sunday, and burned his original autopsy notes, a fact he first defended by saying he did so because he didn't want the notes, spattered with JFK's blood, to become some kind of macabre holy relic. But later we learned he also burned another set of notes that were never in the autopsy room, never spotted with blood.

One of the occipital skull fragments, according to Dr. Humes, contained an exit wound. But to downplay this evidence, Humes testified to the WC that he could not be sure from *which* part of the skull the fragment came. He slipped at another point in his testimony and stated that the rear of JFK's head exhibited *both* entrance and exit wounds. The failure of the government to vigorously cross-examine the autopsist and the autopsy reports, or to pursue the evidence of frontal shots and other inconsistencies, causes even patriots to suspect conspiracy.

Cranial fragments:

Speaking of skull fragments: Not only were there too many *bullet* fragments to fit the Magic Bullet scenario, there were too many pieces of detached *skull bone* to fit the official autopsy photos. Skull pieces include:

1: three pieces of cranial bone found by Secret Service agent Floyd Boring during the official limousine inspection late on the day of the shooting... after many people had already picked up other pieces noted below.

2: a small piece found by Seymour Weitzman.[77]

3: a finger-tip sized piece found on the pavement of Elm Street by Postal Inspector Harry D. Holmes: this respected/credible witness also added, "...there was just pieces of skull and bone ...all over the place...." He later discarded the fragment, so it was in addition to those in the autopsy collection.[78]

4: The "Harper fragment": found on Elm Street by a medical student, William Harper, the piece was large enough that his uncle, a doctor, could identify it as coming from the occipital (rear) area of the skull. Others who have studied the "Harper fragment" also believe it came mostly from the occipital/rear part of the skull (which conflicts with the official photos and X-rays).

5: Deputy Sheriff Jack Faulkner and witness A.D. McCurley picked up a piece of skull bone on Elm Street, but did not turn it in.

6: Dallas Policeman Joseph R. Cody found a piece of bone in the gutter at Dealey Plaza that he said, "apparently came out of the back of the President's head."

7: Secret Service Agent Sam Kinney found yet *another* piece of skull while loading the limo onto Air Force One, lying in the rear seat of the bloody limousine, "a big piece." He believed it to be from "the back of his head," partly because he had witnessed close-up (see below) the gaping hole in the rear of JFK's skull, and partly because the skull fragment had enough size and curvature (Kinney said it resembled a piece of "flowerpot") to come from the back, not the front.[79] Kinney's statements make it clear: "It was the right rear, I saw that part blow out." Kinney had helped remove the injured President from the back of the limousine, viewing close-up the wound on the back of the head, and added, "His brain was blown out, there was nothing left...he had no brains left in his head." Kinney's vivid testimony is in sharp contrast to the Zapruder film and the WC drawings that portray an intact rear skull. Testimony from Kinney and others who saw the rear head "blow-out," plus the quantity and size of bone fragments, destroy the official story of a tiny bullet-hole on the back of the head.[80]

8. Additional tiny pieces were never recovered; some may have fallen onto the freeway as the limo sped up; smaller fragment may have been on the Kennedys clothing and fell off later. The Presidential limo was washed down immediately with a sponge and bucket, destroying potential evidence there.

Trying to fit all these skull fragments into the relatively-small holes shown in the official autopsy photos is like fitting a large square peg into a small round hole.

Dr. Paul Peters concurred that the initial autopsy pictures and drawings which have been belatedly "leaked" to the public are false, stating: "There was a large hole in the back of the head through which one could see the brain."[81]

•Congress has photographic evidence of a shot exiting from the rear of the President's head.[82]

•More signs the X-rays were altered or anomalous: a white patch on the rear of the President's skull does not seem normal, the frontal bone appears to be missing, and on the lateral X-rays, the dark frontal area contains no brain—on either side.

Gerald Posner tries to blame the rushed, flawed autopsy on the grieving Kennedy's: "Jacqueline and Robert Kennedy... [placed] pressure on the physicians to hurry their work" on the autopsy. But neither the ex-first lady nor the Attorney General had any jurisdiction at Bethesda Naval Hospital. The responsibility was upon the autopsy team to take as long as necessary, and for the Secret Service and FBI to insist on the same, once they had (illegally) refused to let the proper Texas authorities/coroner investigate. This was a homicide, and you do not rush a homicide investigation under any "pressure" from family members. Bobby Kennedy might have expressed concern for an exhausted Jackie, but in the end, he knew to let the doctors do their job and it is doubtful that military officers would have felt intimidated by the young Bobby, who had no military authority. Contrary to Posner's claim, we know that Humes was rushed by military officers, an Admiral and a General, who were present *in* the autopsy room—not by the Kennedys waiting on another floor.

Posner next claims that "subsequent panels of leading national forensic specialists" later "confirmed its findings."[83] But **none of them had any basis upon which to "confirm" the autopsy**: the original autopsy notes were burned and the FBI had altered the final report; the autopsy cover page showing wound locations does not match the wound locations reported *inside* the report; the personnel present had vastly different assessments of the wounds; the chief autopsist did not track the bullet hole in JFK's back more than an inch or two in depth; parts of the report/photos are missing from the archives, etc. etc. None of those "expert panels" exhumed the body; none of them had access to *all* the photos and X-rays; none were open to the real possibility that parts of the autopsy report had been forged/altered; none of them cross-examined the various doctors at Parkland and Bethesda. And none of these "experts" fully addressed the medical issues so well-established by Lifton, Groden and others. Posner pretends the alleged JFK autopsy photos and X-rays are authentic. He points out that they were authenticated by two HSCA panels.[84] However, those panels based their "authentication" on a few narrow criteria, admitted the autopsy was sloppy, and failed to explain the discrepancies in the autopsy materials.[85] Moreover, two of the HSCA experts later changed their views after further studies.

Posner attempts to explain only *one* of the many indications of forgery: The disparity between the pictures of JFK's face vs. the skull X-rays. He fails. In the autopsy pictures, Kennedy's face is intact and undamaged. But the X-rays show missing frontal bone just beyond the forehead, i.e., just past the hairline. Dr. Lawrence Angel and Dr. G. M. McDonnel prepared interpretations of the alleged skull X-rays for the HSCA. These experts stated that the X-rays show missing frontal bone—in direct conflict with the photos. Dr. David Mantik, a radiologist and physicist who was permitted to examine the original X-rays at the National Archives, and Dr. Phillip Williams, a neurosurgeon who saw the President's body at Parkland Hospital, likewise noted that the X-rays depict a significant amount of missing frontal (facial) bone. They state this in writing but also on a filmed 1991 conference which included several other medical witnesses who agree that the autopsy is inaccurate. Dr. Mantik, after studying the original X-rays at the National Archives, also determined that a 6.5 mm circular mark on the anterior-posterior X-ray is not metallic. This means someone added it to the X-ray after the autopsy in order to appear to be from a 6.5 mm Mannlicher-Carcano. Since this apparent entrance hole in the X-rays is four inches higher than the entry point described in the autopsy report, we have two reasons to believe the X-ray is fake.[86]

Ballistics expert Howard Donahue has pointed out that it is highly unlikely that the lead fragments seen throughout the X-rays or removed in the autopsy could have come from a full-metal-jacket bullet as is alleged to have been fired from the sniper's nest. Defenders of the X-rays speculate that the fragment "sheared off" from the bullet as it entered the skull. But Donahue observes that if a bullet had been fired from the TSBD, and thus entered the skull at a downward angle, it would have deposited a sheared-off fragment *above* the entrance point, not below it, as the records indicate. He further noted that he had never heard of a full-metal-jacketed bullet shearing on impact. Australian forensic expert Detective Shaun Roach and forensic pathologist Dr. Halpert Fillinger have likewise stated that a fully jacketed missile would not behave in this manner.

Since entire books have been written on this one topic of body and autopsy alterations, we stop here and let the reader investigate further if interested. We have, in brief, shown evidence that an exhumation and second autopsy is necessary. For a more detailed, technical summary of problems with the X-rays and autopsy, see Dr. David Mantik's at: www.assassinationresearch.com/v2n2/pittsburgh.pdf

Lie Number 21: Zapruder Film is Proof: The Zapruder film proves that Oswald was the lone shooter. ~ABC News

The debunkers point to the Zapruder film as corroborative of the autopsy report, refusing to admit the common problem: both pieces of evidence were fully in the hands of government agents who had the means and the motive to alter it. The conspiracy-deniers also fail to explain why— even with the mistakes and alterations in both—inconsistencies still remain. The Zapruder film raises as many questions as it answers.

There is strong evidence that the Zapruder film was altered. But even if we were to accept that the film has not been retouched, we are still left with a hand-held, inexpensive camera with a distorted lens, shaking, and frustratingly blocked by a road-sign at a key moment. And we are left with other questions: Why do we see so much clear and professional video for JFK's arrival at the airport and for most his motorcade journey, but on Elm Street, the TV cameras stop? Why is the only significant footage we have of the Dealey Plaza area a fuzzy, amateur film—and does not show the Grassy Knoll area? The fact that the film was quickly hidden away from the American public, placed in the hands of the CIA film lab, and has different versions now released to the public, makes the film worthless as definitive forensic evidence since the CIA is *one of the suspects!* Our suspicions are also raised by the fact that other film evidence was confiscated and destroyed: Beverly Oliver, a 17-year-old girl at the time, had an 8 mm movie camera confiscated by a man claiming to an FBI agent, and the film/camera was never seen again. She was within 30 feet of the key head shot. Ms. Oliver (now Massegee) gave sworn testimony of these claims to the House Assassination Review Board.[87] Yes, Oliver's story has changed some over the years and is not our most credible witness... but if Oliver's claims were false, and she were not the "Babushka Lady," *some* unknown woman with a head scarf (seen in other photos/films with a camera facing the Grassy Knoll) took pictures that have never surfaced, pictures that almost surely would have included any gunman looking over the fence. Other film also has been reported missing or confiscated: a color photograph by Norman Similas is missing; the original negative of a photograph by Hugh Betzner is missing; Orville Nix took moving pictures of the final shot, turned his film over to the FBI, but when it was returned to him, he reported in 1966, it was not the same film he had originally given them. So the alteration to the Zapruder film is not an anomaly in this case.

When *ABC News* and the *Discovery* channel tried to prove that the Magic Bullet hit both JFK and Governor Connally simultaneously, they put too much weight on the subjective interpretation of a few seconds of fuzzy and half-blocked video. Again, even if we accept the Zapruder film at face-value, we still see Connally reacting *after* JFK. As debunkers finagle the sixth-floor-to-car position and angles and the JFK-to-Connally positions (bending JFK unnaturally), and falsify the wound locations on JFK's back, we are still left with oddities about ballistics, bullet damage through bone, contrary reports by Connally and his wife, mis-aligned holes in clothing, excessive amounts of lead in the bodies and the limo, and provenance of the single nearly-pristine bullet. Therefore, no one's case can rest upon a few Zapruder frames, nor is truth served by trying to pressure a change and parse Connally's words 30 years after the fact (as Posner did).

Posner claims that computer graphics analysis (as seen in documentaries by *ABC News* and the *Discovery Channel*) have proven the Single Bullet Theory. This is simply not true. The company "Failure Analysis" also tries to make this claim—that computer simulations and calculations have verified the Single Bullet Theory. 'Tis hard to argue with a computer. But computers are only as accurate as the information fed into them—by humans. Even *if* the Zapruder film were unaltered, and even *if* it did not have a road-sign blocking key moments necessary for the timing and positioning questions, it can't just be "scanned" into a computer and automatically converted into data. Humans have to view the film, make assumptions about how the two-dimensional images correlate to real 3-D space in Dealey Plaza, and make guesses about the exact positions of moving bodies in a moving car. Failure Analysis Associates used such an assumption-laden hypothetical construction, and projected a cone back to where the bullets might have originated. But since it used data based on a fraudulent autopsy, the study was obviously biased from the start.

Gerald Posner took this inaccurate study one level further from reality by deleting a neighboring building from his book illustration of the "cone." A portion of The Dal-Tex Building was included in the three-dimensional cone that was computer-projected back from the wounds to possible firing origins, but it has disappeared from Posner's version of the graphic.[88] The debunkers also avoid facing the problem that computer simulations can't solve: the missed shot that hit the curb and then grazed James Tague—on the opposite side of the road, hundreds of feet away—does not line up at all with the intended target and the so-called "sniper's nest" in the TSBD. A line from the Dal-Tex building to the mark on the curb goes in a path very near the Presidential limo, while the sixth floor of the TSBD has no such alignment.

Some critics ask, "If the Zapruder film was altered, why does it still show evidence of a frontal shot?" In the pre-computer-graphics era of 1963-64, any changes to film had to be done manually. The conspirators decided to be cautious, adopting a "less is more" approach to the film. All they truly needed to do was delete a few key frames, and then paint a black spot over the back of JFK's head to disguise the rear exit wound. Too many people, including some in the media, had seen the original Zapruder film and thus the conspirators could not risk any further drastic changes.

View the film for yourself... slow motion versions are found online, on YouTube and elsewhere. Stop it frame by frame.

Look for these anomalies that indicate an unreliable film: **1.** Skipped/missing frames as limo heads down Elm; **2.** The Simmons Freeway sign seems to have been increased in size, which would be the only explanation as to why Newsman Dan Rather described JFK's movements behind the sign that are not seen there now. Before it was sequestered for years, Rather had viewed the film once and described President Kennedy rubbing his eye—something no longer visible on the film. JFK's hand-to-eye movement now is obscured by an enlarged sign. The larger sign makes it impossible to exactly time the second shot. **3.** The back of JFK's head was blacked out to mask the size of his rear head wound. Look at Z314-Z318 and you'll see the back of JFK's head has a brief, blurred bump or deformity, but by Z320, it has been blacked out. The color of his hair in the back becomes black, rather than the dark brown elsewhere. And the brain matter and blood (the "blob," see below) exploding out the front of his head is exaggerated. **4.** The frames after Z318 are much more blurry, even though we know the limousine had slowed to a crawl at that point. **5.** Other evidence of film alteration—technical issues such as the lack of "pincushion effect" (a deformed lens-rectangle shape) in some frames— can be found in Robert Groden's work, and here: www.assassinationscience.com/johncostella/jfk/intro/index.htm

Experts who believe the film is unreliable include:
•Roderick Ryan, an expert on cinematic special effects, winner of a Lifetime Achievement Academy Award for the same, points out that the bulging brains seen in Zapruder (sometimes called "the blob") had been painted into several frames, from about Z335 to Z360 [Herein I use the standard abbreviation for frames from the Zapruder film: a "Z" and a three digit number, such as "Z233".] The purpose of the added "blob" was to exaggerate the amount of an "exit wound" from the WC-claimed rear-entry shot—while the true exit wound in the back of JFK's head was

masked.[89]

- Photo-analyst Jack White points out that still photographs conflict with frames in the Zapruder movie, such as a change in position of Mary Moorman: in a photo, she is at the street, but the movie shows her re-positioned on the grass.
- An Australian physicist, John P. Costella, a PhD in the field of electromagnetic waves and the physics of light as applied to evidence of film fakery, outlined film alterations in his paper, "The JFK Assassination Film Hoax: An Introduction."
- An article in *OpEdNews* (February 5, 2008), "New Proof of JFK Film Fakery" also presents multiple indications that the Zapruder film was altered.
- Highly-credentialed scientist Dr. Robert Mantik writes: "Recent work by Hollywood professionals has shown a distinct black, geometric-shaped mask lying precisely over the occipital area in question [after the fatal shot]. This apparent artifact [on the Zapruder film] is highly suggestive of photo tampering. I have observed this geometric mask myself...."
- Dallas Police motorcycle escort Bobby Hargis was riding to the left-rear of the Presidential limo. He reported being hit so hard by the blown-out brains, he thought for a moment that he himself had been shot. The forward speed of the limo and Hargis was about the same (less than 10 mph), the breeze was minimal, so there is no way a rear-entry shot with side "explosion" of skull matter (the blob supposedly exploding from JFK's right temple, far to the right of Hargis) could explain Hargis' experience. The officer even further behind him, B. J. Martin, was also on the left and also splattered with brain matter and blood. The only explanation is that the Zapruder film was altered to cover up the rear-exploding brain/bone matter.

Blacking out the hole in the back of JFK's skull was an easy alteration, even with 1960's technology. But there were limits to how much alteration can be done to a film without computerized technology. What the conspirators could not do in 1964 was drastically alter the movements of JFK's entire body when the shots impacted. This leads to our next "Lie."

Lie Number 22: The Jet Effect: "The jet [effect, of JFK's brain being expelled,] can carry forward more momentum than was brought in by the bullet [from the rear], and the head recoils backward...."
~Dr. Luis Alvarez, in the American Journal of Physics

The Zapruder film was hidden from the American people for years, with the excuse that it was gruesome. It is. And so is the average police drama on prime time TV any given evening. After much pressure from JFK researchers, the Zapruder film was finally released in 1975. The reaction of first-time viewers is usually, "It looks like the President is shot from in front!" Most who view the film—as with those who saw the shooting first-hand—say the President's head and body jerked *backwards* from the impact of a *frontal* head wound. This has elicited the most strained explanation of all: *the jet effect*. Physicist Luis Alvarez ran tests on watermelons, demonstrating that when a bullet hits a sealed fluid/matter, the fluid squirts out, causing a "jet effect" escaping the exit hole—like a rocket engine that pushes the melon in the opposite direction of the bullet's entry-force. There are two serious problems with this: **1.** As we have seen, the best testimony shows the larger exit hole was in the *back* of Kennedy's head (occipital), not the front/side (anterior-lateral). **2.** A human head is not a melon![90]

The obvious problem with "experts" like Alvarez, and even with some ballistics experts, is that they compare apples with oranges—or in this case, melons with men. The reaction of soft-shell melon to a bullet is irrelevant. A bullet hitting a hard skull will cause energy to be transferred into motion **in the same direction the bullet is heading.**

What about other tests, with a block of wood and with the hard skull of a goats, that purported to show the reverse jet effect? Still apples to oranges. The only human head analogous to a block of wood are the *blockheads* who believe this sham science... sorry, I couldn't resist. A light, unattached melon or block of wood is not even remotely analogous to an *attached* human head, making this some of the worst "science" ever sold to the American public.

As for the use of goats to test forensic theories: the shape of a goat head and the angle and manner that a goat head is attached to its animal body is also a poor analog to human anatomy. The observations of shooting goats, shared by Alfred G. Olivier, DVM, with the Rockefeller Commission, are, again, irrelevant. **Shooting a standing, four-legged animal is not correlative to shooting a seated, two-legged human.** Having a veterinarian as an expert witness is as blockheaded as shooting watermelons to "debunk" the notion of a Grassy Knoll assassin.

A panel of ballistics experts assembled by the House Assassinations Committee did not confirm the jet effect. Some of them were willing to accept that the Zapruder film might portray a rear entrance wound, explaining JFK's rearward head-jerk as a neurological reaction. But all of them had been given the *altered* autopsy photographs, and they were led to believe by other presumptive "evidence" that the shot came from behind. Thus their testimony was prejudicial. Moreover, if the Zapruder film had not been doctored, they would likely have drawn a different conclusion, as they would also have seen brain matter propelled out the *back* of JFK's head.

The jet effect is never going to be more powerful than a bullet traveling at 2000 feet per second and exploding on impact with the skull bone. JFK's head was thrown backwards violently and instantly from a frontal shot.

Here we do well to ignore laboratories and artificial reconstructions. We (sadly) can easily find, on the internet, video of actual shootings of humans. The following website (warning: *it's morbidly graphic*) shows real-life (or should we say, real-death) videos of persons being shot in the head: www.educationforum.ipbhost.com/index.php?showtopic=10505

In every case, the **real head of the victim moves *away* from the shooter** with the impact of the bullet, just as Kennedy's did, proving there is no significant "jet effect" strong enough to counteract the bullet's impact. Real-life observations trump lab calculations of melons any day.

Interlude: About Lies and Liars

What constitutes a Lie vs. merely an honest mistake? The answer is the difference between *honest* ignorance and *arrogant* ignorance—a difference of intentionality. A person who refuses to keep an open mind, arrogantly imposing their one-sided opinions on others, has made a choice for deception. A Lie. If a government official arrogantly decides the American people are too stupid or unworthy of truth, and hides the full truth (based on feelings, not facts), that too is a Lie. Such "Father Knows Best" (or "Uncle Sam Knows Best") condescension is also a form of Lie. Our justice system has been predicated upon "the whole truth and nothing but the truth." Most conspiracy-deniers, even on the rare occasions where they tell the truth, still fail to tell the *whole* truth. In this report, I label a statement a "Lie" when the person making the deceptive statement could have chosen to learn the truth, but intentionally ignored or covered-up a part of the story in order to blur the full picture.

This does *not* necessarily mean that when I quote a "Lie" (as in the bold section headings, **Lie Number...**), that I'm therefore calling the source of the quote a "Liar." A Liar is a person who habitually lives by deception, the kind of persons that Dr. Scott Peck called "People of the Lie," who are untrustworthy in almost all they say and do. Vice-President Lyndon Johnson, for example, was a habitual Liar. By contrast, Justice Earl Warren was a generally-honest man who chose, for what he perceived to be the good of the country, to allow a white-wash... not a Liar, but a person who permitted Liars to run the show.

To any honest person falsely-implicated herein: my apologies. My intent is not to attack character, but to assess historical, political, and forensic truth.

~~~

We now have laid out many of the key aspects of the case, with the exception of Jack Ruby. Before we look into Ruby's motives and possible connections to Oswald and to a greater conspiracy, we do well to first circle back and dig deeper into the central figure, the patsy, Lee Harvey Oswald:

Lie Number 23: Oswald's Motives: "...Oswald acted alone. Therefore, to determine the motives for the assassination of President Kennedy, one must look to [Oswald] himself." ~*WC Report*, p. 22

Everyone who has studied the brief bio of Lee Harvey Oswald agrees he led a strange and enigmatic life, filled with contradictions. He demonstrated only admiration for Kennedy, and showed no desire to claim "glory" for the first "successful" assassination since Lincoln's. He: •claimed to be a communist but joined that gung-ho patriotic group, the U.S. Marines •defected to Russia at the height of the Cold War, yet was financially-assisted by the U.S. State Department to return to the U.S.A. •claimed to be pro-Castro yet befriended anti-Castro

Cubans •claimed to be an extreme liberal yet associated with extreme right-wingers: Guy Bannister, David Ferrie, and George de Mohrenschildt.

The most *illogical* conclusion is that Oswald was a stupid, unlucky loser (with a perfect plan, a perfect location, and two perfect shots), and an anti-social loner (who had more friends than a teenager on Facebook: he had all sorts of entanglements with Cubans, CIA agents, FBI agents, right-wingers, left-wingers, etc.). The "official" psychology and motive attributed to him are contradicted by the facts.

Self-titled "reformed conspiracy theorist" Michael Beck asks rhetorically "Why would an innocent man flee, and then kill a cop [Tippit]? He didn't act like an innocent man by resisting arrest."[91] Beck's either/or, black or white thinking is a lazy response to the complexities of Lee Oswald. For a moment, set aside the grave doubts we have about whether Oswald killed Tippit. If Oswald had been framed, and suddenly realized he was being set-up by murderers, his panic in being chased by cops might result in his using a gun in self-defense—*not* because he had killed JFK, but because he realized someone was framing him. And if he knew from his undercover informant work that a some Dallas cops were crooked, he would have been all the more likely to pull a gun on a cop in self-defense. Remember, **Oswald never asserted he was "innocent"; instead, he announced he was "a patsy."** Beck is disingenuous to demand that we either view Oswald as an innocent bystander, merely a victim of mistaken identity, *or* as a lone-nut loser-assassin. This is a false choice. I choose the third option: all the evidence points to Oswald being a contract employee of both the CIA and FBI. We now have compelling evidence (see La Fontaine for starters) that his interactions with Cuba, Mexico and Russia were as a wannabe double-agent, and that his gun purchases were made in his role as a Federal informant—as a mole infiltrating a gun-running scheme. Oswald as a fall guy manipulated/framed by the real conspirators fits the facts like no other scenario.

Despite coming from poverty and a broken family, Lee was able to pass the entrance exam for the Marines and receive the U.S. security clearances to work at Atsugi Air Base, the home of the largest CIA station in the Pacific. This "unstable nut" was issued a Department of Defense ID card of the type given to intelligence agents working abroad.[92] He traveled the world (Japan, USSR, Mexico), landed various skilled jobs including ones that required security clearances (a map-making company funded by the CIA), managed the paperwork required to defect to Russia and to come *back* from Russia, and even managed to bring a Russian wife to America in the midst of the Cold War.

To the point of motive: Oswald never expressed to anyone a hatred or animosity toward Kennedy. Days before the assassination, a full-page ad in the Dallas newspaper accused JFK of being a communist. A true leftist nut would have waited 90 seconds longer to shoot the more-conservative Vice-President Johnson, or travelled elsewhere to kill less-guarded anti-communists like Goldwater or Nixon.

In answering the question of his motive and role in the shooting, who would best know the true nature and identity of Lee? His foreign wife of two years or his mother of twenty-four years? The WC chose his wife: a woman who spoke limited English, who shared a home only intermittently with the peripatetic Oswald, and who had been herself a communist who now lived in fear of deportation. No, they ignored the sworn testimony of the woman closest to Lee, who had known him from birth: his mother, Marguerite Oswald. She testified that her son, Lee, was "an undercover agent for the U.S. government."[93]

When Oswald was a teen, his favorite television show was *I Led Three Lives*, the story of an FBI counterspy. Oswald's interest in the double-agent movie is not a sign of insanity; the movie was not "Cybil," (about a crazy split-personality). Rather, what inspired the young Lee was a real-life story about a secret agent who rationally chose secret identities in order to serve his country. This became Oswald's lifelong ambition, and every indicator shows that Oswald was living out his childhood dream as a spy and informant. Not only is the *evidence* strong that Oswald had a double-life, secretly working for the FBI and the CIA, the *logic* is even stronger. If Oswald's motivation was the pursuit of fame, as the WC claimed, why did he use an alias, "Alek Hidell," to order two guns? When we consider that he sometimes spelled his alias as "Alek James" and "Hydell," it is easy to see that Alek James Hydell is an almost perfect anagram (letter jumble) of "Jekyll And Mr. Hyde." It was his inside joke revealing that he, like Dr. Jekyll, had an alter-ego, just like the drama, *I Led Three Lives*. (Coincidentally, the woman who found Oswald the TSBD job, Ruth Paine, was named "Hyde" before she married.)

To the best of our knowledge, Oswald never committed fraud for personal gain, yet he went to great pains to develop an alias. If, as detractors have painted it, Oswald's obsession was to kill someone famous so that he might *become* famous, why establish an alias? In 1963, unregistered guns were easy to buy, even if you were a defector. If Oswald wanted to trumpet his delusions of historical-significance, why did he "emphatically deny" that he had succeeded in killing the world's most powerful leader? Watch the videos of Oswald in the Dallas Police station: he speaks with intelligence... calmly but justifiably frustrated at being denied due process. If he wanted the world to know him as a powerful man who struck a blow for a Marxist revolution, why did he describe himself as an innocent "patsy"?

Deputy Sheriff Roger Craig saw and heard the captured Oswald close-up in the interrogation room. When Lee realized that his childhood dream of continuing as an undercover agent had now ended, with a sad look, Oswald sighed: "They'll know who I am now." Craig said it was not the triumphant, "smug" proclamation of a crazy killer proud of his crime (as Gerald Posner claimed); it was the sad lament of a man who realized his dreams of a spy career were over. At that point, a future career was the least of Oswald's problems.

Oswald began to realize that he was being railroaded, scapegoated, framed for murder. As mentioned above, the evidence indicates that a Federal agent had asked Oswald to order the Mannlicher-Carcano as a part of a gun-running investigation (and Jack Ruby was a known dealer in illegal guns), and that the FBI had access to Hidell's/Oswald's post office box. It is easy to frame someone when you have advance access to a weapon in his name (or at least in his alias, Hidell).

Lee Harvey Oswald was shot in the Dallas Police Station before he ever spoke to a lawyer. He told the press after his arrest: "I don't know what kind of facts you people have been given—but I emphatically deny these charges!" He was beginning to see that someone had "fed" the police and media bogus facts.

If he had been the killer, he would have known that the rifle and bullets would be traced back to him, as he had the Hidell I.D. in his wallet. The Hidell I.D. matched the Carcano bill of sale, and he knew the police would find the barely-hidden rifle. So if Oswald were the lone assassin, why not raise his fist in the air in front of the army of newsmen and cameras and boast, "I just single-handedly brought down the leader of capitalism! Hail Karl Marx! Hail Castro!"? Instead, he humbly said, "I'm just a patsy." This is the question never answered by the lone-gunman advocates: if he *did* desire to be caught, why spend two days denying his guilt, and if he did *not* want to be caught, why have the incriminating evidence (the Hidell I.D.) in his pocket? If he were willing to kill a police officer to escape, why would he not have carried his pistol to work in a lunchbox? No, he inexplicably wasted time (and money on a taxi) going back to his apartment to retrieve a pistol.

Nothing LHO did or said November 22nd-24th fits the profile of being a glory-seeking assassin or a lone nut hoping to get away with murder. All his words and actions on those days point directly to what he said he was: a framed patsy.

Lie Number 24: Oswald and the CIA: "There was nothing to support the speculation that Oswald was an agent, employee or informant of the.. CIA...."
~*WC Report*, p. 22

How did Lee Harvey Oswald learn Russian so quickly and fluently? Why did he defect to Russia? The Soviets themselves admitted it was *extraordinarily* rare for an American with no family ties in the USSR to do so. Why was he re-admitted to the USA so quickly and easily? How could Oswald be both an anti-Castro activist, and a pro-Castro demonstrator? How did a so-called "nut" like Lee succeed in the military to the point of working in top secret bases? Why did he—or an impostor—visit the Cuban embassy in Mexico a few weeks before the assassination? In that Cold War era, why was this Russian defector and communist "agitator"—who had physically threatened an FBI agent—not considered a security risk by the FBI and Secret Service as they planned the motorcade route? None of the debunkers have offered a reasonable answer to these questions. **Only one answer single-handedly addresses these puzzling questions:** Oswald was, at least for a time, a CIA contract agent and was being "handled" by the Intelligence community.

With all these facts and rumors swirling around, we don't

need a signed memo to know that the CIA was neck-deep in Oswald's life. Allen Dulles, former CIA Director and Warren Commissioner, made it clear that if Oswald had been an agent, no one would officially admit to it. Another Commissioner asked him, "What if we brought a CIA agent in here and put him under oath? Would he lie?" Dulles answered, "A good agent would."

The CIA was all too present wherever Oswald went—New Orleans, Dallas, Mexico City, Japan, Russia. And where he *tried* to go: Cuba. Allen Dulles was fuming mad that JFK had abandoned Dulles' CIA plan to invade Cuba at the Bay of Pigs. Later, with Allen Dulles helping to steer the WC, and with CIA operative E. Howard Hunt a known conspirator, it is absurd to say the CIA was not involved. The CIA had an agent on duty at the Russian Embassy who helped facilitate Oswald's return to the U.S. CIA agent Priscilla Johnson made contact with Oswald in Moscow, and some researchers believe she later helped craft Marina Oswald's "story" post-assassination.

While in the Marines in 1957 and 1958, Oswald was stationed at Atsugi Air Base in Japan, the home of the largest CIA station in the Pacific. Here he was groomed to become a CIA operative, initially with the intent to send him as a sham defector to Russia. He was taught to speak Russian while in Japan (Marina and others in her Soviet town remarked at how well Oswald spoke their language; that he was able to quickly convince Marina to marry him and move with him to the "enemy" U.S. is a testament to his language skill. Jeanne de Mohrenschildt, a friend to the Oswalds in Dallas and a Russian emigre´, was amazed at Oswald's Russian fluency.)

George and Jeanne de Mohrenschildt had their own entanglements with the CIA. Russian-American George de Mohrenschildt befriended Lee in Texas, and was involved with the intelligence community—yet another secret not revealed in the initial investigation.[94] They hosted a small party in their home in February 1963, and in attendance were Lee and Marina Oswald, *and* CIA agent J. Walton Moore. Later, Moore would admit that he knew de Mohrenschildt, but would deny his presence at the party with Oswald just months before the assassination, despite multiple witnesses to the fact. Strangely enough, in the Sixties, Fox news pundit Bill O'Reilly was a local Channel 8 News Reporter in Dallas and went on the air to say, "a recently declassified document now... indicates that Lee Harvey Oswald was employed by the CIA possibly in 1962.... [and] a Dallas CIA agent named J. Walton Moore... told George de Mohrenschildt Lee Harvey Oswald was OK to recommend for a job." (We can only guess why O'Reilly wrote a book claiming there was no conspiracy.) Indeed, it was de Mohrenschildt who landed Oswald a job at the photographic-mapping company, Jaggars-Chiles-Stovall, which routinely did intelligence work, and another attendee at the same party, Ruth Paine, later got Oswald the job at the TSBD. Curiously, de Mohrenschildt was friends with the Bush family and we have warm correspondence between the two Georges: George de M. and soon-to-be CIA Director, George H. W. Bush.

After his arrest in 1963, Oswald's mother immediately asserted that the CIA had sent her son to Russia as a double-agent a few years earlier. Lee's brother, Robert, testified to the WC that their mother emphatically asserted that "...she had knowledge of facts in writing that almost conclusively proved to her that Lee was an agent of the CIA." In that hearing, former CIA Director Dulles quickly changed the subject and called for a recess.[95] Robert Oswald also testified that LHO insinuated to him that he might be a CIA agent. Lee had just returned from an FBI interview where, Lee told Robert, "They asked me was I a secret agent," and when Robert inquired, Lee laughed and said, "Well, don't you know?" Oswald had told his mother, and had assumed she had told his brother, but he was not at liberty to reveal more.

Oswald had curious ties to Cubans, strange contact with the FBI, and an elaborate alias. (We now know the CIA lied to the WC about their assassination plots aimed at communist leaders, including Castro.) The late Jim Garrison, New Orleans District Attorney, linked LHO to Guy Bannister, a former intelligence officer, and to a wealthy international businessman named Clay Shaw, who worked with David Ferrie to send arms to Cuban rebels.[96] CIA Director Richard Helms later admitted Shaw was a contract agent for the CIA. Shaw, David Ferrie, E. Howard Hunt, Frank Sturgis and David Atlee Phillips were all CIA operatives associated with Oswald.[97]

Oswald and Ferrie's connection is strong evidence of a CIA link to Oswald: First, several witnesses have gone on record as having seen Ferrie and Oswald together in Clinton, Louisiana, in 1963. Second, other witnesses saw them together at other times in New Orleans. Third, David Ferrie himself said he knew Oswald. And fourth, the **Associated Press and PBS have both confirmed a photograph of Oswald and David Ferrie standing side by side** when Oswald served in Ferrie's squadron at the Civil Air Patrol camp near Alexandria, Louisiana in 1955 (which may have been when Oswald was first groomed for CIA work).[98]

What kind of work? Mostly infiltrating rightwing anti-Castro groups who were involved in gunrunning—getting weapons and other aid to the anti-communist rebels in Cuba. Four circles of interest overlapped: the Mafia wanted Cuba back for their casinos and other businesses in Havana, the CIA wanted Castro gone and in fact, in 1963, Robert Kennedy and John Kennedy were working secretly toward that goal, having made covert alliances with the third-highest placed official in Cuba: Commander Juan Almeida, head of the Cuban Army.[99] In the overlap of those circles of interest was Jack Ruby, who was attempting to sell arms to the rebels as well as to ingratiate himself to the Mafia casino owners. As we will see in the section on Jack Ruby, there was another layer of overlap, which was Oswald's work at trying to uncover some of this criminal efforts —initially, perhaps, for Naval Intelligence and the FBI, which explains his association with Guy Bannister, formerly with both organizations. At some point, Oswald came to the attention of the CIA (either in his Marine assignment in Japan, or through Bannister's associate, David Ferrie, who was a contract CIA agent). In the end, they realized Lee Oswald would serve them best as a patsy. But they allowed him to believe he was fulfilling his childhood dream of being a double-agent (the sad irony being that everything they asked Lee to do was designed to set him up to appear as a pro-Castro communist sympathizer... when the truth is, he just wanted to serve his country and its President, John F. Kennedy... a man he had expressed great admiration for). He became the perfect fall guy, unwittingly helping the conspirators cover up their own plot. An undercover spy is, of course, going to do his best to cover up even the most trivial evidence of his secret—most do not even tell their own wives the full truth. So it is very difficult to find any other bits of evidence confirming Oswald's secret role... and yet we do:

- Oswald had requested (but never followed through with the paperwork) a formal renunciation of his U.S. citizenship, and he had even told the Russians he would divulge secrets about U.S. radar. Upon return to the U.S., he should have been arrested for treason (with a sentence of life imprisonment or even death). Moreover, the U.S. Immigration and Naturalization Service refused Marina's entrance to the U.S. So despite the fact that Oswald was a self-admitted communist traitor, married to a U.S.-denied Russian citizen whose uncle was in the KGB, they were both allowed back in. According to a Top Secret report to the Warren Commission, the U.S. State Department expedited the Oswalds' return and made, quote, "special pleading... to convince the Immigration and Naturalization Service" to allow Marina to accompany Oswald back to the U.S.A.[100] The U.S. State Department even threw in a $500 "repatriation loan" to facilitate the return trip. This is a "smoking gun" pointing to clear CIA involvement to bring their spy back from Russia. Let those who debate this cite any other case where a traitor was *paid* to return in good standing to this country, with a Russian wife who also violated the INS standards. •Although Oswald was a known defector to Russia, he landed a job with a map and photographic company that required top-secret clearance for its intelligence contracts. •He carried false/alias ID. •A poverty-stricken Oswald owned a rather expensive, miniature Minox camera. The "spy camera" was tiny, easy to hide, and excelled at taking close-up pictures of documents, etc. It was recorded on the Dallas Police's list of evidence but disappeared.[101] Detective Gus Rose reported that the FBI agents "made three different trips to our office to talk to me about this camera," to try to persuade him to change his records. "They said that after they had received all the property they found that I had made a mistake, and that that really wasn't a camera, it was a Minox light meter." Rose was so sure it had been a camera, he refused to alter the records. •Oswald attempted to infiltrate Alpha-66, a Cuban ex-patriate group that planned regular raids and weapons importation aimed at overthrowing Castro. Frank Sturgis, a CIA operative, was not shy in announcing his hatred of Kennedy, and court records (see the *Liberty Lobby* court case) prove his involvement in the Bay of Pigs fiasco and with Alpha-66. This is confirmed by Craig Sheldon of Fairhope, Alabama [incidentally, the town where this author now works] and Kenneth Giddens, a Mobile, Alabama TV-station owner, who were involved in fundraising for the Alpha-66 group. Craig Sheldon was an ex-

Marine well-associated with Antonio Veciana and other CIA-connected Cuban fighters. Sheldon also lived with Jerry Buchanan, who got into a fist fight with Lee Oswald (or his double) in Miami in early 1963. Jerry Buchanan allegedly may have himself used the alias *Oswald* at one point. Sheldon described the CIA of the early sixties as ripe for renegades, saying, "With those fellows, there's never anyone in charge." I spoke with Sheldon's daughter, Megrez Rudolf, who told me that the Cuban freedom groups were highly suspicious of Oswald and cautious of possible infiltration/spying.[102] She cited an example: when her father had travelled to south Florida to meet with them, he coincidentally sported a beard, and when he returned home, he was clean-shaven: the Alpha-66 group had feared that Sheldon's beard revealed a secret pro-Castro sentiment! Sheldon was, in fact, a staunch U.S. patriot and very much anti-Castro. While Sheldon's daughter's knowledge of Oswald is limited, everything her father told her about the Alpha-66 group and its encounters with Oswald indicate they suspected him of duplicity. Oswald's handlers had sent him to spy on the right-wing extremists in Alpha-66; we don't know if the handlers had already identified Oswald as a potential fall guy, but we do know this brought him in contact with Sturgis, spymaster David A. Phillips (aka Maurice Bishop), and Antonia Veciana (the undercover CIA agent who founded Alpha 66).

Lie Number 25: Oswald and the FBI: "There was nothing to support the speculation that Oswald was an agent, employee or informant of the FBI...."
~*WC Report*, p. 22

Within 24 hours of Oswald's arrest, Dallas Police Chief Dallas Police Chief Jesse Curry let this slip in front of TV cameras: "I understand that the FBI did know he [Oswald] was in Dallas." Curry then made it clear that the FBI had not alerted them of the presence of this subversive. A few hours later, Chief Curry tried to retract the statement about the FBI's foreknowledge: "I want to correct anything that might have been misinterpreted or misunderstood regarding information that the FBI might have had about this man." And then, in trying to retract his earlier slip, Curry stuttered and actually repeated the very fact that he was now trying to deny: "I do not know if and when the FBI has interviewed this man... last night someone told me, I don't even know who it was, that the FBI did know this man was in the city, and had interviewed him." (You can view Curry on YouTube... see footnote.)[103]

Oswald's history as a defector and a volatile trouble-maker, and his current job site, were fully-known by the FBI, yet he was allowed access to guns and left unwatched as the President paraded in front of him. This book documents the substantial evidence he was a paid FBI informant (despite Gerald Ford's denial); even the WCR admits the FBI had several interactions with him. Clearly, Chief Curry had been scolded by the FBI or someone for revealing this information, which thus raises the obvious question: *Why would the FBI not have informed the Secret Service that a Soviet defector —in the height of the Cold War— worked in a building overlooking the motorcade route?*

It should also be noted that in the same interviews collected on YouTube, Curry inadvertently revealed that "officialdom" was already imposing their pre-constructed spin-story (of a lone assassin). When asked if a ballistics test had proved that Oswald's rifle was the same one that shot Kennedy, Curry replied, "The ballistics test, we haven't had a final report, but it is... I understand it will be favorable." What a relief to know *in advance* that it would "favor" their railroading of Oswald. Asked again, he repeated, "The ballistics tests are encouraging." Note that this was within 24 hours of finding the rifle, showing it off to reporters Friday evening, and then, as Curry said, having it "shipped to Washington." There had not been enough time to run a full ballistics test, much less report it back to Curry. Even a quick test takes a day, not adding in the time to fly it to Washington, to drive it to and from airports, and then to get word back to a busy Chief Curry. On Saturday, they already know the ballistics test "will be favorable" —*future tense*.

In the "too fast to believe" category: how could the FBI have discovered so quickly that the rifle was ordered from an obscure Chicago mail-order gun shop, under a false name (Oswald's alias, A. Hidell)? Curry admits it was "from a tip." That is a hugely-significant fact that the WC ignored. **Who would have had knowledge of the gun in question,** *and* **of Oswald's secret alias,** *and* **of where it was purchased,** *and* **would want to give that "tip"** to the Dallas police within hours of the crime!? In *Oswald Talked*, reporter Mary La Fontaine presents a strong, documented case that the only person who knew in advance of the *A. Hidell* alias was FBI Agent James Hosty. Hosty knew Oswald, knew of his Russian past, knew he was potentially violent, and, according to La Fontaine, knew of the mail-order rifle. Yet Hosty claims he did not tell any of his FBI colleagues, even as the President made public plans for his motorcade to pass by Oswald's workplace. The point is clear: the FBI knew of A. Hidell and the rifle-order, and of Oswald's defection to Russia, but waited until *after* the shooting to "tip off" local law enforcement.

The FBI's participation in a cover-up continued:
• The FBI mishandled ballistic evidence.
• They denied their knowledge that John Elrod had heard his cellmate, Lee Oswald, speak of Jack Ruby (see Lie Number 33).
• They pressured eye-witnesses to remain silent and/or twisted their testimony to the WC.
• They denied a November 17th FBI teletype warning of an

assassination plot, according to FBI Agent William Walter.[104] And they ignored a warnings by FBI Don Adams and FBI informant William Augustus Somersett, who reported a threat on November 9, 1963, against JFK made by right-wing nut, Joseph Milteer. Milteer had told the FBI undercover agent that JFK was being targeted and that a sniper would strike from the upper window of an office building.

• The FBI destroyed the Department of Defense picture ID... probably because it had been issued to him, strangely, *after* he had defected to Russia.[105]

• The FBI denied the presence of hit-man Mac Wallace's fingerprint on a box from the sniper's nest... despite other fingerprint experts' positive ID.

• They tried to hide the fact that the address Oswald had stamped on his "Fair Play for Cuba" pamphlets also belonged to ex-FBI Agent Guy Banister's office. His office had two door on two streets. Oswald referenced 544 Camp Street, the front entrance; the FBI, in a brief on Guy Banister, used the more obscure address that Oswald and Banister shared on Lafayette Street, to downplay this damning connection. The address commonality was no fluke: Banister's secretary, Delphine Robert, revealed that Banister had told her, "He's with us...."[106] The Banister-Oswald association was corroborated by Delphine Roberts' daughter, and by Banister's aid, Jack Martin... yet "debunkers" still deny the proven connection.

• The FBI disregarded and downplayed their own interview of Jack Martin. Martin was visited by FBI agents Regis Kennedy and Claude Schlager on November 25th, just three days after the death of the President. Martin, a private eye, told them that Banister, David Ferrie and Lee Oswald were all involved in anti-Castro activities together (rather odd for a supposed Communist). This "double-agent" role of Oswald, cavorting with rightwing anti-Communist ex-FBI agent Banister *while* claiming to be pro-Marxist, is consistent with his love of the movie about an FBI double-agent. His paradoxical association with David Ferrie's Cuban exile group is also consistent with what I learned of from Craig Sheldon's family: that Oswald was trying to insert himself into the right-wing Alpha 66 "Free Cuba" movement.

•FBI Director Hoover and Lyndon Johnson were close friends for decades, and lived less than a block away from each other. Hoover had placed pressure on Kennedy in 1960 to put Johnson on the ticket. Hoover hated the Kennedy brothers with a passion. Johnson promised Hoover he would not be forced into mandatory retirement in 1964, while JFK planned to do the opposite. Not surprisingly, then, Hoover orchestrated most of the FBI cover-up regarding Oswald.

•FBI agent Warren deBrueys kept a "confidential informant" file on Oswald. According to ex-FBIer William "Bill" Walter, he and William Sullivan, Deputy Director of the FBI, confirmed that **Oswald was a paid FBI informant**.[107]

Lie Number 26: CIA Involvement in General: "The... Central Intelligence Agency [was] not involved in the assassination of President Kennedy." ~U.S. House of Representatives, Select Committee on Assassinations (HSCA)

The question of the CIA's involvement is, of course, not limited to Oswald. The "fingerprints" of the CIA are found all over this case. CIA agents are the persons best trained to pull off a complex assassination and cover-up such as this.

We are at a disadvantage at pulling back the veil, as it is nearly impossible to reveal much about a super-secret agency like the CIA, whose first talent is subterfuge. Indeed, H.R. "Bob" Haldeman, President Nixon's chief of staff stated, "After

Kennedy was killed, the CIA launched a fantastic cover-up... the CIA literally erased any connection between Kennedy's assassination and the CIA."[108] Haldeman also states in his book that President Nixon asked the FBI to cease investigating E. Howard Hunt (another Watergate conspirator) lest they uncover "that whole Bay of Pigs thing," which Haldeman said was Nixon's reference to the JFK assassination (there is ample evidence the CIA wanted revenge on Kennedy for not backing up the Bay of Pigs invasion with full air power). And we know that the CIA thumbed its nose at the Warren Commission, the HSCA and other congressional oversight committees, stonewalling about Oswald's CIA file and hiding their involvement with him and with the Bay of Pigs fiasco that led up to Dallas 1963.

The Lie above, by the HSCA, is another case of Orwellian double-speak, since we know that Robert K. Tanenbaum, one of the Deputy Chief Counsels for this very same House Committee, uncovered proof of the CIA's complicity and obfuscation (see Lie Number 34).

In addition to inside government sources like Haldeman and Tanenbaum, a few documents survived the paper-shredders and blacked-out sections of FOIA documents, and some witnesses/agents have later come forward, so that we have learned:

• From the late fifties through at least the sixties, the CIA was involved in assassination plots of other world leaders. The CIA had little congressional oversight in 1962-1963; the Agency was crawling with unsupervised divisions and rogue agents who acted with impunity.

• The CIA did work with the Mafia in the early Sixties. Robert Maheu was reportedly the Agency man who negotiated with the Mafia. The overlap of Mafia, CIA, and FBI in the JFK plot and the overlap of Oswald with all three is more than circumstantial evidence.

- We have already mentioned the CIA connections of David Ferrie, David Atlee Phillips, and Oswald. Phillips was a high-level CIA agent who, in the early sixties, worked with anti-Castro Cuban groups (DRE and Alpha-66). Cuban double-agent Antonio Veciana has hinted that Phillips' alias was the agent "Maurice Bishop," who worked with David Ferrie on plots to depose Castro. Ferrie's photo in a New Orleans training camp with Oswald supports Veciana's claim. No surprise, then, that Phillips walked out of a congressional questioning session of the HSCA rather than answer questions that would have incriminated him (or caused him to perjure himself) regarding his involvement with the JFK plot.
- Now we know for a fact that in 1963, the CIA was plotting to kill Fidel Castro... Oswald's associations with Cubans was put into perspective when this was revealed, and the sometimes-too-blind naiveté of patriotic citizens was disabused.
- In addition to ex-CIA director Allen Dulles' work of cover-up on the Warren Commission, we also find that later CIA Director John McCone served on the WC, and CIA deputy director Charles Cabell, whom Kennedy had also fired, was the brother of Earle Cabell, the mayor of Dallas in 1963. Cabell was a close friend to LBJ.
- CIA Deputy Director James Jesus "Jim" Angleton tried to shift blame for the JFK plot to the USSR, saying, without any evidence, that Russian defector Yuri Nosenko was a lying double-agent because he claimed Oswald was not a Russian sympathizer. After glasnost, KGB papers show no evidence that Oswald was a Russian spy. Angleton and Richard Helms, CIA Deputy Director at the time, both knew the truth of the CIA's involvement.
- In a libel trial between E. Howard Hunt and the *Spotlight* newspaper, a jury concluded that Hunt, a CIA operative, was guilty of conspiracy to assassinate President Kennedy. Mark

Lane proved in court that CIA contract agents Victor Marchetti and Robert Morrow said Hunt was involved. The forewoman of the jury, Leslie Armstrong, stated that "Mr. Lane was asking us to do something very difficult. He was asking us to believe that John Kennedy had been killed by our own government. Yet when we examined the evidence, we were compelled to conclude that the CIA had indeed killed President Kennedy."[109] Moreover, Hunt confessed his involvement on a deathbed video (widely available on the internet), and also named Frank (Fiorini) Sturgis as one of the plotters.[110] Hunt and Sturgis had both been convicted of burglarizing the Democratic National Committee headquarters at the Watergate motel in 1972. The Rockefeller Commission admitted that Hunt was a CIA operative in 1963 and that he was out on "sick leave" on November 22nd, but denied that Sturgis was an agent.[111] Yet Sturgis later admitted that he had been an agent, and told a newspaper reporter that Jack Ruby had been part of the plot.[112] The two are connected by their association with the President who followed Johnson: Sturgis later worked for Richard Nixon; Jack Ruby had earlier worked for then-Senator Richard Nixon's staff.[113] Republican strategist Roger Stone, who worked on Richard Nixon's staff in the seventies, confirms that when Nixon was a congressman, Lyndon Johnson asked him to hire on Jacob Leon Rubenstein (alias Jack Ruby) in 1947.[114]

Sturgis was probably **not** one of the "three tramps" arrested by Dallas police, as widely rumored.[115] But he certainly was involved in the JFK plot. Whether he was actually present in Dallas on November 22nd is irrelevant. Jim Buchanan reported that Sturgis had been a CIA operative embedded in the Free Cuba movement, and had met Lee Harvey Oswald in Miami shortly before the assassination.[116] Sturgis also knew Oswald and Ruby and confessed CIA assassin E. Howard Hunt. Another CIA document, declassified in 1993, proves Sturgis had been a paid operative of the agency (proving again that government investigatory committees like the Rockefeller Commission and the HSCA were either fooled by the CIA, or did not dig deep enough).

Of course, we knew this from multiple sources even before the declassified documents and before Hunt spilled the beans in his dying confession. Hunt also named the following CIA (and Mafia) entanglements with Oswald and the JFK plot: Cord Meyer was the CIA agent in charge of the disinformation campaign, Operation Mockingbird, and coincidentally, the husband of Mary Meyer, JFK's mistress (who was murdered shortly after telling people she knew the secret of the assassination plot); CIA agent William Harvey was connected to Mafia figures Santos Trafficante and Sam Giancana; and David Morales, CIA hit man. As with all the testimonies of questionable characters, they are worthless if they do not correlate with other witnesses and other pieces of evidence. But when it comes to CIA involvement with Oswald, the Cuban exile community, and the events of November 22, we have such corroborations in spades. (Also see Lie Number 31)

Lie Number 27: Officer J.D. Tippit's slaying: "There is no question of Oswald's guilt in this case when you look at his murder of Tippit."
~Gerald Posner on *ABC News*

No question? Nothing *but* questions. Most JFK researchers, including this writer, believe that Oswald was an undercover operative who, shortly after the shooting, realized his role was "patsy." As such, it is possible that Oswald shot Tippit in self-defense while running for his life. Thus, it is bad logic to claim that proving Oswald killed Tippit would *ipso facto* prove he killed JFK... yet the WC and its defenders make exactly that jump of (faulty) logic. And in further contradiction to Posner's lie, above, we shall see that **the events surrounding the Tippit slaying point to another cover-up**— not proof of Oswald's guilt in *either* murder. I pity the debunkers like Bugliosi, McAdams and Posner: from their perspective, how frustrating it must be that *every* aspect of the Kennedy mystery is riddled with contradictory testimony, flawed evidence, inconsistencies in timing and three new questions raised for every one question answered. No wonder Posner claims there is "no question" in the Tippit matter: that is their sweet-dream fantasy, to have something—anything—in this case that was open and shut. Pure fantasy. Reality is far more complicated.

Before 1:15 pm, within minutes of JFK's death, Dallas Policeman J. D. Tippit was killed a mile from Lee Harvey Oswald's apartment. At 1:45 pm, Oswald was arrested in a nearby armed with a pistol. Several eyewitnesses later claimed they had seen a man who "looked like" Oswald at the scene of the Tippit shooting. Several of those witnesses picked Oswald out of a line-up. It seems like an easy conviction... but as ESPN's Coach Lee Corso was famous to quip, "Not so fast, my friend!" Upon closer examination, we find a mixed bag of conflicting testimonies and flawed physical evidence. Eyewitness statements differ greatly as to how many shots were fired, how many men were present, the description of the assailant, etc. Picking him out of a line-up is irrelevant: •First: it is possible that Oswald was at the scene but not guilty of the shooting: if Tippit and Ruby were co-conspirators with Oswald, Tippit may have been another fall guy in the conspiracy. Patsies—scapegoats—usually end up dead, but not at the hands of another patsy. As Oswald was herded past reporters in the Dallas police station, he stated, "I didn't shoot anybody." His denial was later analyzed using a lie-detecting device that measures truth by voice stress, the Psychological Stress Evaluator (PSE). The PSE has been shown to be as reliable as a polygraph in several studies, and is used by law enforcement agencies—even acceptable as evidence in court. PSE tests done years later on the news-tapes of Oswald's statement indicate he was likely telling the truth: he had not shot anyone. •Second: the line-up was rigged (see Lie Number 4). Most eyewitnesses were unsure, expressing serious doubts even as they pointed out Oswald. •Third: the only witness who actually saw the shooting up close was Helen Markham—and a WC Counsel made a note in his report that she was not a solid witness. Fourth, other witnesses described an entirely different-looking suspect. So it is unlikely that Oswald would have been convicted of Tippit's murder based on "eyes." Fifth and sixth: next we will see there were other serious problems in the Tippit case with **ballistics** and **timing**.

An Interlude and Apology: Let me be careful not to impugn the character of any law enforcement officer—they have my utmost respect. Across the years, I've personally known many fine policemen and FBI agents—noble heroes. But as with all humans and all institutions, a few bad apples are in the law enforcement barrel. We would be foolish to investigate a complex crime like this and have blind trust of officers when so much went wrong. With apologies to anyone we may wrongfully accuse via "guilt by association," we must say: the actions of *a few* of the Dallas Police and Sheriff's department, and the FBI and Secret Service, were certainly not ideal. And often suspect. In the case of officer J. D. Tippit, many people view him as a hero, the first to attempt to arrest Kennedy's killer. But all honest cops are heroes the moment they put their badges on... they all risk their lives for us. With that said, we cannot be forbidden to ask questions in this case. To inquire as to what prior connections Tippit may have had with Jack Ruby, Oswald and others does not necessarily make him a co-conspirator. Maybe he just knew too much and had to be silenced, or maybe he was an unwitting dupe... or maybe he took a bullet trying to do the right thing. Since Tippit, Ruby and Oswald are all dead, we just don't know.

What we do know about the Tippit shooting: J. D. Tippit had begun the last day of his life by hugging his son, Allan, while saying, "No matter what happens today, I want you to know that I love you." No dangerous assignment awaited him, and he had never before made such an expression of morbid tenderness to his son on the way to work.[117] This was only the beginning of Tippit's odd behavior that day. Before and after the assassination, the Officer's patrol behavior was abnormal: he was seen at times driving very slowly (even stopping at a record store and making a personal phone call), at other times in a frantic hurry, making unexpected stops. Though taking time for a personal phone call, he was surprisingly quiet with his police radio—even when spotting a suspicious suspect. Though Tippit was assigned to the Oak Cliff area, which included the section of town where Oswald lived, it is a huge area of Dallas, so it is quite a coincidence that Tippit just happened upon Oswald—at a spot closer to Jack Ruby's apartment than to Lee's rooming-house. Did he drive up to Oswald and speak to him based on the vaguest of descriptions? He had not been given Oswald's name or address. Or was the suspect whom Tippit questioned someone else, someone who looked a bit like Oswald, or even a prior acquaintance of the Officer's?

The "smoking gun" in the Tippit affair—indicating a conspiracy—is found within this piece of WC testimony by Oswald's landlady, Earline Roberts. She saw a police car pull in front of the rooming-house and beep its horn twice, as if summoning Oswald (which is impossible, because the police department did not yet send out this address to the squad cars):

Mr. BALL. Did this police car stop directly in front of your house?
Mrs. ROBERTS. Yes--it stopped directly in front of my house and it just went "tip-tip" [two short horn blows]....
Mr. BALL. Where was Oswald when this happened?
Mrs. ROBERTS. In his room.
Mr. BALL. It was after he had come in his room?
Mrs. ROBERTS. Yes.
Mr. BALL. Had that police car ever stopped there before?
Mrs. ROBERTS. I don't know--I don't remember ever seeing it....
Mr. BALL. You remembered the number of the car?
Mrs. ROBERTS. I think it was 106, it seems...like it was 106."

The number "10" on the side of Tippit's patrol car was much smaller than the text curved around it: "DALLAS POLICE"... and since Mrs. Roberts was blind in one eye and weak in the other, a slight double-vision of the zero could have appeared to her (looking from a distance as well as trying to remember after the fact) to be a "6." Since **no other patrol car was anywhere near her home at that point in time**, the odds seem very, very high that this was Tippit's car. She did say there were *two* men in the car—but Tippit had a police jacket on a hanger in his car that day, and again, at a glance from a distance looking through reflective car windows, her bad eyes may have mistaken the hanging jacket for a second officer. Or there may have been another person in the car, considering several witnesses saw, minutes later at the shooting, *two* men with Tippit. Ms. Roberts also states that the FBI changed her statement from saying the car number was "106 or 107" to "**2**07." Did the FBI change the number "1" to a "2," to make the number less like Tippit's Number 10? Whatever the case, bad eyesight or not, there can be no doubt that Earline Roberts saw a black police car. According to police records, all cars in the area were accounted for—only Tippit's black car was known to be within blocks of Oswald's rooming-house at that time. This alone is strong evidence pointing to a conspiratorial plan: without prior association with Oswald, how and why would anyone—within 25 minutes of the assassination—know to send a police car to Oswald's rooming-house, where he was registered with the alias, O. H. Lee? (In fact, the first address searched by police was Marina's lodging with Ruth Paine, not the rooming-house.) This does not exonerate Oswald of Tippit's murder, but it does tell us that something is rotten in Denmark... that some member of the police department knew Oswald intimately (to have advance knowledge of his "alias" address and his timing). The rooming-house visit and horn-blow and the encounter with Oswald (if it happened) on an irrelevant side-street points to the likelihood that Oswald was being set-up to be shot by a policeman while "fleeing."

Witnesses to Tippit's shooting say that when he stopped his squad car to speak with a man who roughly matched the broad description sent out by police dispatch radio just minutes earlier, the officer and the suspect seemed calm. Instead of running, the suspect bent into the window, leaning on his hands that rested partway inside the car. If this "fugitive" had not known Officer Tippit, he would have run away at first sight of the patrol car, knowing the officer would have to open the driver's door, climb out and run around the car to catch him. Or, why did he not initially shoot the officer through the window while he still had the element of surprise? If Tippit did not know the man, and if he believed him to fit the description of the fugitive assassin — possibly a man who just killed the President—then why did he not report to dispatch, quickly by radio, that he was about to leave his car and question a possible suspected *killer*? An hour earlier, the officer had done exactly that—reported to HQ that he was leaving the car for a moment—but on a non-hazardous call: speaking to a woman before the Dealey Plaza shootings. But now, pursuing a killer, he calmly pulls up to a strange man, keeps his gun holstered, and fails to report in. After speaking to the man through the window and determining the suspect was worth further questioning, why did Tippit (patrolling alone) not draw his weapon as he got out of the squad car? But as he calmly began to walk around the front of his squad car, Tippit was shot three times in the chest and fell to the concrete, unmoving. The assailant then coldly walked over and shot the fallen officer, execution style, in the head. This behavior does not match the behavior of a fleeing fugitive, full of panic and eager to run away as quickly as possible: he had to walk around the car to waste another bullet—and Oswald was arrested with only a few bullets left. **These *four* shots seem more like the action of someone whose chief concern was silencing Tippit and/or trying to further frame Oswald.** This murderous behavior does not match the personality of Oswald, according to his mother, wife and brother, who refused to believe he was a cold-blooded killer (temper, yes, hate-filled violence, no). Buell Wesley Frazier, who regularly drove Oswald to work at the Depository, said this about Oswald when interviewed for the documentary, "The Men Who Killed Kennedy": "The individual that I know as Lee Harvey Oswald, I don't think had it in him to be a person capable of committing such a crime as murdering the President of the United States. I'll always believe that. The side I saw of him was a very kind and loving man." The extra, unnecessary shot to Officer Tippit does, however, fit the profile of a cruel and trigger-happy Mafia hit man... and such a man lived just a mile from the shooting: Jack Ruby. Ruby also fits the description of Tippit's killer as given by a woman named Acquilla Clemons, who described the assailant as "short and kind of heavy... kind of chunky." Thus begins a list of several *non sequiturs*, lies and misleading "conclusions" by the WC and its defenders regarding the evidence surrounding Tippit's murder... including our next, related Lie: *Timing*.

Lie Number 28: Timing of the Tippit Shooting: Officer Tippit called the Police Dispatcher at 1:08 p.m., therefore Oswald had time to arrive to kill him at 1:15 pm. ~Vincent Bugliosi, in *Reclaiming History*

The first Dallas police department transcript of radio transmissions was released in 1964 and falsely attributed two transmissions made at 1:08 pm to Officer Tippit, Unit 78. If true, this would mean he didn't encounter his assailant until *after* 1:08—which would support the other timing lie: the WC Report tells us Oswald shot Tippit at 1:15 pm. But once again, the WC had to gerrymander the facts to place Oswald at the crime scene in time. Four months later, the FBI released a more accurate transcript that correctly attributed the transmissions to two other policemen, Unit 58 and Unit 488—not Tippit.[118] In the seventies, copies of the actual Dallas police radio recordings became available which **confirmed** the FBI transcript was correct—the two 1:08 pm transmissions had *not* come from Tippit's squad car, Unit 78. For whatever reason, this lone cop did not call-in to dispatch as he slowly pulled over to talk to a possible assassin.

The best evidence points to the Tippit murder happening *before* 1:15, making it impossible for Oswald to have been there. Until apprehended by police in a theatre, Oswald was last seen headed a different direction from the Tippit murder: waiting for a bus, a mile away, at about **1:04 pm**. The timing established by radio dispatch and by the best witnesses indicates that Tippit first encountered his killer at the *same* time Oswald was at his bus stop. This we can be sure of: Oswald and his near-twin were repeatedly spotted in TWO places *at the same time*. From the moment the motorcade started until the time Oswald was arrested, there are reports of simultaneous sightings in different locations. The striking thing is, the people who had prior associations with Oswald and truly knew what he looked like did NOT see him fire the weapons involved in either murder, but saw him elsewhere. The dispatch record and at least six people place the Tippit shooting at about 1:06 pm, which means he would have first driven up alongside his assailant at 1:02. And to repeat: Oswald had been sighted by his landlady at 1:04 pm.

    The contemporaneous affidavit by Tippit murder witness Helen Markham places the shooting at **1:06 pm**. Markham was walking to catch the 1:12 pm bus for work and thus had studied the clock before leaving her home. A second person arguing against the Commission's late-shooting-time was Deputy Sheriff Roger Craig, who testified that when he heard the news that an officer had been shot, he looked at his watch and noted the time was **1:06** pm. A third witness: T. F. Bowley's sworn estimate of the timing matches Helen Markham's within a minute. He looked at his watch when he stopped his car near the fallen officer: 1:10 pm (Commission Exhibit #2003). But witness Domingo Benavides' statement tells us that the actual shooting was committed a few minutes *before* Bowley's arrival, thus still placing Bowley's timing of the shooting at, again, **1:06**. There are more timing confirmations: after an ambulance was summoned and Tippit's body was loaded and driven to Memorial Hospital a mile and a half north, and after the doctors tried to revive him, Doctor Ligdori declared him dead at 1:15 pm... a fourth corroboration that he was shot closer to **1:06** pm than at the later time claimed by the WC. Yet a fifth timing collaboration comes from Mrs. Donald Higgins, who lived near the Tippit shooting. Because she was watching TV and heard the time announced just before hearing the shots, she felt confident in also placing the time of the officer's death at 1:06 pm. She saw a man running away with a handgun who did not look like Oswald.

    And a sixth timing collaboration is the police dispatch record.

Tippit pulled up to a pedestrian, had a brief conversation at the window, then got out of his squad car and took several steps, whereupon he was shot, and then his killer walked closer and shot again. These events took time. After that, all of the witnesses (who were at some distance away or came upon the scene in progress) reacted slowly, out of fear, waiting for the shooter to casually empty his gun and leave the scene at a fast *walk*. The witnesses sat frightened and horrified, waiting until the gunman was out of sight before going to Tippit's aid. When Benavides was finally brave enough to do so, and saw that Tippit was likely dead, he climbed inside the police car to use the radio to call for help. But he did not know how to work the police radio, so he then had to slide back out of the car, whereupon another late-arriving witness climbed into the car and began to work the radio, and Dispatch recorded his call for help at 1:16 pm. All of this took several minutes, so moving backwards in time from the police radio log, the best estimate for **an initial encounter with the pedestrian is at 1:04 pm**. But Oswald was a mile away, within eyesight of his landlady at that time.

This would utterly destroy the WC house of cards, so they proclaimed the timing of the shooting of Tippit to be 1:15. Their time is based on Benavides calling the dispatcher at lightning speed upon witnessing the shooting—but that is not what happened. Benavides reported—three times in the WC transcript—that there was a delay before anyone contacted Dispatch: he had ducked down on the floor boards of his truck for a few minutes to wait for the murderer to flee, so as to not be shot himself. Then Benavides had trouble operating the police radio. A later arriving witness, T. F. Bowley, got out of his car and walked up to the patrol car, where he discovered Benavides struggling to operate the police radio. Bowley took the microphone from Benavides and radioed in the distress call, which confirms that several minutes had passed after the shooting before dispatch was reached... and not surprisingly, Bowley was never called to testify by the WC.

All of this establishes beyond any doubt that **Tippit had encountered his assailant by 1:05 pm at the latest.** So is there anyway Oswald could have made it "in time" from his rooming-house to the police car window—a distance of over a mile?

A good, trained athlete who runs daily can run a mile in 5 minutes; an average young man in street shoes would take about 9 minutes to jog it... but if Oswald were trying to keep a low profile, he would not have been running (and no one saw him running). WC counsel David Belin made the walk himself and timed it at 17 minutes to get to the crime scene; a "debunker" claims the shortest route would only take 13.5 minutes.[119]

As stated, Oswald had been last seen waiting for a bus at the corner of Beckley and Zang at **1:04 pm**, by his landlady, Earline Roberts—who was quite confident about the time.[120] Thus, even if we generously accept that Oswald walked briskly in only 13 minutes, the earliest possible arrival time he could have encountered Tippit would have been 1:17... by which time the officer was already laying dead in the street.[121] Even if you discount Earline Roberts' testimony, every bit of evidence (including the WC's own report) points to Oswald not having had enough time to: flee the Depository (at 12:34) on foot for blocks, board a bus near the TSBD (at 12:40) and ride until stalled in a traffic jam, then walk back to the bus station and transfer to a taxi, then exit the taxi blocks from his boarding house (at 12:54), head south on Beckley, but since his apartment was north, shortly reverse course and head home, then go inside (1:01) to change clothes, grab a pistol and bullets, throw on a different jacket, then go the opposite direction and wait at a bus stop within eyesight of his apartment (1:04), then reverse direction and hustle over a mile's distance to end up on Tenth

Street... simply impossible to arrive by 1:04 or even 1:06 pm, when he was first spotted by Officer Tippit. This last appointment is impossible, but even the above times are "optimistic," possible only if Oswald was moving very, very quickly at every step in his journey. Most of the reports often mention him pausing, waiting, standing, offering his cab to a lady. So the times given have finite time limits supported by hard evidence and the realities of the distances involved. The only way Oswald could get from the bus stop at 1:04 and magically to Tenth Street to be seen by Tippit before 1:06 is to be beamed there by Scottie and the Star Trek transporter beam.

There is a simpler explanation: cabdriver William Whaley's description of "Oswald" was so changeable and unclear, he may well have had the "Oswald double" in his cab. This passenger left Whaley's cab at 12:54, not far from where Tippit was shot: the perfect time and distance for this conspirator (not needing to detour to a rooming house) to have walked to the spot on Tenth and shot Tippit in an effort to frame Oswald further—knowing that bullet casings would later be swapped in evidence to implicate Oswald's gun...which leads to our next Lie.

Lie Number 29: Tippit continued: Ballistics: The four shells found on the scene "were matched, to the exclusion of any other gun, to Oswald's revolver."
~WC Report, p. 278

Oswald "speaks to Tippit through the right window vent. He is hostile... Oswald pulls out his .38 and fires four bullets in rapid succession."
~Bill O'Reilly in Killing Kennedy, p. 280

In 2012 and 2013, the lies continue. With his new book, Bill O'Reilly was not attempting to prove the lone gunman theory...

he was just selling sensationalistic old lies and throwing in new ones on the eve of the 50th Anniversary of the crime. He is *Killing Truth*. His statement above is one of several invented fictions in his "non-fiction" book; witnesses report the exact opposite of O'Reilly's claims. Whoever was speaking to Tippit through the patrol car window was not described as "hostile," but as calm and familiar (see Lie Number 27). Nor did the assailant fire four bullet in rapid succession... the witnesses say he fired three shots, paused, then walked around the car to make a fourth shot into the officer's head (like a Mafia hit). Why does O'Reilly tell this and other lies? What is his motivation to contradict witnesses and create accounts out of whole cloth?

Just as with every piece of evidence in this case, there are more ambiguities and mistakes in evidence-handling than there are definite answers:

• The initial police report from the scene said the bullet casings were from an "automatic" pistol; Oswald's gun was a manual revolver. The bullets from these two disparate weapons are noticeably different.

• Only one of the four bullets from Tippit's body was able to be even *partially* matched with Oswald's gun... an iffy match at best. Firearms expert Cortlandt Cunningham examined the one bullet removed from Tippit's body (referred to by the Commission as exhibit Q13). Cunningham reported: "The bullet Q13 is so badly mutilated that there are not sufficient individual microscopic characteristics present for identification purposes."[122]

• The shell casings in evidence did not match the casings found on the scene by Barbara and Virginia Davis and by Domingo Benavides, handed over to Officer J.M. Poe. Poe had marked the empty shell casings with his initials, "JMP," but the shells held in evidence that matched Oswald's revolver had no such markings.[123]

- The WC never asked Benavides to view/ identify the shells in evidence to see if they matched the ones he had found. And "Barbara and Virginia Davis could not identify their shells when asked to do so."[124]
- Oswald's gun misfired in a struggle with a police officer in the movie theatre. Settled into a cinema seat with time to think, Oswald had realized that he was being set-up as a dupe, likely to be "shot while escaping." So he pulled his gun on Officer Maurice McDonald in the theater in self-defense. If Oswald's intent was to kill the officer, he had ample time to have shot before the officer reached him—he was seated five chairs in from the aisle. The officer's hand actually hit the gun's hammer and made it pull back and release, but not with enough impact to explode the firing cap.

So again the Warren Commission scenario is hard to swallow: that Oswald, running for his life, saw a police car moving slowly toward him and instead of dashing sideways through yards with a head start from an officer seated in a car, he calmly walked over to the window and chatted with him, his hands on the window sill rather than keeping one hand behind him near his gun; the officer calmly got out with his gun initially holstered and began to walk toward him; Oswald shot him three times in the chest and Tippit collapsed to the concrete; then Oswald took time to walk around the car to shoot the slain officer in the head... they claim.

Domingo Benavides was another witness to the murder of Officer Tippit who described a man who did not resemble Oswald: "I remember the back of his head seemed like his hairline sort of went square instead of tapered off...it kind of went down and squared off and made his head look flat in back." This is the opposite of how most people would describe the back of Oswald's head and hairline.

Here we must make an additional point: Posner and other

Warren defenders dismiss as "not credible" the witnesses who indicate someone besides, or in addition to, Oswald, was present at the Tippit shooting. He relegates Acquilla Clemons, who described Tippit's assailant as "short and... chunky," to a footnote, merely claiming "such statements... have internal inconsistencies" without offering any support for his dismissal of her. The usual justification Posner gives for ignoring testimony is that some witnesses changed their accounts over time. Perhaps in a normal case, this might be a reason to disregard testimony. But the pressure brought to bear on these contrary witnesses was great: the media and official story line were claiming it had to be Oswald, and even more ominously, reports of witnesses being beaten, killed or threatened created a climate of fear. This is a salient aspect of the Tippit case:
• Domingo Benavides reports that he has been repeatedly threatened by police, and advised not to talk about what he saw.
• Benavides' look-a-like brother was shot in the head. Domingo's father-in-law, J.W. Jackson, was shot at in his home two weeks later. Warren Reynolds, the amiable used car man, was making history. • Another witness, Warren Reynolds, was not able to identify Oswald as the slayer of Tippit... until he was shot at, whereupon he changed his mind. • A young hoodlum named Darrell Wayne Garner was arrested for the murder attempt on Benavides, but he had an alibi, a girlfriend named Nancy Jane Mooney, a stripper at Jack Ruby's Carousel Club. Garner was freed but his alibi. Mooney, was not so lucky: she was found dead, hung, in the Dallas city jail. In such a climate of fear, we should not be surprised that many witnesses altered their testimony—and in light of that fact, it makes far more sense to believe their earliest testimonies (before fear/pressure caused them to waffle). And in almost every case of fluctuating eyewitness reports, the earliest testimonies point to a conspiracy, and the latter, fear-induced, statements tend to support the

slanted Warren Commission.

The WC never called Acquilla Clemons to testify. Admittedly, she was not watching the exact moment the shots were fired, but she had observed the police car, Tippit, and his assailants, immediately before and after. Clemons did not seek publicity: independent investigators found her when knocking on doors in the neighborhood of the shooting. She was initially reluctant to speak, as she had been threatened, she says, by two armed officers who warned her that if she spoke to the WC she "might get killed." Her testimony would have given a jury great pause in trying to convict Oswald as a lone perpetrator: she saw *two* men near the police car just before the shooting, one which she described as "kind of chunky... kind of heavy," a description which does not fit Oswald at all. Mrs. Clemons said the man with a gun went off in one direction and the second man in another. She described the man with the gun as "short and kind of heavy" and wearing "khaki and a white shirt" —a description which does not fit Oswald at all. The second man, she said, was thin and tall rather than short, a description which could refer to Oswald... or any number of other young men in the 1960's.

Just as at the JFK crime scene, someone wanted us to believe that Oswald had been at the Tippit scene. FBI Agent James Hosty stated that FBI agent Robert Barrett showed him a wallet, picked up at the Tippit murder scene, that contained both an Oswald ID and an Alek Hidell ID card. Obviously, if true, this was another planted piece of evidence, since Dallas police arrest records show that Oswald's real wallet **was on his person when arrested** at the theatre. A TV video of the Tippit crime scene shows a wallet being picked up from the street. Critics claim it to be Tippit's, but do not explain why anyone would have removed Tippit's wallet yet just left it laying on the pavement, nor do they explain how Agent Barrett saw a second Oswald wallet.

Some eyewitnesses described a second man present who did

not match Oswald, and other witnesses were more inclined to believe it was a man whose size resembled Oswald but with darker hair and a different color jacket. Next Oswald fled to a movie theatre where he was apprehended. As a policemen moved toward him there was ample time for this "bloodthirsty" Oswald to shoot, but he did not. He instead waited until several officers surrounded him and grabbed him before he pulled his weapon, and as a policeman's hand was grabbing his revolver, the hammer on the gun was flipped and the gun was wrested from his hand. Again and again, we see "two Oswalds," with different behavior patterns: one seemingly blood-thirsty, rash, impetuous; the other calm and polite. No doubt Oswald had a temper—but that's far from abnormal for a young Marine! Until November 22nd, Oswald had never hurt anyone. The WC presents an oscillating scenario of a man who is calm at times, panicked at other times, trigger-happy and ruthless with one cop, but moments later slow to fire on another; shooting the President one minute, assisting someone to find a telephone three minutes afterward or offering his taxi cab to a lady shortly after that.

Jack Tatum, sitting in his red 1964 Ford Galaxy a block east, noticed a man turn and walk toward the police car. Tatum turned left onto 10th Street and drove slowly west past Tippit's car. Tippit was then talking to the man through the passenger side car window. Tatum said, "it looked as if Oswald and Tippit were talking to each other. There was a conversation. It did seem peaceful. It was almost as if Tippit knew Oswald [or his double—*ed*.]," Tatum said. Which leads to our next Lie.

Lie Number 30: Tippit, Ruby & Oswald: There is "no evidence that Officer J. D. Tippit was acquainted with either Ruby or Oswald." ~*WCR Summary*, p. 369

Several credible witnesses claim Ruby knew Patrolman J. D.

Tippit and/or Oswald: •Dallas Police Lt. George Arnett said that Tippit and Ruby knew each other. •Harold Richard Williams, a chef at another Dallas club, had also seen them together in Tippit's patrol car. The Dallas Police told Williams not to repeat this, with threat of arrest. •Andrew Armstrong, an employee of the Carousel, testified that Ruby knew J. D. Tippit. •Larry Crafard, an employee of the Carousel, testified that Ruby knew Tippit. •Jack Hardee, Jr., said Tippit was "a frequent visitor to Ruby's night club" •Eva Grant, Ruby's sister, said "Jack knew him, and I knew him (Tippit)." The Commission's denial of this was later proven false; there was another policeman with the last name of Tippit, but most of the witnesses knew the difference. The other Tippit did not go by the name/initial, "J.D." •Reporter Thayer Waldo and author Mark Lane were both told of a two hour meeting held in Jack Ruby's Carousel Club about a week before the assassination, with three men present: Ruby, rightwing activist Bernard Weissman, and J.D. Tippit. George Senator told reporters that Ruby had tried to contact Weissman after the assassination.[125] •Dorothy Kilgallen, a columnist and TV personality (famous for the show, "What's My Line?"), interviewed Jack Ruby privately... he told friends at his trial that she was the only reporter he trusted. Kilgallen told friends that Ruby and Tippit had indeed been associates, seen talking business together at Ruby's club. Within days of saying this, Kilgallen was dead of an overdose.[126] •Tippit had been employed part-time as a security guard at Austin's Barbeque, and the owner of the BBQ was a good friend of Ruby's. •Mary Dowling reported that two days before the assassination, J.D. Tippit was having coffee at the Dobbs House Restaurant where she was a waitress. Another customer complained loudly about his order of eggs. Tippit, a frequent customer, noticed the incident but said nothing. The man complaining was later identified by the owner and employees of the Dobbs House as

"Lee Harvey Oswald," and that Tippit and Oswald (or his double) were there many times.

Photographer Al Volkland and his wife, Lou, both knew J. D. Tippit. They reported that 15 or 20 minutes after the assassination, they saw (and waved at) Officer Tippit sitting in his police car at a Gloco gas station in Oak Cliff, watching the cars coming over the Houston Street viaduct. Three employees of the Gloco station verified the Volklands' account. They said Tippit stayed at the station for "about 10 minutes, somewhere between 12:45 and 1:00, then he went tearing off down Lancaster at high speed" in the direction of the apartments of Ruby and Oswald in Oak Cliff. Police radio logs do not show any contact with Tippit at that point, and no specific description of Oswald had been issued, so what prompted Tippit's shift from placid to frantic? Cabdriver Whaley testified that he drove Oswald across the Houston Street viaduct, right past the Gloco station, at approximately the same time Tippit was there. Another meaningless coincidence in the case? Or instead, is it an explanation? If Tippit, Ruby and Oswald had been entangled in a plot of some sort, it is quite possible that the officer spotted Oswald (or Oswald's near-double) in the cab and chased after him for a rendezvous —not knowing that he was marked for death just as Oswald was.

Here I ask the reader to indulge the speculative nature of the previous paragraph, because, to again state the obvious, Ruby, Oswald and Tippit took the absolute facts about what transpired to their grave. No one, not me nor Posner, can know the absolute facts and details of the Tippit murder. But this we do know: the evidence to convict Oswald as a cop killer was flimsy, based on conflicting and vague eye-witnesses and suspicious ballistics, with unsolvable timing issues. If anything, the trails around Tippit lead to Ruby. And a short trail it literally was: Tippit died within a few blocks of Ruby's apartment.

Lie Number 31: Ruby as Rube: "There is no credible evidence that Jack Ruby was active in the criminal underworld."
~*The Warren Commission Report*, Appendix 12

Gerald Posner (who also loves the phrase, "no credible evidence") and the WC would have us believe that Jack Ruby was just an ordinary rube like me or you who let his emotions get the best of him, who had a freak one-in-a-million chance to be at the right time and place to kill Oswald and "be a hero." And they would have us believe that his many associations with Mafioso members in multiple cities over a lifetime is mere coincidental trivia. Personally, because of my various very-public careers (pastor, author and rock musician), I have known literally *thousands* of people—including many, many nightclub owners—but **not a single one of them is in the Mafia**. Ruby, by contrast, had a multitude of connections to "the Mob," and in many cities (Chicago, Dallas, New Orleans, Havana), beginning in childhood and continuing even past the moment he shot Oswald. His first visitor in jail was a Mafia leader (to reassure him that if he kept his mouth shut, nothing bad would happen to his family?). Considering the plethora of "one-in-a-million" coincidences in the JFK nexus, we have to ask: Is it just sheer coincidence that Oswald was "hit" by a man who had friendships with other "hit men" and with the kind of people who order "hits"?

Seth Kantor was a highly-respected Washington correspondent for Scripps-Howard newspapers and accompanied President Kennedy on the Dallas trip. He had encountered Jack Ruby at Parkland Hospital during the time the "pristine bullet" was found on a hospital stretcher. Kantor personally knew Ruby before the shooting. He shook hands and spoke with Ruby at the hospital, so he had no doubt.[127] Yet the WC refused to believe his testimony. Wilma Tice told the FBI that she, too, had seen Jack Ruby at Parkland. The WC encouraged her not to testify to this, but she did anyway— boldly. Contrary to the Commission's denial, she saw Ruby face-to-face from three feet away, around 1 pm that day, and even heard him being called "Jack." Tice said she had been threatened by phone callers not to testify.

Since the WC refused to believe his testimony, newsman Kantor spent more than a decade investigating the background of Ruby, culminating in his 1978 book, *Who Was Jack Ruby?* In it, this outstanding reporter accused the WC of ignoring evidence that Ruby was connected to the Mafia. His ironclad proof was totally disregarded by Posner in his chapter on Ruby (though eventually Posner was forced to admit that Kantor *had* seen Ruby at Parkland). Neither Posner nor the WC ever satisfactorily answered these questions:

•Why was a member of the Marcello crime organization dining with Ruby the evening before the JFK assassination... and why was the same Mafia-member the first person to visit Ruby after he had been jailed for killing Oswald?

•Why was a known and armed criminal, Jack Ruby, allowed to be within a few feet of Oswald in the Dallas police station on *three* occasions?

•Why would Ruby throw his life away just so, as he claimed, "Jackie Kennedy would not have to return to Dallas for a trial"?

•Although Ruby was an ethnic Jew (real name "Rubinstein"), he was a strip joint operator, not an active Jewish worshipper; why, then, should we believe his "confession" to a Rabbi of his innocence in a plot? Posner spends pages trying to use the Rabbi as a form of alibi for Ruby, never considering the obvious: Ruby lied to the Rabbi because he knew a religious figure on his side could be a real asset in court.

•Why did many witnesses report seeing Ruby in key places: in New Orleans and Cuba, at Dealey Plaza before the assassination and after, in Parkland Hospital, at the police department, in Oswald's company a variety of times? Was there a connection between Ruby's trips to Cuba, LHO's membership in the New Orleans "Fair Play for Cuba" committee, and the CIA's Cuban operatives in New Orleans?

There are four cities that keep coming up in the assassination plotting: Castro's **Havana** (where Mafia bosses Trafficante and Marcello made millions with casinos, and where Oswald was supposedly trying to visit); **Chicago** (another Mafia stronghold and the location of an aborted plot to kill JFK, until JFK's plans for a campaign trip there were changed); **New Orleans** (where Marcello lived, where Oswald lived, and where Jim Garrison found many other conspirators); and of course **Dallas**. Jack Ruby had lived in, or made frequent visits, to all four of those key cities! Again and again we are asked to disregard these facts as insignificant coincidences. My brother, who is a scientist, would say that you cannot prove a case based on coincidences. And yet, most scientific proofs are built upon the statistical significance of "incidents": you observe a phenomenon repeatedly until you eventually see a pattern pointing to something beyond mere coincidence. What I am doing in every facet of the JFK-Oswald-Ruby nexus is observing a *reality of relationships*... **not random coincidences but co-*incidents***.

Three witnesses reported they had seen Jack Ruby near the Book Depository and the railroad tracks minutes after the shooting. This includes Victoria Adams, who saw Ruby in front of the Depository. Malcolm Couch, TV news cameraman, testified that an employee for another broadcast station, Wes Wise, saw Ruby near the Book Depository soon after the assassination. What was Ruby up to?

One answer came when the House Select Committee on

Assassinations took a closer look at Jack "Ruby" Rubinstein. The committee found that Ruby's relationship with Joseph Campisi, part of the Carlos Marcello crime family, was no anomaly. Ruby had many ties to the Mob. Ruby was a friend and business associate of Joseph Civello's, Marcello's deputy in Dallas. Yet another friend of Ruby's with a connection to the Marcello mafia in Dallas was James Henry Dolan: he was a close friend of Marcello's lieutenant Nofio Pecora (and he knew mob boss Santos Trafficante). Ruby's connections with the Marcello organization extended back to New Orleans, where Ruby met with New Orleans nightclub operators and Marcello associates Harold Tannenbaum, Frank Caracci, Cleeve Dugas, and Nick Graffagnini in June and October 1963. New Orleans resident David Ferrie was an associate of Marcello. Ruby was seen with Ferrie—and both men are quite distinctive in their appearance, so the multiple witnesses tying them together are credible. Marita Lorenz is a proven repeat liar. She testified in court that she saw CIA agent Frank Sturgis meeting with Oswald and Ruby. Is this a rare moment when (under oath) she *did* tell the truth? She is far from alone in seeing connections between CIA agents Ferrie, Sturgis, and Hunt that overlap with Ruby and Oswald (see more on this in Lie Number 26).

Posner tries to exonerate Ruby by claiming his phone records fail to reveal a conspiracy. Does he really think the Mafia would have discussed an assassination plot or "hit" over phones that they knew were bugged?[128] Even if there had been an incriminating phone call, the FBI could have covered that up, as we know that the FBI and CIA destroyed an abundance of records from 1963. The House Committee also established that Ruby was acquainted, as a young man in Chicago, with two Mafiaoso hit men who had worked as executioners for the Chicago mob and closely associated with Sam Giancana. Giancana and Marcello had multiple reasons to be eager to assist rogue CIA agents in a plot to kill JFK, and most importantly, to help cover-up the crime by a classic Mafia "hit" on Oswald before he could talk.

Lie Number 32: Ruby just another crazy killer:
"Lee Harvey Oswald and Jack Ruby acted on their own [independently] in November 1963."
~David Von Pein

The Warren Commission and its defenders downplay the significance of Jack Ruby, painting him as a silly little man who shot Oswald in an impetuous act of emotion. Ruby was eccentric and volatile, yet this did not stop him from being a successful businessman, nor would it stop him from being used by the Mafia. 100% healthy-minded, well-adjusted people do not become Mafiosa.

Much ink has been wasted on red herrings in this matter, first to discredit witnesses who saw Ruby and Oswald together before November 24th. It is irrelevant on this point: Ruby was ordered to silence Oswald, and it does not matter whether Oswald was an associate or a stranger. More ink was wasted trying to prove that Ruby could not have known the exact **time** Oswald would be transferred (the time was changed at the last minute). Ruby had *several* opportunities to shoot Oswald, having been seen lurking among the reporters in the police station all weekend—but either lacked the nerve, or was unsure he could get close enough, to take a shot. Whether Ruby was let in a side-door to the police department by a co-conspirator, or allowed down the parking garage ramp, is also irrelevant; Ruby was allowed to be within a few feet of Oswald on *numerous* occasions and the end result was a planned inevitability. Perhaps a bit of luck was involved in the timing of Ruby's shooting of

Oswald in the police department basement—but is there *any* scenario where his success could have been perfectly insured? Again, I refer the reader to the final pages of newsman Seth Kantor's book, which makes a convincing argument that Officer Blackie Harrison placed a last minute phone call to Ruby that Sunday morning, alerting him that Oswald was about to be transferred.[129]

The details of Ruby's final success in "hitting" Oswald are less important than these questions: if Ruby was just another lone nut, why did the WC deny so vehemently that he had been present at Parkland (so well proved by Kantor's book), and why did Ruby himself deny he had been at Parkland? That was on Friday and had zero relevance to his shooting of Oswald on Sunday. What transpired at Parkland that has to be covered up? I don't know... perhaps the planting of a "magic bullet" (that would ballistically match Oswald's rifle) on a hospital stretcher, or a fallback instruction from the conspirators, like, "Jack, you get to Parkland and if our patsy, Oswald, ends up there wounded, you shoot him, or if JFK isn't dead, you might have a chance to finish him off." It all sounds strained, but I've yet to hear a better answer to: "Why was Ruby at Parkland, why did the Warren Commission want to hide Ruby's presence at Parkland, and why were the aggressive investigators, Hubert and Griffin, pulled off of Ruby's trail and not invited to his soft interrogation by Gerald Ford and Judge Warren?" Whenever we find the WC and a suspect sharing a common lie about something (as with Ruby at Parkland), that is a sign something important is being covered-up.

Publicly, Ruby said all the right things—if anything, a little *too* tightly-rehearsed, a melodramatic actor—to try to make his killing of Oswald appear to be an act of temporary insanity mixed with sympathy for the widow Jacqueline Kennedy. By doing so, Ruby expected a grateful, sympathetic jury to impose a light sentence for a charge called "Murder without Malice," and he hoped that once out of jail on probation in a few years, he would receive a huge cash payoff from the Mafia. The conspirators double-crossed him and he never saw the money... nor the light of day. When he finally realized he was, just like his victim, another patsy, Ruby talked. In a brief interview with the WC in the Dallas jail, Jack Rubenstein encouraged the Commission to investigate his presence at Parkland more deeply, and begged them to take him to Washington to testify. They refused. He implied that his life was in danger, and that for him to reveal the full truth "about my motivations" and of "the people who benefitted," the WC would need to take him to a safer place. Chief Justice Warren cut the interview short and left. Ruby died in jail three years later. But before his death, in a TV interview with reporter Harry Kendall, Ruby talked yet again:

```
Ruby: "Everything pertaining to what's happening has
never come to the surface. The world will never know
the true facts of what occurred, my motives [for
killing Oswald]. I'm the only person in the
background that knows the truth."
Kendall queried: "Do you think it will ever come
out?"
Ruby: "No, because unfortunately the people that have
so much to gain and have an ulterior motive to put me
in the position I'm in will never let the true facts
come above board...."
Kendall: "Were these people in very high positions?"
"Yes," Ruby concluded.[130]
```

    This interview alone might have convinced the American public of conspiracy had it ever been broadcast on network prime-time.

    How can Gerald Posner and others possibly explain away Ruby's clear statement that he was part of a conspiracy? First, they claim we've taken bits of his testimony out of context (even as *they* take quotes out of context to make their claim). Read for yourself the full transcript of Ruby before Earl Warren and

Gerald Ford, and watch the Kendall video, and you'll see that Ruby was a torn man: at once trying to maintain that his crime was not pre-meditated (so as not to ruin his chances at appeal), and also clearly promising that if spirited out of Texas and given safety and immunity in Washington, he would further spill the beans.

Second, if the "out of context" defense fails, Posner and Bugliosi next claim that Ruby was just a lone, crazy lunatic—the same script used for Oswald. The video interview with Kendall, however, shows a calm, sane Ruby—though frustrated by his predicament. The later episodes of schizophrenic and paranoid behavior—during which Ruby believed they were "killing Jews" in the prison floor below him—are so bizarre and inconsistent with his normal state, either: a) he was faking it to try to get declared insane or b) it is possible that the CIA "doped" him with LSD. Please don't scoff: we know for a fact that the CIA, in the early sixties, possessed potent LSD hallucinogens and administered LSD to unsuspecting victims—including prisoners. Ruby's rants and hallucinations sound more like an LSD experience than "dementia," as Posner called it. The LSD Mind Control Project MK-ULTRA was partially exposed by Congressional Committees (Rockefeller's and Church's in the seventies), but CIA Director Richard Helms had ordered all MK-ULTRA files destroyed shortly before those investigations. Nevertheless, though other documents we learned that at least one man, biochemist Frank Olson, died as a result of the experiments. MK-ULTRA had been originally approved by Allen Dulles, the CIA Director fired by Kennedy and chosen by President Johnson for the Warren Commission cover-up.[131] Think about it: with Ruby saying all too boldly that there was a conspiracy and that he wanted to squeal, the conspirators had few choices... if they killed him in prison, even a faked suicide, the American public would insist on a new investigation. Ruby was the man who shut up Oswald by killing him, so for Ruby to die by anything other than a natural cause was not an option. So the best choice is to make him appear insane.

From all the evidence, and with the cautious, measured answers Ruby gave to newsmen and his tormented pleadings to the Warren Commission, we can reasonably conclude that **a)** Ruby was an eccentric yet calculating hit-man who knew more than he had been allowed to tell; **b)** There were several conspirators in "high positions" who did not want him to speak, and Ruby was referring to government, not Mafia; **c)** the conspirators "will never let the true facts" out, so evidently they had threatened Ruby and/or his family with death should he squeal.

After that revealing interview, Ruby's health declined precipitously and he died in jail before his appeal could be heard in court.

Lie Number 33: Ruby and Oswald: "[The Commission] was unable to find any credible evidence to support the rumors linking Oswald and Ruby directly or through others."
~The Warren Commission Report, Appendix 12

In addition to the similar discussion (Lie Number 30) about Tippit's cross-connections with Ruby and Oswald, consider Ruby and Oswald's concatenation:

•Dallas is one of the largest cities (in area) in the world, covering over 300 square miles. Ruby and Oswald lived within walking distance of each other... just 1.3 miles apart (the WC was forced to admit that...see Appendix 12). In flight from his boarding house, Oswald was headed in the direction of Ruby's apartment and only blocks away when he encountered Officer Tippit (either shooting Tippit himself, or witnessing Ruby do it... there is evidence for both) and detoured to the theatre. A dozen witnesses, at different times, had seen Oswald in Ruby's club or with Ruby in motel rooms and restaurants... some of the witnesses are more credible than others, but collectively, added to a long list of other indicators, the picture becomes clear: Ruby and Oswald knew each other and had common criminal associates, like David Ferrie and Carlos Marcello.

•Ruby and Oswald both had a keen interest in Cuba. WC investigators Burt Griffin (later to become a respected judge) and Leon Hubert wrote memos on March 19 and April 1, 1964, reporting "substantial evidence" that Jack Ruby had odd Cuban associations, which we now know were connected to Ruby's visits to New Orleans, Miami and Havana, to pursue gambling and gun-running schemes. Ruby met with Texas-to-Cuba gunrunners, and with Mafioso connected to casinos in Havana run by Trafficante and Marcello.[132] So Ruby had extensive contacts with the Dallas police, the Mafia, gun-runners, New Orleans and Cuba. But Posner, Bugliosi, and the WC want us to believe his "hit" on Oswald was merely the work of an oddball nightclub owner who just wanted to be a hero.

Oswald also had entanglements with gun-runners, Cubans, Mafiosa, and he lived in New Orleans shortly before his final move to Dallas. Either he, or his impostor, met with Cuban exiles in Miami. What are the odds that Ruby's varied geographic paths and nefarious acquaintances have a dozen intersections with Oswald's, leading up to their "final intersection" in the Dallas police station basement?

•In the 1969 memoir, *Retired Dallas Police Chief Jesse Curry Reveals His Personal JFK Assassination File*, Curry wrote, "Witnesses to the shooting [of Oswald] wondered if there wasn't a gleam of recognition in Oswald's eye when Ruby stepped out from the newsmen." Curry knew that many of his police officers knew Ruby well (raising the question, "Since they knew he wasn't a newsman, why *did* they let Ruby near Oswald... twice?"). The former Chief came to believe that the rumors of an association between Ruby and Oswald were true.

•Eugene "Jim" Brading, Joseph Milteer, and Jim Hicks—all suspicious characters reportedly on the scene in Dealey Plaza—had connections to Ruby.[133]

•In 1959, Ruby made contact with Louis McWillie in Cuba for the purpose of exploring opportunities for weapons sales—possibly while serving as an informant for the FBI regarding gunrunning. During the same period, Ruby met Robert McKeown, one of the major Castro gunrunners associated Frank Fiorini Sturgis.[134] A few years later, after the American casinos were closed in Havana, McWillie found work at a Las Vegas Casino. Ruby made numerous phone calls to Louis McWillie at the Thunderbird Casino in Las Vegas from May to September of 1963. Ruby visited Vegas just a week before the assassination.[135] This is not the only indication that Ruby was involved in gun-running. A confirmation of that fact, and of Oswald's undercover work to investigate gunrunning for the FBI, comes by way of petty criminal, John Elrod. Elrod briefly shared a cell-area with Oswald and heard Oswald say he knew Jack Ruby. We might dismiss "criminal" testimony were it not for the fact that a good deal of law enforcement convictions have always depended on the testimony of criminals. And what makes Elrod's story compelling is that it matches up with a long list of similar reports regarding Oswald, Ruby and gun-running.

To keep this report somewhat brief, we will not rehash all the good, detailed work of Bill and Mary La Fontaine in their 1996 book, *Oswald Talked*. Instead, we summarize: they offer solid documentation of Jack Ruby's involvement in gunrunning, of FBI Agent James Hosty and other FBI agents in New Orleans and Dallas investigation of gunrunning—and the fact that

Oswald crossed paths with them all, as he was hired by the government (ostensibly) to infiltrate gunrunning operations and be an informant. The La Fontaine's present multiple proofs of this from multiple sources, but the clincher is their discovery of John Elrod's jail-cell encounter with Oswald on November 22nd. For thirty years afterwards, the Dallas police denied that Oswald had a cell-mate... but in 1992, when the Dallas records were finally released, reporter Mary La Fontaine found records confirming that John Elrod shared cell-block "F" with Oswald, and had heard Oswald say he knew Jack Ruby. Elrod reported that he saw Lawrence Miller, arrested for illegal gun sales, being escorted into the Dallas jail, whereupon Oswald told Elrod that he knew the man, and that Miller was conspiring with another man named Jack Ruby, along with Ruby's friend, Donnell Whitter, to traffic stolen guns.[136] The arrest of Miller was not publicly known when Elrod first shared this account in 1964 with the FBI in Memphis. Every important aspect of his story has been verified via corroborative testimonies, FBI records/recollections, and the Dallas arrest records. I suspect that Oswald, seeing Miller being brought in for questioning, began "thinking out loud" in Elrod's presence about the frame-up unfolding before him. After Miller was paraded in front of them in cellblock "F," Oswald told Elrod that he knew the man from a motel meeting with Ruby. If Oswald had been involved in a gunrunning scheme, he would not have spilled the beans to a stranger about his presence at that clandestine meeting. No, he had been there as an *informant* (and indeed, the reason Miller was arrested was because of an informant's tip). Moreover, if Oswald, a reasonably smart fellow, had shot the President and Tippit, he would not have had on his person the fake Hidell I.D. that linked him to both of the guns *and* his own personal Oswald I.D., even a bracelet identifying himself as "Lee."

    This presents a compelling scenario: Oswald was misled to

believe he was investigating Jack Ruby (and possibly J. D. Tippit) for gunrunning—first with guns being funneled to Cuban exiles in Louisiana and Florida, then later with the theft of a weapons cache from a National Guard Armory near Dallas. As part of a general investigation into the flow of guns from gun-dealers in Chicago and California, through Texas, to Louisiana, to Cuban rebels, Oswald had been instructed to order a mail-order rifle and pistol under his pseudonym, Alek Hidell, in order to build the government's case against the illegal gun sales. The famous "backyard photo" of Lee posing with those very guns and artificially holding a Communist magazine is thus explained: his handlers told him to make this silly pose/picture as part of his double-agent role. (Jack White and other photographic experts make a strong argument that the photos were composite fabrications. The HSCA disagreed, but their findings have flaws, so that debate rages on. Either way, the contrived photo of Oswald holding a rifle *and* a Communist magazine screams *frame-up*.

In the "House of Mirrors" built by the intelligence agency, they had Oswald sometimes portray himself as a right-winger (when he worked with Guy Banister and when he tried to infiltrate Alpha-66) and sometimes present himself as a leftwing Communist (passing out pamphlets for the Fair Play for Cuba charade). Once his possession of those guns was established by the photo and by fingerprints, it was an easy task to frame him with those very guns and with his record of (feigned) Communist associations. The powerful conspirators brought the Presidential motorcade by his workplace, a building owned by Lyndon Johnson's good friend.

Lie Number 34: Thoroughly Investigated: Subsequent investigations —House Select Committee on Assassinations, Church Committee, *et cetera*— rectified the WC's mistakes and supports the lone gunman theory. ~party-line of modern news media

In recent years, this lie has become a mantra in mainstream news media, and repeated on JFK chat rooms by those who are not willing to admit they were wrong. They claim the Warren investigation was flawed, but that subsequent investigations, like the 1976-78 U.S. House Select Committee on Assassinations (HSCA), confirmed that there was no conspiracy. First of all, the HSCA did indeed conclude there was "likely" a conspiracy but would not name names (and they tried to divert attention away from a government conspiracy by blaming an amorphous crime syndicate). Digging beneath the surface of the HSCA press "spin," we find substantiation for much of what the conspiracy community has been asserting for years. But yet again, those who tried to draw attention to the dirty truths were slapped down... proof of this is shown in the resignation of several key HSCA lawyers. In the end, an after-the-fact admission by the final head of the HSCA that it lacked integrity and credibility should be enough to silence those who claim the HSCA confirmed the WC.

Ironically, the HSCA investigators came very close to the truth. Pressure from on high stopped them from following through with criminal charges, which could have begun with perjury/contempt of Congress charges against several who testified on behalf of the CIA and FBI. When an investigation tolerates perjury, it is on a pointless, Quixotic chase after windmills.

The HSCA was thorough in some areas, but they failed to pursue some of the most damning evidence. For example, they refused to take a thorough look at the leaked autopsy photos. The HSCA would not address the conflict between the JFK autopsy photos vs. the oppositional eye-witness testimony. About twenty people had seen major damage to the rear of the President's head (an exit wound). David Lifton and Robert Groden's work presented irrefutable truths in this matter—a photo speaks a thousand words. An untrained eye can see that in one photo, the hair on the top and back of JFK's head is close-cut, yet in another, it is several inches long (the photos were supposedly taken at the same time, at the beginning of the autopsy, before any hair was trimmed or skull excised). Douglas P. Horne was HSCA's Chief Analyst for Military Records, tasked with studying the medical evidence and autopsy, as well as the Zapruder film. In 2009 he published a detailed five-volume work, *Inside the Assassination Records Review Board*, which presents documents, testimony and evidence. His work exposes government chicanery in both the medical evidence/autopsy and in parts of the Zapruder film. But his conclusions never made it into the public report released by Congress.

Thoroughly investigated? No... though admittedly, each subsequent inquiry became privy to more information (thanks to independent JFK researchers like Mark Lane and Mary Ferrell), and thus each inquiry found more pieces to the puzzle. Like the WC, the House Committee spent a great deal of time and money taking testimony, but they failed in the same manner: ignoring the conflicts and refusing to draw the obvious "big picture" conclusion that someone had been actively altering evidence. For example, Dr. John H. Ebersole, one of the autopsists, testified before the HSCA and stated unequivocally that the "back of the head" was missing when the body arrived; that the shot came "from the side," not the rear; that a piece of bone was given to them by the Secret Service that had been "removed"—

occipital bone (rear of skull). Yet, no one on the committee pursued these blatant contradictions with the official autopsy photographs that portray only a tiny entrance wound and a fully-intact back of the skull (occiput).[137] They then sequestered this damning testimony for 50 years. We would still be ignorant of this had it not been for the JFK Assassination Records Act, which brought some documents out of hiding after 1992.

The pressure that prompted the JFK Records Act stems in part from other Congressional committees having stumbled upon proof of CIA and FBI lies regarding related issues (assassination plots against Castro and Central American leaders, Mafia entanglements, obstruction of justice/file shredding). Other definitive, titanic documents exposing the JFK plot have been long ago buried, and we assume we have only seen the tip of the iceberg. The congressional investigations never pursued the ramifications of this fact: governmental agents lied to us, and lied to its own investigators.

While the HSCA did several things right, in other ways it seemed like *déjà vu*—a Warren Commission redux. Just as the WC had its CIA mole (Allen Dulles), the HSCA had its own CIA mole: George Joannides. Mr. Joannides was the CIA's "special liaison" to the HSCA, but it was discovered later that he was likely complicit in the original assassination plot! He had been a leader in the very organizations that Lee Harvey Oswald had become suspiciously entangled in the year leading up to the assassination, including a CIA-created anti-Castro group, the DRE [Revolutionary Student Directorate] and the related Alpha-66. The HSCA's Chief Counsel, G. Robert Blakey, later admitted that Joannides and the CIA were guilty of obstruction of justice. But at the time, for a variety of reasons, the HSCA remained in a state of denial and left many matters unexamined. For example, in early 1977, JFK's personal physician, Dr. George Burkley, sent word through his attorney to HSCA counsel Richard A. Sprague that he had serious misgivings about the "no-conspiracy" claim.[138]

Dr. Burkley wanted the HSCA to know that he had never been interviewed, but that he had "information in the Kennedy assassination indicating that others besides Oswald must have participated." Unfortunately, the staff of the HSCA did not pursue this point with Burkley. Though some leads had turned cold after a decade, the HSCA still had a chance to pursue the truth about the autopsy, and about LBJ's nefarious connections... and it did neither.

The HSCA went through three Chairmen, two Chief Counsels, and two Deputy Chief Counsels. In the end, the House committee lacked consensus and tried to straddle the fence: on one hand, they gave a weak and ambiguous nod to conspiracy theorists, saying it was "likely" there was a second shooter with a possible Mafia-connection, but on the other, they then disavowed any involvement of the U.S. government in the conspiracy, exonerating the CIA and FBI yet again. This was another lie—a rather egregious lie.

Eventually, the *de facto* leadership of the HSCA fell to a Cornell law professor, G. Robert Blakey. It is not clear how many of the changes in leadership were caused by someone trying to get a committee that would be favorable to a rubber-stamping of the Warren Commission's findings. But one clear example of that kind of pressure is seen in the case of Leslie Wizelman. Professor Blakey had brought with him to the project four hand-picked law students from Cornell; although originally devoted "teacher's pets," they were quickly disillusioned and smelled yet another cover-up. One of them, Wizelman, (now a highly-respected attorney), had sent Blakey a memo early in the investigation in which she wrote: "I find myself greatly frustrated about my role on this Committee. I will have very serious difficulties writing a report that concludes the Warren

Commission was right. I simply do not believe it. It appears that certain theories have been [pre-]developed and conclusions have been [pre-]established. It would be interesting to have someone...tell us upon what they are based."[139]

Twenty years later, in 2003, it seems that Blakey came to see the error of his ways, as he issued a statement that reveals the utter failure of the House committee: "I no longer believe that we were able to conduct an appropriate investigation of the [Central Intelligence] Agency and its relationship to Oswald.... We now know that the Agency withheld from the Warren Commission the CIA-Mafia plots to kill Castro.... We also now know that the [CIA] set up a process... designed to frustrate the ability of the [HSCA] in 1976-79 to obtain any information that might adversely affect the Agency. Many have told me that the culture of the Agency is one of prevarication and dissimulation and that you cannot trust it or its people. Period. End of story. I am now in that camp."[140]

This provides vindication for Robert K. Tanenbaum, an early Deputy Chief Counsel for the HSCA... until he, like Leslie Wizelman, also resigned in disgust. Tanenbaum wrote in 2011:
"Based upon the evidence adduced during the [HSCA] investigation, I had reason to believe that David Phillips, the third-ranking member of the CIA in charge of Western Hemisphere operations, employed a *nom de guerre*, Maurice Bishop. Bishop had significant involvement with anti-Castro Cubans and Lee Harvey Oswald. I had him [Phillips *aka* Maurice Bishop] subpoenaed to appear before our committee in executive session. I asked him under oath where we could locate the tape of the so-called Oswald conversation of October 1, 1963, while inside the Russian embassy in Mexico City. Phillips stated that it was CIA policy at the time to recycle the tapes every six or seven days and it was no longer in existence after... October 1963. I then handed him the Hoover memo which... clearly revealed that the tape was available in Dallas on November 22 and 23, 1963. Phillips read the memo, then folded it, placed it in his jacket pocket, arose, and walked out of the meeting. I immediately urged the committee to recall Phillips... [under threat of] perjury. There were

many more questions that he needed to answer.... They chose to do nothing. Thereafter, our... staffers' pay was withheld... [Congress] played politics with our investigation and subverted it. [Congressmen on the committee had] assured me that whatever the facts revealed would be forthrightly presented to the public. Regrettably, that was false."[141]

Tanenbaum is one of a long list of HSCA insiders who were unhappy with the committee's final results. The HSCA may have begun with good intent, but in the end, it was co-opted by the "powers that be" and became just another obfuscation, another lie.

In the first 34 Lies, we've made an irrefutable case for conspiracy. Now the cake is baked, we are just adding the icing... let's re-visit the Oswald question.

Lie Number 35: Oswald in the TSBD, Part 1: Just before the assassination, "Oswald was seen on the sixth floor... and no one... saw Oswald anywhere else in the building until after the shooting."
~the WC Report, p. 156

The Warren Commission proves its complicity in a cover-up by asserting absolutes about things that are highly debatable, and in most cases, dead wrong. Here's another example where the WC overstates its case: no one saw Oswald anywhere other than the sixth floor. Actually, *six* **witnesses** (mostly Oswald's co-workers/bosses) saw him elsewhere, and gave testimony to the FBI and/or Warren Commission and others about Oswald's whereabouts between 11:45am and 12:35 pm. These were all consistent in saying Oswald was on the first and second floors, not the sixth, around the time of the shooting:

•**Charles Givens** first told the FBI (sworn statement on November 23rd) that he saw Oswald reading a newspaper in the second floor "domino room" at 11:50 am. Unbeknownst to Oswald, the motorcade was running late... if it had been on time or a few minutes early, Oswald would have missed his chance to shoot while reading the newspaper on the second floor! Months later, the Warren Commission reported a different version of Givens' statement: suddenly the time had been changed to 7:50 a.m. This is obviously altered testimony —a lie—because we know from other reliable testimony that Oswald did not enter the building until *after* 8 a.m.[142] Indeed, most everything Givens testified to was self-contradictory—though it is impossible to know how many of the contradictions were because of Givens' confusion or because of later "creative typing and editing" of his words in the official record. And we can't rule out the possibility that Givens lied; he may have been eager to see Oswald convicted in order to save his own skin because he was one of the few other suspects ever pursued and the **only TSBD employee with a criminal record** other than Oswald. In fact, his record was *worse* than Oswald's. Contrary to the Commission's claim, Oswald was not the only employee who left the TSBD after the shooting. Indeed, before 2 pm, the police had issued an APB for Charles Givens, finding it suspicious that he was missing from the gathering of employees *and* had a criminal record.[143]

•**William Shelley**, another TSBD employee, told the WC he saw Oswald on the first floor "near the telephone" about "10 or 15 minutes before" noon.

•**Eddie Piper** also saw Oswald on the first floor "at 12 o'clock."

•**Carolyn Arnold**, in her first interview with the FBI, said she caught a "fleeting glimpse" of Oswald as she was walking out of the TSBD to see the motorcade "a few minutes before 12:15." She said he was "standing between the front door and the double doors leading to the warehouse." Again, this is consistent with the others who saw Lee in that vicinity before and after the shooting. Like so many witnesses who didn't say what the WC wanted them to say, Ms. Arnold was never called to testify before them.

•**Officer Baker** and **Roy Truly** saw Oswald within seconds of the final shot (discussed in great detail elsewhere in this section.)

These witnesses who saw Oswald on the first and second floors at lunchtime and near motorcade time make a compelling case; equally important are those who did *not* see Oswald on the *sixth* floor. **Mr. Bonnie Ray Williams** was on the sixth floor eating lunch from noon to 12:20, and "didn't hear anything." Allen Dulles asked him again, "You were all alone?" "I did not see anything," he replied. Then, he told the WC that he went downstairs to the fifth floor to join his friends at a window there.

•**Mrs. Ruby Henderson** told the FBI on December 5, 1963 that just before the motorcade arrived, she was standing on the east side of Elm Street near Houston Street, and glanced up at the TSBD, where she saw two men in a window on an upper floor: one was dark-complected, possibly a "Mexican or Negro" (or Cuban?!), the other white. (The WC never deposed her.)[144]

•**Arnold Rowland** also told the WC that he saw two men on the sixth floor at about 12:15, one with a scoped rifle at one end of the building, and another, a black man (which could have been Bonnie Ray Williams finishing his lunch). We thus know the man Rowland had seen with a rifle on the sixth floor at 12:15 could not have been Oswald: he was on the first floor. Vincent Bugliosi dismisses this testimony without due cause: Rowland's testimony is corroborated by his wife, and by Ruby Henderson (above).

~~~

The Commission had to prove Oswald had moved, unseen, from the 6th floor sniper's nest to the alcove of the 2nd floor lunchroom in 75 seconds, where he was seen by Officer Baker at

12:31, calm and not winded.[145] They failed.

Victoria Elizabeth Adams felt that her life was in jeopardy when she contributed to their failure. After Adams testified to the Warren Commission that she had been on the stairwell at the same time they claim Oswald was descending, the WC not only failed to question her further, they ignored other witnesses who bolstered Adams' story. Instead, the WC coerced an unreliable witness to change his story to discredit her. Elsie Dorman and Dorothy May Garner were standing with Vickie Adams in the TSBD at a fourth floor window overlooking the area of the first two shots. Ms. Adams, a smart (*summa cum laude*) and articulate young witness, testified: "...it seemed as if [the shot] came from the right below rather than from the left above." In her case, "right below" was the Grassy Knoll, and to the "left above" was the sniper's nest, two stories above her.

After the final shot, Adams and Sandra Styles went immediately down the same stairwell that Oswald supposedly used within 90 seconds of the same shot. They neither saw nor heard anyone on the stairs, despite being in the stairwell during the same time-span. Sandra Styles confirmed Adam's statements—but the WC never called Styles to testify. Ms. Adams said that they left the window within "15 and 30 seconds" of the fatal shot, which is how long it would have taken an adrenalin-rushed Oswald to stand up from his crouched position, pause and savor his "success," cross the long diagonal of the sixth floor, hide the gun, and begin descending down the same stairway. He would have likely been a bit behind her (behind in time because he was above her in location, coming from from the sixth floor as she came down from the fourth), but the wooden stairs, even though not an "open" stairwell, were noisy; she would have heard him if not seen him. In her testimony before the WC, she was interrogated by WC counsel David Belin, and it includes this exchange:

Mr. BELIN – 'How long do you think it was between the time the shots were fired and the time you left the window to start toward the stairway?'
Miss ADAMS – 'Between 15 and 30 seconds, estimated, approximately.'
Mr. BELIN – 'How long do you think it took you to get from the window to the bottom of the stairs on the first floor?'
Miss ADAMS – 'I would say no longer than a minute at the most.'
Mr. BELIN – 'You heard no one else running down the stairs?'
Miss ADAMS – 'Correct.'[146]

    She also stated—confirmed by others—that the elevator was not running. (Others—Luke Mooney, Geneva Hine, Roy Truly— stated the power was mysteriously cut to the elevator and to some of the floors.) None of the women coming down the stairs at various times, nor the policeman coming up the stairs, saw Oswald in the stairwell. Dorothy Garner had been watching at the same window with Ms. Adams, but did not go to the stairs as quickly as Adams and Styles. She stayed on the 4th floor a moment, and then as she went down the stairwell, she saw Office Baker and Roy Truly coming up—but no Oswald coming down.[147] A letter stating Garner's assertion was found in the WC files, but was never shared with the public; it confirms Vickie Adams' account/timing.

    Though the elevators had been stuck on the 5th floor, the door opened manually, so around 12:30 pm, Jack Dougherty was already loading books into the west elevator; Dougherty did not see Oswald crossing the landing between stairwells on the 5th floor, even though it is adjacent to, and visible from, the west elevator opening. Within moments of the last shot, it regained power and Dougherty took it down as Officer Baker came up the nearby stairs. This timing is well-established: Baker and Truly came first to the elevator, found it stuck on 5th, went up one flight of stairs, found Oswald in the lunchroom, resumed their stair-climb and then saw the elevator had moved (with Daughtery on board). So at the same time Oswald would have had to descend those stairs from the sniper's nest, several people were on or around the stairs, yet none saw him.

According to the WC re-enactment of Oswald's movements (with the *a priori assumption* that he was the killer), the fastest he could have made it to the door of the second floor lunchroom was 74 seconds; new evidence points to *over* 90 seconds. The lunchroom is where motorcycle policeman, Marion Baker, accompanied by Oswald's boss, Roy Truly, encountered the supposed-assassin... over thirty feet away from the stairwell on the second floor, near the Coke machine in the lunchroom. By the WC's own admission, Baker and Truly were on the second floor in less than 90 seconds of the first shot; one "test run" made it in 75 seconds, but let's give the WC the benefit of the doubt: compare the *fastest* of "Oswald's test run" (74 seconds) with the *slowest* of Baker's "test run" (90 seconds). Thus Oswald would have beat Baker by a mere 15 seconds. But they compare apples to oranges: timing from the *first* shot for Baker to the *last* shot for Oswald. Moreover, the WC did not factor in the testimony of witnesses on the ground (and this is found in their own Report) who testified that the shooter was **slow to leave the window**: he had to eject the final shell (three empty shells were found), bolt-load a fourth shell (found in rifle, loaded but unfired), pause and watch the results of his actions, stand up from his crouched position, wipe his fingerprints, and then go hide the gun. So adding 11 seconds (5 seconds for two more shots, then 6 seconds for final shell ejection/reload, fingerprint wipe, gun hiding, etc.), that means Oswald would, in the "best WC case scenario," have beaten Baker to the second floor by a scant *four* seconds! Is this "best case scenario" believable? This best-case scenario, (best for the WC's case, that is) would require Oswald to be moving much faster than a walk to make it to the lunchroom ahead of Baker and Truly—but there are three reasons that is doubtful: 1. Oswald was not winded after his four flight journey. 2. Moving faster than a casual walk might have aroused suspicion and certainly would have made noise on the stairway for Ms. Adams to hear. 3. When Officer Baker saw Oswald, he was on the other side of a door (seen through a window) with his back turned to the officer, so Oswald had no idea anyone was watching him, yet Baker says the suspect was just "walking."[148] Although the WC Report uses the word "walking" to describe Oswald, it uses "run" and "trot" to describe Baker and Truly: Officer Baker "ran" into the building, continued "at a good trot," and Truly "had run up" ahead of him.[149] So we are to believe that Oswald managed to *walk briskly* across the sixth floor and down FOUR floors faster than the officer *ran* into the building and up ONE floor?

But it gets worse for the WC case: there is evidence that Oswald had taken a few more seconds to get a Coke from the drink machine. Even a few seconds added to this already-improbable timing issue ruins the WC's case. We would not be surprised to learn that the WC and FBI tried to remove the Coke reference after their re-enactments showed how tight the timing was. And that is exactly what happened: someone deleted a signed statement by Patrolman Baker that declared: "I saw a man standing in the lunchroom drinking a Coke." A mark-out line has been drawn through the phrase "drinking a Coke," and Baker's initials mark the "correction." The evidence strongly indicates that the phrase should not have been deleted:

•In addition to Baker's statement, Dallas Police Chief Jesse Curry mentioned this detail—Oswald calmly drinking a Coke as Officer Baker encountered him—to reporters the day after the shooting.

•Immediately after the shots rang out, TSBD clerk Mrs. Robert Reid bumped into Oswald on the second floor, coming from the

lunchroom with a Coke bottle in his hand.
- Did Baker or the WC later change his testimony on this matter? It appears so, because during a radio interview on December 23, 1966, WC counsel Albert Jenner slipped and said, "...the first man this policeman saw, was Oswald with a bottle of Coke." Of course, this conflicts with what Jenner's own WC testimony claimed: that Oswald bought the Coke *after* his encounter with Baker and Truly.
- Dallas Police Captain Will Fritz wrote in his report about his early interrogation: "I asked Oswald where he was when the police officer stopped him. He said he was on the second floor drinking a Coca-Cola when the officer came in." This casual remark does not seem like something Oswald would have invented, knowing that Truly and Baker had seen him. Why invent a lie that, at the time, he had no way of knowing it was crucial to his defense?
- The early news-media accounts reported that when police first encountered Oswald, he was drinking a Coke.

The significance in this "Coke" issue is not only that it adds 8 seconds to his "flight from the sixth floor" time (to put coins in the mechanical machine, have it operate, pop the top and then turn to face the policeman), but it also shows yet another attempt to jigger the police records in order to fix the blame on Oswald.

If the timing isn't already so tight as to exonerate Oswald, we have yet *another* problem for Posner's followers: author Barry Krusch, using photos taken at the time of the shooting, makes a thoroughly-convincing argument that the assassin took even *longer* to leave the window. He reminds us that the House Special Committee analyzed two photos taken immediately after the shooting. The Committee's photographic panel concluded: "There is an apparent rearranging of boxes within 2 minutes after the last shot was fired at President Kennedy."[150] Based on eyewitnesses and photos of the sniper's window (one by James

Powell, one by Tom Dillard), it is very likely that two people were in the sniper's nest: one a sniper, another his spotter. The spotter may have moved the boxes and then hidden the rifle as the sniper dashed downstairs, thus giving him—supposedly Oswald—enough time to meet Baker on the second floor... but of course, two men in the nest constitutes conspiracy. So if we stick with a lone assassin theory, the photos show that the sniper paused a few more seconds to rearrange the boxes. The WC's "star witness" regarding the sixth floor assassin, Howard Brennan, said of the sniper: "He did not seem to be in any hurry..." after the shots were all fired.[151]

To review, the following scenario is the fiction foisted upon us by the WC: A generous 90-second clock starts ticking as Officer Baker reacts to the first shot. Oswald reloads and shoots twice more, takes time to eject the final shell, gets up from a crouched position, pauses ("he did not seem to be in hurry") to observe the damage in the limo, then moves a few boxes, wipes most of the fingerprints off of the rifle, walks briskly in a serpentine path (dodging book stacks and columns) over 100 feet across the entire diagonal of the sixth floor, bends over and hides the gun behind/between boxes, then dashes quickly but quietly down four flights of stairs (each stairwell separated by ten feet of landing), goes through two doors another 25 feet of distance to the Coke machine —where Baker sees a calm Oswald through the door-window to the lunchroom, a Coke bottle in his hand. The mechanical door was not swinging. 90 seconds. Baker, a trained officer who knows a murder has just been committed, steps through that door to confront Oswald at gunpoint. A calm Oswald shows not a hint of breathlessness. Roy Truly was already ahead of Baker up the stairs, but realizing he'd lost Baker, turned around and joined the officer to assure him that Oswald is an employee. Officer Baker saw no reason to detain him further.

Oswald more likely had been walking to the lunchroom from another direction, having come up from the "domino room" where he said he had eaten lunch moments earlier. Here's Officer Baker's sworn testimony:[152]

Representative BOGGS: "When you saw [Oswald], was he out of breath, did he appear to have been running or what?"
Mr. BAKER: "It didn't appear that [way] to me. He appeared normal you know."
Representative BOGGS: "Was he calm and collected?"
Mr. BAKER: "Yes, sir."

So Oswald showed no signs of being breathless despite rushing down from the far side of the sixth floor? The WC claimed the Secret Service Agent re-enacting this "was not winded," but try if for yourself and see if that is believable—dash nearly the length of a football field (this was not a straight path—the curves, steps and turns add to the distance). Also, first watch a horror movie to simulate the adrenalin-pumping that must have accompanied having just assassinated the President of the United States! Are you "calm and collected" and breathing easy?

Seeing how crucial this information about the gunman's escape was, we would expect an impartial Commission to investigate further. But they never re-called Ms. Adams, and spent very little time with her testimony compared to other less-critical witnesses. Adams also testified, in very articulate and intelligent language, that a few minutes after the shooting, she had seen Jack Ruby standing near the front of the building. Belin never dug into this juicy tidbit, but abruptly ended the interview. The WC never called Sandra Styles to corroborate Adams, nor did they try to re-create Victoria Adams' stairwell journey, despite the vital importance of Oswald's and Baker's timings on the same staircase. Vickie Adams goes further: she said that years later, when she read the WC record of her testimony, she saw that it had been altered to "soften" her clear and firm recollections. And the Report now claimed she had spoken with co-workers Billy Lovelady and William Shelley upon coming to the ground floor... something she denies. The WC had twisted the vague testimony of Lovelady and Shelley to discredit her. Ms. Adams said law enforcement coerced her silence. The House Special Committee also ignored her strong testimony.

We cannot now determine to what degree Oswald was involved, but after examining these timing problems, we know one thing: he could not have done it alone. Perhaps if he had immediately handed the gun off to an accomplice, who inexplicably ejected the final shell, then wiped the fingerprints, moved some boxes, and hid the gun, *while* Oswald was making an unimpeded dash to the lunchroom... but that would still constitute conspiracy. *Murder + crime scene cleanup + cross-building dash + four flights of stairs ÷ 90 seconds = calm and not winded*. That is the fictional math of the WC.

Lie Number 36: Oswald in the TSBD, Part 2:
"Oswald, at the time of the assassination, was present at the window from which the shots were fired." ~WC Report Summary, p. 156

Contrary to reports, no one outside the building could positively identify the sixth floor sniper. Of all the employees and police *inside* the Book Depository, **no one saw Lee Harvey Oswald on the sixth floor or on the stairwell or elevators during the 15 minute time span of the assassination preparation, execution and flight time span** (approx. 12:20-12:35). To repeat: **no one!** When he *was* seen within moments of the shooting, he was nowhere near the sixth floor.

And Oswald was not the only employee to remain inside the building during the motorcade: over twenty people stayed inside (many, but not all, watching from the windows). We've mentioned several, but there are more:

- **"Junior" Jarman and Harold Norman** ate lunch together in the domino room on the first floor, which served as an alternative eating spot to the second floor employee lunch room. Neither would go on the record saying they saw Oswald there that day, but Harold Norman admitted, "there was someone else in there," though he couldn't remember who. After seeing his picture, Norman would not rule *out* Oswald as that person (with 75 employees, most did not know every single name of their co-workers). Oswald told the police that during the assassination, he ate lunch in the domino room without interacting with anyone, but he did remember two men walking through, and Oswald described them correctly: a black man named "Junior" and a short, black man whose name he did not know—which had to be Norman, as the description matches fully and we know "Junior" Jarman and Norman were indeed eating lunch together in the domino room. Mr. Jarman and Mr. Norman left about 12:20 pm to go upstairs to watch the motorcade from a vantage point above the gathering crowd.
- Three witnesses—**Eddie Piper, Bill Shelley, and Charles Givens**—reported seeing Oswald on the first floor between 11:50 and 12:00 pm.
- Another TSBD employee, **Carolyn Arnold**, stated in 1978 that she had seen Oswald just before she went to watch the motorcade, exactly where he said he had been, on the first floor (likely having finished lunch and heading for the second floor drink machine). Thus his location, like most everything else Oswald told the police, was consistent and corroborated by multiple witnesses.

From outside the building, **no one gave an ironclad ID of Oswald** at a window: •The "best" eyewitness claiming to be able to identify Oswald as the sixth floor sniper, **Howard Brennan**, could not say if the shooter was, or was not, wearing a jacket, and described the man as *standing*, when in fact the sniper had to kneel down in order to shoot out of the nearly-closed window. That's a poor observer who can't tell if a man is standing or crouching. Yet the case against Oswald rests on Brennan's observational skills—or lack thereof. Photos from that day show the windows were very dirty and shadowy, so seeing the sniper clearly after he stood up would have been difficult... and Brennan had no way of knowing the distance from the window sill to the floor, so therefore he could not have even made a *guess* at the man's height. He also described the sniper as wearing a light colored shirt, when Oswald was wearing a dark colored shirt (before he went home and changed out of his work clothes). To repeat this critical point: Brennan was over 90 feet away, six floors down and across the street, peering up through a mostly-shut, dirty and shadowed window. Yet so-called debunker Vincent Bugliosi writes that Brennan saw Oswald with striking "clarity." Pure bunk, Mr. B.

If any witness' credibility should be questioned, it would be Brennan's, since (according to the WC) he gave the police a description of the man's height when **he could see only the upper half of his body!** Though Brennan identified Oswald in the police line-up, Oswald was then distinctive with a bruised eye and a scruffy, disheveled look, in contrast to the other folks in the line-up. Most importantly, according the FBI, Mr. Brennan specifically told the police that **he was not sure if Oswald was the man he'd seen** in the window, only that LHO looked *more* like him than anyone else in that particular line-up!![153] His exact words to the WC were that Oswald merely looked "more like a closest resemblance to the man in the window than anyone in the lineup... I told them that I could not make a positive identification." This flimsy nonsense is what the WC uses to make its claim that Oswald was seen on the sixth floor during the shooting, and it is upon this inaccurate witness that Vincent Bugliosi builds his book. Read more of his original testimony in the *WCR, Volume 3*, pp. 147-148:

```
Mr. Belin: "Now, is there anything else you told the
officers at the time of the lineup?"
Mr. Brennan: "Well, I told them that I could not make
a positive identification."
Mr. Belin: "In the meantime, had you seen any
pictures of Lee Harvey Oswald on television or in the
newspapers?"
Mr. Brennan: "Yes, on television."
```

At a later time, Brennan tried to claim differently —that he had been afraid for his life and therefore was hesitant to make a positive I.D. But his actions make this statement even more fishy... see www.giljesus.com/jfk/brennan.htm. If he was so fearful, why even tentatively point out Oswald in the line-up? Even if we attribute Brennan's waffling to fear, we still have a man with poor eyesight and poor memory whose long-distance description was inconsistent and failed to match Oswald.

•The WC ignored better witnesses. A boy named **Amos Euins** saw the rifle fire and testified to the WC:

```
"I seen a bald spot on this man's head, trying to
look out the window. He had a bald spot on his head.
I was looking at the bald spot.... And I could see
his hand ...on the trigger."
```

Oswald had no bald spot. The WC later tried to correlate this to Oswald's receding hairline, but Euins referred to a bright "bald spot," not a hairline, and **pointed to the top of his head**, about "two and a half inches" back from the hairline. Euins testimony exonerates Oswald, so the WC was left with no choice but to discredit and disregard his testimony... despite the fact that *The New York Times* wrote at the time, "No one's recollection about the first shot was more precise, though, than that of a ninth grader named Amos L. Euins."

•Even worse for the WC's lone-gunman case is that we have a variety of testimony that *more* than one man was on the sixth floor, and **neither matched Oswald's description**. As mentioned, **Carolyn Walther** told the FBI she had seen two men in a window of the TSBD, one with a rifle (though she was confused about which floor). Yet she was not called to testify by the Commission.

•**Arnold Rowland** confirms Walther's report: he told the WC that he saw two men on the sixth floor: about 15 minutes before the first shot, he saw a man with a scoped rifle at the west window (closer to the Grassy Knoll side) and another man—a black man, so obviously not Oswald—near the "sniper's nest" at the east side of the building. The WC chose not to believe Walthers or Rowland, but instead accepted the weak eyes of Howard Brennan, whose description was obviously inaccurate (see above). Likewise, the WC accepted the words of **Charles Givens**, the only eyewitness from within the Depository who claimed to have seen Oswald on the sixth floor —but *before* the motorcade began— even though Givens' various statements had multiple flaws and alterations (see previous section).

•While the WC embraced Brennan and Givens, they ignored the conflicting testimony of **Richard Randolph Carr**. Carr saw a suspicious man on a top floor of the TSBD who did not match Oswald's description. Carr was working as a steel welder on the seventh floor of the under-construction courthouse building over a block away from the TSBD. Shortly before the first shot, he saw a heavy-set man with horn-rimmed glasses and a tan sport jacket on the sixth floor of the TSBD. The distance involved makes it hard to put much faith in Carr's description—but it must be noted that on his seventh floor job, he was looking across at a near-horizontal. People on the street were looking up in a long diagonal at a shadowed window. And after the shooting, Carr got much closer and saw the same man emerge from the building. Carr followed the man and thus was able, later, to make this report to the FBI: "This man, walking very fast... got into a 1961 or 1962 gray Rambler station wagon which was parked just north of Commerce Street on Record Street." This corroborates the similar claims about a Rambler station wagon made by Sheriff Roger Craig. Both Carr and Craig described one person in the car as being dark-skinned, which also matches up with those who reported Cuban involvement in the conspiracy. Yet both Craig's and Carr's matching stories were disregarded by the authorities. The Warren Commission did not call Carr as a witness nor was he mentioned in any of their published evidence. Carr reported that an FBI agent had told him: "If you didn't see Lee Harvey Oswald in the School Book Depository with a rifle, you didn't see" anyone.[154] Helen Forrest, James Pennington, Roy Cooper and Marvin Robinson all saw the Rambler station wagon stop to pick up a man or men—all ignored by the WC in their rush to discredit Sheriff Craig's trouble-making testimony.

Above we listed several witnesses to the fact that **two men—not matching descriptions of any TSBD employees—were on the top floors**. More than one witness saw one of the two holding a gun. This rules out a "lone gunman" theory... but then raises another question: How likely is it that two assassins could escape the sixth floor without being noticed? Not as hard as you may think. There were several unguarded doors leading out of the back of the TSBD. Amos Euins, mentioned above, said, "...he seen another man... he seen a man run out the back [of the TSBD]... he had kind of a bald spot on his head." Several people reported seeing "officers" or "secret service agents" on November 22nd who were later suspected of being impostors. So the sixth floor gunmen could have possessed identification (forged or real; CIA, FBI, Secret Service or police) ready to flash to any civilian who might bump into them as they headed out the back doors. Indeed, the first to go up the back stairs other than Officer Baker was Dallas Deputy Sheriff Luke Mooney—and he reported that on his way up to the sixth floor, he saw two men coming *down* the stairwell, who he assumed were "plain clothed deputy sheriffs." These may have been the two mystery men spotted on the sixth floor. Deputy Sheriff Roger Craig also went to the Depository about the same time, and bumped into a man in a suit who told Craig, "I'm with the Secret Service."[155]

The sniper could have easily been disguised as one of these fake agents/officers. Or, after Vickie Adams descended, the sniper may have started down the same stairs, heard Truly and Officer Baker coming up, and from the fourth floor landing, detoured across to the fourth floor *front* elevator. The stair landings on both the fourth and fifth floors were partly blocked by books. The layout of the offices on the fourth floor could have allowed a sniper to walk by unseen, as most of the people on that floor either headed downstairs immediately or were in the front offices looking out the windows. Other less-believable theories have been suggested as to other ways men could escape the sixth floor: using the fire escape, or climbing down inside the elevator shaft (and it is peculiar that the power was cut off to the freight elevators at the same time as the assassination).

Find those possibilities hard to swallow? Believing Oswald was the shooter requires accepting even stranger propositions:
• This "crazy and unstable" young man was amazingly brave/cool, though he had no forged police "I.D." yet ironically, carried his fake A.J. Hidell I.D. and his real I.D. If Oswald was the assassin, why would he carry a fake I.D. into a situation where he very likely would be arrested in the presence of 50 people who knew him as Oswald, not Hidell?
• Some suggest he wanted to be caught, but once it began to dawn on Oswald that he was likely being set-up as a fall guy, he fled and tried hard to avoid capture for awhile, even fighting with police officers. If he wanted glory/notoriety, why claim innocence after being arrested?
• Oswald had left his rifle in the building, where it was easily

found, a rifle he had asked his wife, Marina, to photograph as he held it, a rifle bought by "A. Hidell" ...and he still carried the Hidell fake I.D. on his person that tied him to it!

• If he had planned to escape capture, why not carry his pistol to work inside his lunchbox as a contingency plan... rather than have to return home to grab it?

• He had left $170 cash with Marina (not at his nearby boarding house), and had only $17 on him... he had no travel bag packed, no car, no plan for escape.

Lie Number 37: Oswald's Run to Mexico: Oswald had a plan to flee to the country after the shooting. ~David Belin, WC Counsel, in a 1964 draft that never made it into the final WC Report

Oswald had visited Mexico just weeks before the assassination. If we believe, as the evidence indicates, that the CIA and/or FBI were manipulating him with the promise that they were making Lee into a "spy" (his lifelong aspiration), it was a simple trick: tell him to go to the Cuban embassy in Mexico for the purpose of baiting them into hiring him to assassinate the President. Years later, Castro publicly stated that entrapment is what they suspected Oswald had been attempting. (The irony here is that Oswald thought he was on an assignment to "entrap" Cuba, when actually he was assisting in his own entrapment/framing.) Oswald's involvement with Cuban politics is well-documented—including the fact that he associated with *both* pro-Cuban and anti-Cuban groups. This is one of several signs that he was a fledgling spy.) For good measure, the conspirators also sent an Oswald impostor to very visibly "make a scene" at the Soviet embassy. Unfortunately for their plan, a picture of the impostor was taken, which proved the man claiming loudly to be Lee Oswald was not him.

Originally, some in the CIA may have planned on a *fake*, near-assassination, to be blamed on Cuba, to provide a rationale for another invasion of that communist island. And Belin may have tried to use Oswald's Mexico/Cuban visit as a way to smear Cuba, as well as to bolster the claim that Oswald had acted on a pre-meditated plan. But Belin's scenario was rejected in the end, probably because the conspirators—LBJ in particular—decided that stirring up war with Cuba and Russia was too risky, and chose instead to paint Oswald as an impetuous, lone nut. So they excluded Belin's scenario.

Attorney Belin does us a service: he shows how low the WC would stoop in framing Oswald—"low" as in their "low IQ." As shown above, Oswald had no plan to assassinate anyone because, as savvy as they try to portray him, he made zero provisions for a fast getaway. The few dollars left in Lee's pocket (vs. the $170 he gave Marina), Belin claimed, was enough to buy a bus ticket to Mexico. So picture this: when Oswald initially "fled the scene of the crime," he had on his person no gun, no belongings or provisions (not even a toothbrush and an extra pair of underwear!), no car or travel plans, and almost no money. The taxi ride, soft-drink, etc., had quickly used up a third of his pocket money, and the rest would have been exhausted in a day: after paying for a bus ride all the way to Mexico, a drink and a meal, he would have found himself in a foreign country without a visa or passport and not enough money for even one night in the cheapest motel. He would have ended up with no food, no money, no lodging, no job, no papers, in a country where he could not speak the language and would need to pay for safe drinking water.

Since Belin is not an idiot, his idiotic proposal here must have been a purposeful deception. Maybe Oswald had an accomplice ready to meet him at the border with a large cash payoff... but if so, that spells CONSPIRACY, which is exactly the opposite of what Belin was claiming (and probably why his idea was rejected in the end by the WC).[156]

Lie Number 38: Oswald's Apprehension: The identification and arrest of Oswald by Dallas Police was not odd.
~The Warren Commission Report and its defenders

How did the police, within minutes of the shooting, know to look for Lee Oswald near his apartment, in the library, and at the movie theatre (his regular hangouts) even **before his name was broadcast**? The description that supposedly lead to the capture of Oswald first went out over the radio in less than 14 minutes of the last shot—the most amazingly-quick I.D. of a man only seen briefly and in a darkened window from six floors down. The eyewitness description of the possible suspect was so vague as to have applied to thousands of young men in Dallas that day: white, brownish hair, average height, average build, no distinguishing characteristics. And yet, how and why did the police broadcast just *one* particular description out of so many possible descriptions turned into them in those first few minutes? Again we must say: only one witness (Brennan) gave a description akin to Oswald's, while others described sighting suspects variously as: a "heavy-set" man; a "bald" or balding man; a "black" man; a "Latin or Cuban-looking" man; a man wearing horn-rimmed glasses, a plaid coat, and a rain coat.

Police soon apprehended a suspect running into the nearby library, and released him as the "wrong man." Minutes later, police arrested Oswald in a theatre just blocks away. He resisted arrest and vigorously denied having shot anyone.

Lee never received legal counsel, nor was read his rights. This author had dinner with the son of Oswald's public defender. He said his father was never given a chance to meet with Oswald, and was given the runaround of delays by the Dallas police department. When it became known that the New York attorney Oswald had requested would not show, they appointed a public defender, but before he received any information about his client, Oswald was shot.

Something else odd happened within the first two hours of Oswald's arrest: the CIA-managed anti-Castro organization, DRE, released to the news-media their documentation of Oswald's pro-Castro activism in New Orleans activities.[157] Police had not released the name "Oswald" as a possible suspect until *after* 3 pm.

In "Lie Number 3," we've already seen how the Dallas police rigged the line-up to make Oswald stand out as "guilty."

More than a dozen other suspects were detained and/or arrested on November 22nd, some of whom matched the eyewitness descriptions of shooters. They were all released on the same day.

No notes or recordings have ever been found of his two days of interrogation. Within 48 hours, LHO was himself murdered in the Dallas police station by Jack Ruby. All told, it was history's quickest APB description, manhunt, arrest, and termination of a murder suspect based on a shadowy glimpse from six floors down!

Lie Number 39: National Security: The hearings and the evidence must be kept secret for reasons of national security.
~Presidents Johnson, Nixon and Ford

To protect "national security," most of the Warren Commission's hearings were conducted behind closed doors. Mountains of evidence were locked away in the National Archives for an unprecedented length of time: 75 years! But this presents another contradiction. If, as the WC claimed from the outset, Oswald was the lone assassin and an unaffiliated nutcake, how could the case possibly be an issue of national security? Why was so much documentation classified "Top Secret" when this was, supposedly, a case that did not involve espionage or conspiracy? In the few documents (such as his Russian defection) where names of foreign agents or other proprietary information rightfully *should* be concealed, the names could have been redacted. But instead, **entire files were hidden away**. One weak excuse for hiding the Zapruder film and the autopsy pictures was that the pictures were gruesome and might upset the Kennedy family. But such pictures are commonly available in other murder cases. Later we are told that some documents were hidden in order to conceal U.S. plans to overthrow Cuba... but with four million documents hidden away, most of which had nothing to do with Cuba or Castro, that excuse does not explain such a vast, mass burial of documents.[158] And to this day, though we know Oswald had entanglements with pro and anti Castro Cubans, we have never been told the full extent of these entanglements. The fierce secrecy surrounding the issue adds to the evidence that Oswald was a contracted CIA agent.

There has never been a satisfactory answer to the stonewalling that JFK researcher's have encountered when seeking access to records in recent years, approaching fifty years out. Besides protecting the guilty conspirators, some of the evidence obstruction and document redaction serves to protect government agents/officers/leaders from public exposure of their incompetency. It's a lie, regardless of the reason.

And despite the demand for secrecy and discretion, the

Commission itself, beginning with WC member Gerald Ford in his own book on Oswald, leaked a good deal of inside info to the press. Why? The answer is that they leaked information that bolstered their official "lone nut" story or enhanced their public relations. In the years since, thanks to FOIA and the *John F. Kennedy Assassination Records Collection Act of 1992*, we have seen a lot of the previously-classified info, and in most cases, the things that were hidden did not support a lone gunman. The documents tend to erode Warren Commission claims, or show complicity in a cover-up, or reveal government incompetence, or all of the above. At the least, each new revelation raises more questions.

A cover-up is the same as a lie, and Presidents Johnson, Nixon and Ford were all guilty of it.

Lie Number 40: Deaths of Witnesses: The deaths of a hundred witnesses can all be explained away.
~Gerald Posner

Why did so many witnesses die in unnatural ways? During the initial investigation and Warren Commission work, over twenty witnesses were murdered and 50 others found dead under strange circumstances. The years that followed brought more killings and mysterious suicides among those closely connected to the case. And in the seventies, when the House of Representative re-opened the case, key witnesses again began to drop dead unnaturally or prematurely, so that the number now exceeds a hundred. The national murder rate, each year from 1963-1973, was less than 10 persons per 100,000. But here we have over 100 deaths out of a pool of just 1,000 or so (witnesses and others closely related to the case). That is a remarkably higher rate... **statistically astounding**. Here's a partial list of the deaths:

- Oswald (murdered before ever seeing an attorney).
- Lee Bowers, key eyewitness, a rail-yard worker who had the best view of the train yard and who saw two men behind the knoll fence (died in a one-car accident).
- Officer J. D. Tippit, who may have been to Oswald's apartment around 1:00 pm on Nov. 22nd, beeping his horn (murdered).
- Edward Benavides, brother of a witness to the Tippit slaying (murdered).
- George McGann, husband of eyewitness Beverly Oliver, an outspoken Dealey Plaza witness known as the "Babushka Lady" (unsolved murder in 1970).
- George De Mohrenschildt, Oswald's Russian friend and CIA contract agent, was shot (supposedly suicide) the day the House Committee on Assassinations was scheduled to interview him.
- William B. Pitzer, Navy Commander who filmed the autopsy (another "mysterious suicide"...the evidence pointed to murder: he was shot in the right temple, but was left-handed).
- Gary Underhill, a CIA agent who claimed knowledge of the assassination (mysterious suicide just before his House Committee interview).
- Guy Banister, New Orleans FBI/naval intelligence man who knew too much about Oswald (murdered).
- Hugh Ward, Banister's partner (died in a plane crash).
- Hale Boggs, contrarian WC member (mysterious plane crash, never found).
- John Crawford, knew Ruby, Oswald, and Wesley Buell Frazier (died in plane crash in 1969).
- Deputy Roger Craig, a Dealey Plaza eyewitness who gave testimony indicating a conspiracy (car-bombed, shot at, and finally died of a highly-suspicious suicide).
- Police Captain Frank Martin told the Commission he "had better not talk," and that "there's a lot to be said but probably

better if I don't say it." (He died of an unidentified cancer in 1966).

- Deputy Sheriff Buddy Walthers, who reportedly found a bullet in the grass at Elm Street and turned it over to an unidentified FBI agent (shot through the heart).
- Warren Reynolds testified that he had seen a gunman running away just after the Tippit shooting—but Reynolds did not think it was Oswald. Shortly after he refused to identify Oswald, he was shot through the head with a rifle, yet miraculously survived. After other attempts to terrorize him, he finally changed his testimony.
- Darrell Wayne Garner admitted to his sister-in-law that he shot Warren Reynolds. However, when arrested for the crime, he had an alibi witness, Betty Mooney MacDonald, who said he was with her, and the charges were dropped. She had been a stripper at Jack Ruby's Carousel Club. Eight days after her involvement with Garner, she was arrested, soon found hanging dead in her Dallas jail cell.
- William Whaley, a taxi driver who had transported Oswald (or his look-alike) on November 22, 1963, was killed in a car crash in 1965, when the WC critics were beginning to arouse the American people to conspiracy.
- Harold Russell witnessed the fleeing Tippit assailant. He was killed by a policeman in 1967. This death may be unrelated to the conspiracy, but we include it for statistical reasons: the sheer number of deaths of key witnesses are unlike any other comparable case in history.
- James Koethe, a newspaper reporter who met with Ruby's roommate in Ruby's apartment on November 24, 1963, was strangled to death less than a year later.
- Bill Hunter, the other newspaper reporter who had met with Ruby's roommate on November 24, shot to death less than a

year later.

• In 1963, Nancy Carole Tyler, a friend to Teddy Kennedy's girlfriend, and a Washington secretary to Bobby Baker (LBJ's crony). Allegedly, she told Baker of the Kennedys plan to dump LBJ from the ticket in '64. She died in a plane crash May 10, 1965.

• Ralph Reppert, newspaper reporter who assisted theorist Howard Donahue (carbon monoxide suicide... one of several in the case).

• Dorothy Kilgallen, a columnist and TV personality (famous as a regular guest on the show, "What's My Line?"), came back to New York from Dallas after interviewing Jack Ruby, and told friends she could solve the case. Five days later, she died, another mysterious suicide. Ms. Kilgallen was found sitting fully dressed, the coroner found she had died from ingestion of a lethal combination of alcohol and three barbiturates—she had a prescription for Seconal, but not for the other two sedatives in her system... and no empty bottle for them was found. All her notes for the Ruby article had disappeared.

• Thomas Howard, at Ruby's apartment the night Ruby shot Oswald (that makes four out of the five with Ruby who were dead within two years).

• Marilyn April Walle, one of Ruby's dancers, was planning a book on the assassination (shot to death in 1966).

• James Worrell saw an assassin run from the back of the Book Depository and also claimed he heard four shots, not three. Died in a motorcycle accident in 1966.

• Thomas Killam lived in the same boarding house as Oswald on North Beckley. His wife worked for Jack Ruby. (Killam's throat was cut in early 1964, before the Warren Commission could interview him).

• Teresa Norton/aka Karen Bennet Carlin/aka Little Lynn: yet

another of Ruby's strippers (shot dead in 1964).
- Rolando Masferrer, a Cuban who worked with CIA agents Hunt and Sturgis (killed by a car bomb after Watergate).
- Manuel R. Quesada, a Cuban involved with Alpha 66, threatened to rat out conspirators (murdered on a fishing boat).
- Eladio del Valle, a CIA liaison, Ferrie associate and anti-Castro Cuban (shot and head split by an axe, shortly after Ferrie died).
- Cuban ex-President Carlos Prio Socarras (shot dead just before a planned interview with the House Assassinations Committee).
- Clyde Johnson, a witness for the Garrison case (beaten the day before he was to testify; days later murdered by shotgun).
- Robert Perrin, husband of Nancy Perrin Rich, a witness in the Garrison case and Ruby associate (died of arsenic poisoning).
- Rose Cherami, who knew Ruby, warned officials that someone was going to kill JFK in Dallas (she was killed by a hit and run).
- Karyn Kupcinet, connected to Ruby, talked about the assassination 2 days before it happened (murdered two days after it happened).
- Joseph Milteer, a Miami right-winger who told a police informant of a plot to kill JFK in Miama in Nov., 1963 (died in an explosion in 1974 before the House Select Committee could interview him).
- Maurice Brooks Gatlin, Sr., a CIA pilot who knew Banister and who had seen Oswald with Ferrie and Banister (fell from a window and died in 1964).
- Joseph Ayres, chief steward on Air Force One, where some say JFK's body was secretly removed from the coffin to alter clues (shooting accident).
- William Pawley, a supporter of the anti-Castro Cubans (gunshot suicide).
- Robert Kennedy, who knew more than he said publicly (assassinated with multiple gunshots).

- Marilyn Monroe, the famous actress who allegedly had affairs with Jack and/or Bobby Kennedy. Shortly before her supposed "suicide," she had told her hairdresser, Sidney Guilaroff, that she knew "a lot of dangerous secrets about the Kennedys." Her home was later found to have contained eavesdropping devices so sophisticated that the bugs were likely to have been planted by the FBI as part of Hoover's attempt to get dirt on the Kennedy brothers.
- Albert Bogard, working at a Dallas Lincoln-Mercury dealership, had tried to a sell a car to an "Oswald double" days before the assassination. Bogard was found dead in his car in 1966 (yet another carbon monoxide suicide).
- Mary Meyer was murdered less than one year after the JFK assassination (her slaying is still unsolved), because she was beginning to tell people she knew who killed JFK. "De-bunker" Gerald Posner downplays this by saying "except for her reported liaison with the President [she was allegedly one of JFK's mistresses], she was not associated with any aspect of the case." Not true. She was the ex-wife of Cord Meyer, an upper-level CIA man and associate of LBJ's, and she was sister-in-law to reporter Ben Bradlee of the *Washington Post*, and CIA Deputy Director James Jesus Angleton was found in her home after her death, stealing her diary... which he burned.[159]
- Malcolm Wallace, purported to be LBJ's hit man, and whose fingerprint was found on the sixth floor of the TSBD, was supposedly killed by carbon monoxide (a frequent method for faking a suicide).

And that is not the complete list... I've left off most "deaths by natural causes," even when the timing was suspect, and have not counted all those where a witness was *almost* killed. An example of the latter is Antonio Veciana. Three months after his testimony to the HSCA was released, he was shot at four times while driving his pickup truck home... two shots struck Veciana, but he survived.

Debunkers chip away at the list, and likely some of the deaths were unrelated happenstance… but cut the list in half and we still have more deaths than in a Mafia informant's trial! The bigger point: even if we were to accept that these shootings and deaths were "accidental" or just amazing coincidences, once witnesses started dying, other witnesses clammed up in fear. One example of several: Oran Brown, a witness to a "double Oswald," cited witness William Whaley's death and the beating of co-worker Albert Bogard and said, "I am afraid to talk." Over a dozen key witnesses have gone on record saying they have been threatened with harm if they talk, and no doubt many more were intimidated. Some we've mentioned, like Acquilla Clemons. A man with a gun told her that it would be best if she didn't say anything to anyone or she "might get hurt." Others who say they were threatened include Amos L. Euins, Jean Hill, Gail and Bill Newman, Paul O'Connor, and Charles Brehm.[160]

If you find it hard to believe that the government would intimidate and threaten witnesses, consider what the CIA does, even to this day, to its own employees, as reported on *CNN* in 2013: "Some CIA operatives involved in the agency's missions in Libya [re: the Benghazi attack] have been subjected to frequent, even monthly polygraph examinations, according to a source with deep inside knowledge of the agency's workings. The goal of the questioning, according to sources, is to find out if anyone is talking to the media or Congress. It is being described as pure intimidation, with the threat that any unauthorized CIA employee who leaks information could face the end of his or her career. In exclusive communications obtained by CNN, one insider writes, "You don't jeopardize yourself, you jeopardize your family as well."[161] In the JFK case, the fear of losing a job was minor compared to the threat of losing one's life.

Lie Number 41: the Kennedy Family Lies: "I would not reopen the Warren Commission report . . . . I have seen everything that's in there. I stand by the Warren Commission." ~Robert Kennedy

This has been one of the best defenses by the no-conspiracy crowd: "If there had been a conspiracy, Attorney General Bobby Kennedy or others in the Kennedy family would have gone public with their concerns." Not true. In later years, the surviving Kennedy clan *admitted* they had been lying. Publicly, Robert, Edward and Jackie Kennedy accepted the Warren Commission Report. But it was a political pretense. They were afraid for their own personal safety. They also had their own skeletons in the closet, so they remained quiet also to avoid political embarrassment. No longer in control of the highest offices, Robert and Edward could not risk taking on Hoover, Johnson and the CIA, who were playing hardball, willing to blackmail... willing to murder.

Within the Kennedy inner circle, everyone knew it was a conspiracy. They suspected Mafia, FBI and CIA involvement. With her closest friends, Jackie blamed LBJ. Years later, Jackie's memoirs revealed more of her true suspicions. In a series of interviews with writer-historian Arthur M. Schlesinger, Jr., kept private by the Kennedy family for decades, she revealed how much they hated and feared LBJ. She shared on tape her belief that LBJ was a part of the conspiracy.

In 2013, Robert Kennedy, Jr. publicly confessed—in a speech in Dallas of all places— that the Kennedy clan had misled the public. He reported that his father, while still Attorney General, had secretly asked his own staff in 1963-64 to quietly investigate. The result, RFK, Jr. said, is that RFK's press secretary Frank Mankiewicz reported back that "there was a link" between "Mob" conspirators and the president's death.[162]

RFK's investigators had discovered phone records between Oswald and Jack Ruby for the months leading up to the assassination and, RFK, Jr. now reports, they read "like an inventory of the Mafia leaders they had been investigating for the past two years.... They had bugs on a lot of these [Mafia] guys and they were the same characters." RFK Jr. said that his father "was fairly convinced, at the end of that, that there [also] had been involvement by... rogue CIA" agents. He added, "The evidence at this point [early 2013] I think is very, very convincing that it was not a lone gunman."[163] Robert Junior's recent statements give credence to the earlier report that Richard Lubic, a campaign worker for Bobby Kennedy in 1968, heard RFK say that when elected president, he would reopen the JFK assassination inquiry.[164]

Why did the Kennedys initially lie? RFK, Jr. claims it was because, "At that time, cities were burning, the Vietnam War was happening. He [the elder RFK] needed to focus on those [things] to be effective.... There was really nothing he could have done about [the assassination cover-up] at that time anyway. As soon as Jack died, he lost all of his power." That seems like a weak excuse, because as Attorney General, he had every right and duty to look into the crime. The same goes for Ted Kennedy as a Senator. But they remained silent because they knew that Hoover might blackmail the Kennedys concerning their sexual infidelities. Moreover, Robert had been involved with the CIA's plans to kill Castro, and initially was tricked into believing that Castro had gotten revenge via Dallas. Thus Robert himself felt some culpability in his brother's death… and did not want the Cuban secret known.

As powerful as they Kennedys were, their wealth had not saved John, so they may have feared yet another "hit" on a family member. Indeed, sadly, their silence did not prevent Robert's assassination a few years later.

Lie Number 42: Hoover as Co-Conspirator: The FBI "tested the fact you could fire those three shots in three seconds...we have proven it could be done by one man." ~FBI Director J. Edgar Hoover

Did Hoover know that Oswald was an FBI informant? Hoover knew everything. And lied about everything. Historians now agree that Hoover was a perennial liar, sexual deviant, blackmailer, and master manipulator who had dictatorial control over the FBI. President Harry S Truman, a man not prone to overstatement, stated "we want no Gestapo or secret police. The FBI is tending in that direction. They are dabbling in sex-life scandals and plain blackmail. J. Edgar Hoover would give his right eye to take over, and all congressmen and senators are afraid of him."[165] Why, then, do the debunkers still cite FBI evidence to prove their case? If they wish to debate my description of Hoover, they will be debating universally-accepted, historically-documented facts. Knowing that this thoroughly-untrustworthy man hated the Kennedys and was partnered with LBJ, yet to still rest one's case on evidence controlled by Hoover's FBI, is willful blindness to truth.

Here's proof that Hoover was a lying co-conspirator: in a memo sent to key leaders on November 29th, 1963, he reported on his conversation with the new President he had held immediately after the assassination: "I further advised him [LBJ] that we have also tested the fact you could fire those three shots in three seconds."[166] This was a lie, because firing, bolt loading, firing, bolt loading, firing would take over three seconds even without taking a moment to aim. To manually bolt load the old Mannlicher-Carcano requires a vigorous action that cannot be done with an eye pressed against the scope. We must remember (according to the official cover-up story) that two of "those three shots" were amazingly accurate, hitting a moving target—a veritable bulls-eye—from a great distance. No one has ever replicated this feat in less than *eight* seconds. What Hoover claimed they had done—test fire three shots in three seconds–is physically impossible. Hoover overplayed his hand: he did not know that his claims would later be so thoroughly examined, tested, and disproven. His zeal to foist the lone-gunman cover story onto us instead reveals his complicity.

More proof of the government and media cover-up was quietly released in *Newsweek*, October 13, 1997. Brief excerpts of the "Johnson tapes" were printed in that and other national news-magazines. Just like the famous Nixon tapes, tape-recordings of Lyndon Johnson's presidential phone calls and meetings also were preserved—and while LBJ knew his conversations were being taped, he would sometimes forget and become careless with what he said. As only a small part of a lengthy article, *Newsweek* casually mentions the subject of the JFK shooting. LBJ: "How many shots were fired? Three?" Hoover (head of the FBI): "Three.... All three at the president.... He was hit by the first and third. The second shot hit the governor."[167] *Newsweek*, without fanfare, states "Hoover's report clashes with the later official version that one bullet missed...." (*Newsweek*, October 13, 1997, p. 58.) In other words, Hoover did not know at that point which shot missed; later, when the Tague bullet was discovered, the "magic bullet" theory had to be invented to explain away that fourth shot. But there is more: *Newsweek* states that "Johnson and Hoover go on to speak as if the gunman were firing from in front, with Connally obscuring his view of JFK.
LBJ: 'Would the president've got hit with the second one...if Connally hadn't been in his way?'
Hoover: 'Oh, yes, the president would no doubt have been hit.'"

In a later taped conversation (also mentioned in the *Newsweek* story), LBJ expressed his disbelief in the magic bullet theory.

Newsweek also wrote: "Johnson is told by FBI Director J. Edgar Hoover the next day [after the assassination] that covert surveillance reveals that the accused assassin, Lee Harvey Oswald, visited the Cuban and Soviet embassies in Mexico City in September 1963.

Hoover: 'We have up here the tape and the photograph of the man who was at the Soviet Embassy, using Oswald's name. That picture and the tape do not correspond to this man's voice, nor to his appearance. In other words, it appears that there is a second person who was at the Soviet Embassy.'"[168]

Please understand the significance of this *Newsweek* article. **Here is a mainstream media report of an official confirmation at the highest levels of government: that someone was using Oswald's name just two months before the assassination, apparently in order to frame Oswald as a Russian/Cuban sympathizer.**

How did someone know, two months in advance, that this "nobody" was going to shoot at Kennedy? Who would have gone to the trouble to travel to Mexico and impersonate Oswald? Obviously, a **conspirator**. Someone wanted to frame Oswald, and at the same time, smear the communists as responsible for the shooting. The fact that Hoover reported it to LBJ without a word of concern of how this points to conspiracy indicates that Hoover was already in the "inner circle."

Four people—a cook, a chauffeur, a seamstress, and LBJ's mistress Madeleine Brown—are on record stating that there was a secret meeting, on the eve of the assassination, between Hoover and wealthy Texas tycoons at a large, remote ranch home owned by the Murchisons. Supposedly, LBJ dropped by late in the evening for a moment. LBJ's attendance would have been difficult, but not impossible. The Vice-President made appearances at various places throughout the evening, his whereabouts largely accounted for, but it is possible he slipped out of the motel without a Secret Service entourage, after midnight, for the clandestine meeting.

Alternatively, it is possible Madeleine Brown mixed up LBJ's attendance at a previous party in her memory of the event, or it may be that LBJ participated by telephone. Either way, Brown has been consistent across the years in stating unequivocally that the purpose of the meeting was to give a final go ahead on the assassination plans. LBJ told her that Kennedy would "never embarrass" him again.

May Newman, a seamstress and part-time maid to the Murchisons, has been recorded on video with her poignant recollection about Hoover's attendance: she said he he was referred to as "bulldog." Her account on the History Channel series, "The Guilty Men," is very credible. Her words are supported by writer Penn Jones, who said the chauffeur, Warren Tilley, corroborated Ms. Newman's story, having driven Hoover from the airport to the ranch. Bugliosi tries to dismiss this Texas meeting by claiming Hoover never went anywhere without his FBI-provided chauffeur. However, for a quick, in-and-out clandestine meeting in Texas, it would make no sense for Hoover to drag his chauffeur along on the plane when Murchison had already offered his own chauffeur to pick him up from the airport.[169]

•The investigation of the homicides of JFK and Oswald were, legally, under the jurisdiction of Texas law. Within hours, the autopsy was moved illegally to Washington, and within days, LBJ illegally ordered *all* the evidence to be turned over to Hoover's FBI. From that moment on, the investigation was filtered through Hoover. And in another White House tape, we hear Hoover encouraging LBJ's plan to circumvent the impending Senate and House investigations, which Hoover said "would be very, very bad." LBJ shared more of his plan to set-up the Warren Commission cover-up team, and the first name he ran by Hoover's ears was former CIA-Director and Kennedy-hater, Allen Dulles. Hoover emphatically agreed. He knew their secrets would be safe with Allen Dulles as one of the handful of LBJ-selected Commissioners.

One of the arguments of those who defend the WC, including Judge Earl Warren himself, is that it is absurd to suggest we can't trust governmental agencies like the FBI, CIA or even the Executive Branch. Watergate revelations should have made us all disavow the creed of "Trust the government," but Posner, Bugliosi, Von Pein, McAdams and the other "debunkers" continue to chide us: "Look at the hard evidence!" The only hard evidence is buried in a grave at Arlington; everything else has been tainted by organizations that are now proven to be untrustworthy.

In the previous 40 Lies, we've seen many examples of evidence and witness tampering. What career FBI agent would dare speak out against the dictated official fable, when hovering over him was a boss with the twisted morality and iron-fisted control of J. E. Hoover—a man who threatened to ruin careers with illegal wiretaps and cameras? The few who did raise questions were ignored or quickly silenced. Some were brave enough to speak out strongly but never given a voice in mainstream media, such as FBI agents Francis O'Neill, James Sibert, and Donald A. Adams, all who smelled something rotten, all who were ignored. Sibert said of Arlen Specter and his Magic Bullet Theory, "What a liar." Adams called the investigation "bungled" and "riddled with numerous mistakes and I believe that many of those mistakes were intentionally made." Adams was one of the agents who had investigated Joseph Milteer's prediction of an assassination. He was told to "be careful what you say." Adams called the WC "a bunch of liars."

Lie Number 43: Conspiracy Theorists are Amateurs and Quacks: Amateur "assassination researchers... lack the relevant knowledge to do an independent investigation." ~Fred Litwin

Some anti-conspiracy journalists and forensic experts have an elitist notion that "amateurs" are stupid and have nothing to contribute. "Leave this up to professional law enforcement," is another protest heard against conspiracy researchers. There are four problems with this arrogant dismissal:

1. Many of the investigators for the Warren Commission were, themselves, not criminologists; they were young lawyers unskilled in detective work. And even the official law enforcement officials had zero experience with a political assassination or *coup d'etat*. Most of them began with the premise that they could fully trust the FBI and CIA. The Dallas Police, the ones closest in time and proximity to the witnesses and the evidence, were stopped soon after their investigation began, forced to hand their unfinished work over to the FBI and Secret Service. Even if one were to accept that the FBI, CIA and Secret Service had no rogue or untrustworthy agents, we must still admit that cross-communication among all the investigatory agents was poor.

2. Most of the "amateur" investigators are intelligent people with advanced degrees who have a passion for the case. Some *are* in law enforcement. Collectively, we amateurs have devoted far more hours to the investigation than the "professionals."

3. "Amateurs" are just as capable of consulting experts in the various fields needed to weigh the facts (ballistics, acoustics, forensics, etc.), and no one has a monopoly on common sense or an understanding of human nature.

4. And ironically, **the WC ignored the professionals**: Parkland doctors, Sheriff's department, Secret Service agents... their contrary testimony was disregarded.

Let's look at the credentials of just a few of these so-called "amateurs" who say loudly and boldly, "Conspiracy!":

•**Doctors and Scientists:** the WC and others certainly have found their share of experts (some who had ulterior, financial motives) to support aspects of the Establishment's "lone-gunman" case... though in most cases, their testimony is taken piecemeal and out of context. But don't think for a moment that those who believe in conspiracy are ignorant, amateur whack-jobs. From the majority of doctors and medical personnel on the scene at Parkland and Bethesda, to most doctors and scientists who studied the case in depth later, over the past 50 years the best and the brightest have gone on record saying, "There's a cover-up."

•**Dr. Cyril Wecht:** forensic expert with law *and* medical degrees, past President of the American Academy of Forensic Science, past President of the American College of Legal Medicine, Chair of the Board of Trustees of the American Board of Legal Medicine; a County Commissioner, a Coroner, and the Medical Examiner of Allegheny County. It would be hard to top his credentials in the field of criminal forensics; take note that he was elected to be Chair of the Academy of Forensic (Crime) Science by his peers... the best of the best. Dr. Wecht stated emphatically, under oath, that the Single Bullet Theory is "absolutely impossible."

•**Dr. John P. Costella:** holds a PhD in the field of electromagnetic waves and the physics of light; he found alterations in the Zapruder film.

•**Dr. James Fetzer:** a distinguished university professor at several prestigious colleges. Graduated *Magna Cum Laude*, Princeton; PhD from Indiana. He has published over 20 books on a variety of subjects, and written extensively to expose the lies in the JFK case. His theories do go beyond the mainstream, but his scholarship is impressive.

- **Dr. Robert Mantik:** holds a doctorate in physics from the University of Wisconsin; medical doctor (radiation oncology); clinical fellowship with the American Cancer Society. After studying the autopsy records at the National Archives, he is convinced the autopsy was faked.
- **Mark Lane, Esq.:** an accomplished attorney, one of the first to publicly challenge the Warren Commission. Though controversial and oft-criticized (because his zeal perhaps made him a bit too eager to embrace wild theories at times), his intelligence and ability cannot be doubted, as proven by the fact that his opponent in the JFK debate, Gerald Posner, author of *Case Closed*, hired Lane to defend him in a plagiarism case against a Miami newspaper. Posner said, "I've always believed that had Mark Lane represented Oswald, he would have won an acquittal." Indeed, Lane won a case in court that proved Howard Hunt was involved in the JFK plot.
- **Law Enforcement Officials:** Deputy Sheriff **Roger Craig** was one of the first—and not the only—professional officers on the scene who smelled something rotten on November 22nd. Many more law enforcement professionals have come forward since then: **Donald A. Adams**, who has written extensively to expose the conspiracy, has 40 years of law enforcement experience, including 20 years as a Special Agent with the FBI. Part of the initial investigative team for the Commission, he reported that the FBI and WC tried to manipulate his report. **Ed Martin** was a Montana law enforcement officer in the Sixties and Seventies who had direct experience with the security procedures—and negligence—surrounding President Kennedy in 1963. **Brian K. Edwards**, who has written books on JFK, is a well-educated police officer who served for years with the Lawrence, Kansas Police Department, and was a senior member of their Tactical

Response Team. Again, just a partial list, but all of these officers have something in common: they all are convinced there was a conspiracy and a cover-up.

•**Journalists:** there is a long list of reputable, award-winning journalists who saw through the government facade, beginning with **Seth Kantor** (Scripps-Howard newspapers), **Jefferson Morle**y (writer/editor at The New Republic, The Nation, Washington Post, etc.), **Gaeton Fonzi, Geraldo Rivera, Mary La Fontaine** and others. Unfortunately, the list is not long enough. (For the credentials of this writer, go to the bio in the final pages.)

Lie Number 44: No Cover-Up: It's not logical to believe that so many different organizations (FBI, CIA, news media, politicians) could conspire together to keep a secret this big.
~a long list of so-called debunkers repeat this lie

"It's almost impossible to keep a secret... two massive conspiracies, not one word, one syllable, has leaked out in over forty years."
~Vincent Bugliosi, in *Reclaiming History*

Vincent Bugliosi is one of many who tries to trumpet this myth, failing to admit the obvious: **the secret has NOT been kept**, or he wouldn't have written a 1600 page book defending the secret, nor would a thousand others—like me—have written books exposing parts of the secret. My report has detailed over 50 proofs of a government cover-up, including witnesses who separately reported that the FBI and WC altered their testimonies or pressured them to change their wording, such as Vickie Adams, Richard Dodd, Roger Craig, James Simmons, J.C. Price, Jean Hill, Nolan Potter, Clemon Johnson, and more.

Even Police Chief Jesse Curry, after retiring, admitted he had felt pressure to change his "story." And he did so: within seconds of the assassination, he sent a radio message to direct officers toward the Triple Underpass... but the next day, told the press there were just three shots coming from the TSBD.[170]

Other lies under this heading by Bugliosi (his words, from the first chapter of his book *Reclaiming History*, are in quotes):

1. "Not one word, one syllable, has leaked out in over forty years." Bugliosi apparently believes that hyperbole is an effective rhetorical tool... however, knowing that all sorts of hard evidence and substantial rumors have indeed leaked out, he is just destroying his own credibility with his "not one syllable" baloney. The truth is, the JFK conspiracy has **not** been kept secret! Polls show the majority of Americans don't buy the Oswald-only theory. Despite the best efforts of the WC to bury the truth, much of the truth has come out.

2. "No ex-wife or mistress has decided to get even by talking...." This lie first of all ignores the "talking" by LBJ's mistress, and Frank Sturgis' girlfriend, Marita Lorenz. Each is quite convincing in telling us that their lovers were indeed involved in the conspiracy. The lie also ignores the fact that not every spy or assassin blabs everything to his wife.

3. "Not one of the [conspirators] has wanted to clear his conscience on his deathbed." Another lie from Bugliosi... there have been several, the most convincing being the deathbed confession of E. Howard Hunt.

4. Bugliosi claims that it is "silliness" to believe a secret of this complexity could be kept. Untrue. The Manhattan Project was kept secret from the American public, despite the fact that it involved millions of dollars and thousands of employees... hundreds of scientists and government leaders were "in the know."

In addition to the Manhattan Project, consider that Hitler kept the systematic massacre of six million Jews a secret from most of the world for many years. Duping the Red Cross—who inspected concentration camps—required a conspiracy of silence involving hundreds of soldiers and leaders.

A conspiracy of this scope requires collusion by several persons in various positions of power—in spy agencies and law enforcement and elected office. That does not mean *everyone* who contributed to the cover-up is necessarily an inner conspirator or aware of the full truth. Earl Warren is an example: it is highly unlikely the liberal judge would have wanted to see JFK harmed, but it is clear that he blindly helped in the cover-up, heeding Johnson's threat about impending nuclear war.

•Bugliosi, Posner, McAdams and their ilk refuse to concede that government could be corrupt or that witnesses could have been coerced (by bribes or by threats) to alter their testimony. Yet many witnesses have told similar stories of threatening phone calls, stern warnings from FBI agents, and we see so many cases of mysterious homicides and "suicides." How can anyone dismiss this possibility? Bugliosi is either a lousy investigator or disingenuous when he says that eyewitnesses favorable to his side of the debate "had no motive for lying." If someone has threatened the lives of your family, even an honest person would have a motive to lie. (And of course, when witnesses go *against* Bugliosi, suddenly they *are* lying, in his view.)

There are many logical explanations why so many people (the WC, the Dallas Police, the CIA, the FBI, the Secret Service) might not tell the whole truth—or simply fail to investigate the matter fully– with or without evil intent:

•Ignorance, incompetence, or inexperience by investigators/officials, many who had no experience with this type of investigation.

•Mass confusion and chaos at the crime scene made it difficult to get a clear picture of what happened, thus making it easy to cover up the truth.

•Many humans have an innate desire to trust authority, to obey authority, and to try to please those in power. Coupled with a naiveté about the extent of government corruption, this yielded a good number of compliant dupes.

•Misplaced Patriotism: some feared that JFK was dangerously soft on Communism, and others felt that too thorough an investigation might uncover and weaken the methods used by the CIA in their fight against Communism. Even the media felt some allegiance to secrecy during the Cold War era.

•A related fear of communism and of nuclear war, and a concern that if the trail led to Castro or Russia, a world war could follow (LBJ used this threat to convince Earl Warren to be cautious in what was told to the public.)

•Peer pressure from others on the WC to follow the party line; peer pressure upon doctors to support a fellow professional's opinion.

•Complicity in the CIA's illegal plot to assassinate Castro, which made Allen Dulles and even Bobby Kennedy hesitant to dig up too much dirt.

•Threats of death or threat of career-damage— fear that talking too much could get a witness killed or a media or government underling fired. Which is connected to our next Lie....

Lie Number 45: Media, Part 1: "Trust us, we won't lie to you." ~the establishment media

The Feds began immediately to influence the media, to slant stories so that reporting aligned with the "lone crazy gunman" myth. On November 22, a reporter for the *Dallas Times-Herald*, Connie Kritzberg, interviewed Parkland doctors and wrote a story that spoke of a large wound in the back of JFK's head (implying that it was an exit wound) AND an "entrance" wound in the neck. But when the story ran the next day, she found her story had been altered. An additional sentence had been added, stating, "A doctor admitted that it was possible there was only one wound." When Kritzberg asked her editor, Tom LaPere, who had changed it, he told her the FBI had.

In the Seventies, CBS news anchor Dan Rather, reflecting on the Watergate scandal, admitted the media can be subject to pressure and intimidation: "The word was out [that if] you start to mess with this... you're going to end up paying the price. The White House was working very hard on publishers, editors, bureau chiefs—your bosses."

Did similar pressure exist in 1963? Evidently. The CIA ran Operation Mockingbird in the late fifties, an effort to build propaganda outlets via Philip Graham at the *Washington Post*, and made inroads with TIME/LIFE, CBS, NBC and other media.

In the Eighties, *ABC* Reporter Geraldo Rivera was forcefully told by his superiors not to unveil new evidence given to him about JFK's assassins (according to a good friend of Rivera's).

In 1997, *Newsweek* magazine published brief excerpts of the "Johnson tapes,"[171] and includes, but downplays, this telling conversation between LBJ and Hoover:

LBJ: "How many shots were fired? Three?"
Hoover: "Three.... All three at the president.... He was hit by the first and third. The second shot hit the governor."[172]

Newsweek, without fanfare, stated, "Hoover's report clashes with the later official version that one bullet missed...." In other words, at that point in time, Hoover did not know about the shot that had missed (and hit bystander James Tague). Later, when that extra bullet was discovered, the "magic bullet" theory had to be invented to explain away a fourth shot. But there is more:

Newsweek reported that "Johnson and Hoover go on to speak as if the gunman were firing from in front, with Connally obscuring [the gunman's] view of JFK. LBJ: 'Would the president've got hit with the second one...if Connally hadn't been in his way?' Hoover: 'Oh, yes, the president would no doubt have been hit.'"

In a later conversation, also mentioned in the *Newsweek* story, LBJ expressed his disbelief in the magic bullet theory (the same theory which Dan Rather and Gerald Posner continue to defend to this day). So those confessions by LBJ and Hoover could have destroyed the lone gunman notion. All these blockbuster revelations should have been the lead/cover story for every news outlet, rather than buried fifty pages in, as with the *Newsweek* article—or in most places, completely ignored.

In the decades to follow, *Time*, *NBC* and *CBS* have all failed to publish the truth, the whole truth and nothing but the truth about the JFK assassination. Add *Fox News* to the list, since Bill O'Reilly recently released his book that paints Oswald as the crazy assassin. Faithful to the official story spoon fed them by government, mainstream newsmen have failed to investigate... and said some dumb things across the years. One network news reporter said this upon the 30th anniversary of the shooting: "I went out to Dealey Plaza, and the place is so small, I don't see how all the witnesses who claim they were there could have fit into that tiny square." This is a perfect example of the kind of absurd, unscientific, blatantly-false statements the media makes about the JFK case. Dealey Plaza is an open park much larger than a standard city block—surrounded by high rise buildings with hundreds of windows. An overpass held several witnesses. About fifty witnesses were in the motorcade itself. The streets were lined with people. There is ample space in and around Dealey Plaza and in its buildings to easily hold thousands of potential witnesses. The buildings and grounds overlooking Elm Street are *in toto* roughly the size of a football stadium —which holds 80,000 fans with just 22 men on the open field. Indeed, the City of Dallas has plans for over 5,000 spectators to gather in Dealey Plaza for its 50th Anniversary memorial service. An absurd statement by an established journalist.

Another example: in its May 14, 1995 issue, *Parade* magazine chose to promote Norman Mailer's book, *Oswald's Tale: An American Mystery*, as the cover story. For whatever reason, Mailer tries to dismiss the possibility of a conspiracy. In attempting to explain away much of the testimony which indicates there were more shots than possible from a lone-nut Oswald, he gives an absurd rationale: TWO unrelated lone-nuts firing at the same time! He wrote: "It is not inconceivable that two gunmen with wholly separate purposes both fired in the same... few seconds of time." *Not inconceivable!?* The mathematical odds of two unconnected persons coincidentally/randomly shooting JFK in the same six second window of time (out of three years as President) is a gazillion to one against. *Parade* wasted ink on this silly nonsense, desperately trying to find *any* explanation other than conspiracy. What is the purpose of such stupid and misleading statements other than to support official government propaganda? This is irresponsible journalism. It is the *absence* of journalism.

With all their resources, network news programs never investigated the case with a fraction of the ferocity and thoroughness of independent researchers. Instead, they aired slanted "documentaries" purporting to "prove" the lone-gunman theory. Using computer-generated graphics (which prove nothing because they are not *photos* but manipulated animations/images), they "proved" that one bullet could have hit Kennedy and Connally. One bullet might have hit them both, of course, if you line up the car, the passengers, the *wounds*, and the lone gunman in exactly the perfect angle. What *cannot* be proven is that those positions/angles ever existed on November

22nd. They all failed to show that an identical bullet could pass through a similar amount of bone and flesh without becoming seriously deformed. They also lied about the location of the wound on JFK's back, rather than aligning the wound using the bullet-hole in his coat and shirt.

Documents released in July of 1997 revealed that Gerald Ford changed the initial wording of the Warren Commission's comments about JFK's back wounds in order to bolster the Magic Bullet Theory. This is an astounding fact, but it never made headlines.[173] The Commission's initial draft had written, "A bullet had entered his back at a point slightly above the shoulder and to the right of the spine." Ford admits to having changed the draft, so that the final report reads, "A bullet had entered the base of the back of his neck at a point slightly to the right of the spine." [emphasis mine] But neither statement was consistent with the FBI and Commission's own "reconstruction" photo, which shows one entry point well below the neck and another (supposedly the fatal shot) at the hairline, neither corresponding to Ford's wording. One autopsy photo clearly shows a back entry wound in JFK's shoulder, close to the spine but a good two inches below the neck (House Assassinations Committee Exhibit F-20). Ford knew back in 1964 that autopsy photos would not be released to the public, so he could change the wording with impunity. Now that we have some of the autopsy photos, there is no question that one of the shots hit JFK in the back. It would have been impossible for such a wound to then exit the front of Kennedy's neck and still go through Connally in three locations...yet, this is the heart of the magic bullet theory. Despite these clear facts, *The Dothan Eagle*, like many newspapers, defended Ford, stating that "he was merely clarifying," not covering anything up. How a bald-faced lie can be called a "clarification," especially in 1997 with all the evidence available, is beyond my understanding of responsible journalism. (Ford had the audacity to still claim, at the close of the millennium, that the Warren Commission's "judgments have stood the test of time.")[174]

But the myth of Oswald as the lone assassin continues to this day. In August 2013, the New York Times still referred to Oswald as "the man who killed Kennedy," even though, as we have proven here, it was quite impossible for Oswald to have fired the fatal shot.[175]

The bias in reporting was never more obvious than in *CBS'* 1993 30th Anniversary Special: "Who Killed JFK: The Final Chapter?" starring Dan Rather... which leads to our next lie:

Lie Number 46: Media, Part 2: The shots were easy, and Oswald's marksmanship (speed and accuracy) in Dallas has been replicated. ~mainstream news-media

Some writers claim, falsely, that Oswald was a bad shot. The record shows he was an average-to-good shot. Yes, some of his Marine buddies observed him missing the entire target, but likely that was when he was just kidding around or perhaps hung over from a night of drinking... young men his age can occasionally be cavalier on the shooting range. In his actual Marine *tests* for marksmanship, he achieved good—though not excellent—scores. So he likely could have made *one* of the shots from the sixth floor window. But that is not the issue. The issue is more complex. Experienced marksmen doubt he could have struck the moving target *twice* under the limits of the *circumstances and timing* Oswald faced. Even the FBI report admitted that the gun had a misaligned scope. Network reports, however, rarely mention that; they ran rigged tests to try to make the shots look easy. A lie.

In 1967, Dan Rather and company "reconstructed" the

shooting to show that it was possible for Oswald to fire three shots in less than seven seconds, with two hitting the target. Rifle expert Col. Edward B. Crossman had tried several times, but was no match for the timing and accuracy attributed to the sixth floor assassin. So CBS set up eleven more marksmen in their rigged test—a no-pressure reenactment with ample set-up time, shooting at a target traveling in a **straight line** at a steady speed (unlike JFK's limo on a curved road with varied speed). The 11 volunteer marksmen made 37 attempts to fire three quick shots at a moving target. Most failed both in time and accuracy, and **none succeeded on their first try**. To make the CBS non-reenactment even easier, their marksmen were allowed to test fire the weapon with the non-aligned scope in advance, on site. So the marksmen had a chance to compensate for the scope error at the distances and angles involved, something which Oswald did not have the luxury to do. The best of their marksmen was Howard Donahue, who "succeeded" on his third try. Donahue, after the test, was so unconvinced of the one-gunman theory he went on to write a book refuting it.[176] The media ignored his work, and *CBS* concluded that Oswald made the shots.

 CBS trumpeted the flawed work of young Gerald Posner, who, thanks to healthy cash infusions from an establishment publisher and a large staff, did the impossible: he defended the Warren Commission's conclusions. When quoting or consulting with "experts" and authors, *CBS* generously gave Posner the bulk of the air-time. Not a single conspiracy researcher or WC critic was given an opportunity to rebut the many false assertions made by the program's lone-gunman narrative. Critics of the single-shooter theory were quoted out-of-context or in such short clips their arguments were rendered weak and incomplete. For instance, in a discussion of the magic bullet, *CBS* quoted forensic expert Cyril Wecht saying, "The magic bullet is the *sine qua non* of the case," but then failed to let him explain *why* he believes that exposing the fallacy of the magic bullet proves a cover-up. Instead, the narrator spoke for him, presenting an incomplete, watered-down version of Wecht's case.

CBS is not alone. *The Discovery Channel* aired a "scientific" program, stating the shot could not have come from the Grassy Knoll because "it would have killed Jackie Kennedy."[177] Photographs prove that statement is utter nonsense, unbecoming of a so-called "science channel." This lie is repeated (and left unchallenged) on the *National Geographic* special, *JFK: The Lost Bullet*, quoting debunker Larry Sturdivan (author of the untrustworthy book, *The JFK Myths*) who says a shot from the Grassy Knoll "probably... would have gone into Jackie." *National Geographic* could have used computer graphics to easily disprove this lie... but chose not to, and let the lie stand as "truth." Look at the Zapruder film, frame 313: when the President's head explodes with the final (Grassy Knoll) shot, Jackie was leaning forward of JFK, looking back to examine his face with concern over the first shot's effect on his throat. Even if Abe Zapruder himself had fired the shot, it would have missed Jackie's head... but the shot actually came from the far *right* of Abraham Zapruder, which means the shot angled back to the Kennedys' left rear even more (relative to the camera lens' position). Take a look at the Moorman photo. Snapped from behind just as the fatal shot is exploding JFK's head, this picture clearly shows that Jackie is leaning forward of her husband, proving beyond a shadow of doubt any shot from the Knoll would have come nowhere near her head.[178] It doesn't take a computer or an expert—just honest eyesight—to see that a shot from the fence on the Grassy Knoll would obviously have gone *behind* the First Lady. Moreover, that fatal shot from the Knoll exploded and fragmented so thoroughly that **no bullet came out the back** of Kennedy's head... only exploded skull did. And the "dodging Jackie" trajectory of that rear-projected skull was proven in two ways: one, in a frame of the Zapruder movie, we can see a sizable piece of white bone on the far back left-side of the limo's trunk (it missed Jackie by a mile), and two, by the fact that the motorcycle policeman in this same line I'm describing was hit hard with flying brain matter. So we have multiple proofs that a bullet from the Knoll would *not* (and did not) hit Jackie... so we have to ask again, **Why did a "scientific" program repeat this absurd lie, blatantly contradicting all the photos/evidence?**

Is the *National Geographic* organization overly-cozy with the CIA? To answer that, consider that an excellent cover to help CIA spooks infiltrate and explore other countries it would be to work for a company that assigns persons a job to travel the globe, to always have cameras and other investigative equipment (often using boats and planes), to be inquisitive and explorative, to have a press pass and to have easy access to media. As one blogger put it, "If you want to know which countries the Pentagon is about to invade, look at the *National Geographic*..." itinerary in the years and months just prior to a war. So I was not the least bit surprised to find the *Geographic's* documentary was one of the most one-sided "pro-lone-gunman" pieces out there... one in which not a single reasonable pro-conspiracy researcher is quoted, and in which the word "CIA" is never mentioned.

The "computer re-creations" and "scientific proof" presented by documentaries by supposed "science channels" like *National Geographic* and the *Discovery Channel,* and by supposedly-factual *ABC* and *CBS* "news documentaries," are not scientific at all. They make assumptions that the facts don't warrant. If you input false assumptions, then you arrive at false conclusions — no matter how "scientific" the rest of your methods are, nor how fast your computer is. The perfect example of this, the above-mentioned *National Geographic* absurdity about a Grassy Knoll shot hitting Jackie, was not an anomaly: it was also asserted by the *Discovery Channel* "documentary." Science or propaganda?

The lies in these so-called documentaries are easily refuted, yet because they claim to be computer-generated, viewers assume they are factual and unbiased... forgetting that a human can make a computer say anything if the wrong data is input or the interpretation of the output is fudged. *Pink-spotted Martians have landed, that's a fact*. That statement must be scientific, since my **computer** sent those words to your Kindle or to the publisher to print, right?

Conspiracy theorists would be happy if the mainstream media presented an honest debate, with equal time from the best experts from both viewpoints. Unfortunately, most of the documentaries and "news investigations" have been exclusively one-sided to the point of absurdity, with no disclaimer given. In this book, from the title onward, I've made no secret in saying that I'm convinced it was a conspiracy. Although I do present both sides of issues, I don't pretend to be a dispassionate news observer—my aim is to present a persuasive argument. But most of the television documentaries and news reports from the mainstream media do the opposite: **they *claim* to be objective news, yet present only one side of the evidence.**

Another case in point is the *BBC* program, "The Kennedy Assassination: Beyond Conspiracy," originally broadcast in Britain on November 23rd, 2003 and later shown on American TV. It presents *only* the opinions of that small minority of researchers, authors and officials who still toe the party line— again, Gerald Posner in particular. Only near the end of the program does it look at two pro-conspiracy voices: Jim Garrison and Oliver Stone. But they were set-up as straw men, only to ridicule them. Stone is a movie producer, not a genuine researcher. It was as slanted as a campaign commercial, full of bald-faced lies, such as stating as fact that Oswald was the only employee missing from the TSBD, when the record proves otherwise. It twice mentions Oswald's visit to Mexico to the Russian embassy... but never mentions the incredible fact that the pictures and tapes recorded there by the CIA show an impostor of Oswald. More cover-up. And to the question of Oswald's marksmanship, the "Beyond Conspiracy" piece stated, "The shot was well within his ability." An irrelevant argument. We concede it was possible for *one* of the shots to have hit the President. But that does NOT mean it was possible for Oswald to have fired exactly three shots, and hit two "bulls-eyes," in the short time-frame and other variables. And there is overwhelming evidence of at least *four* shots.

ABC News did their own version of "Beyond Conspiracy," using the same writer and the same biased approach. *ABC* Anchor Peter Jennings narrated, and his nefarious agenda is clear in his hyperbole: "In all these years, there has not been a single piece of credible evidence to prove a conspiracy." Not a single piece? We have at least a hundred pieces. Jennings might respond by saying, "But you can't *prove* it," and quibble about the definition of proof. How do you demand we prove this? In court? Mark Lane proved it, winning a jury verdict in the Howard Hunt slander case. With science? We've included several pieces of scientific proofs herein. With government records? We have the White House tapes where Hoover admits a fake Oswald. Which leads us to ask, *Why? Why would Peter Jennings, Dan Rather, ABC, CBS, Discover, Geographic, BBC and other news/science programs approach such an important topic with a pre-set agenda of cover-up? Why have they lied?*

Lie Number 47: The Secret Service: The Secret Service could not have prevented the assassination. And it was JFK's own fault that the agents were not riding on the back of the Presidential limo.

~the WC Report, and Gerald Blaine in *The Kennedy Detail*

Vince Palamara is demonstrably the best expert on the early-sixties Secret Service; he has met, interviewed and/or corresponded with over 80 former agents and their family members in the process of writing his book, *Survivor's Guilt: The Secret Service and The Failure To Protect The President*. I agree with Vince's statement, "I am a great admirer of the Secret Service... [with the exception of] the events related to November 22, 1963." We all agree that most Secret Service agents are brave patriots who love their country and who work grueling hours... but some failed to protect President Kennedy. Palamara is authoritative when he repeats what other writers have said before him: it was an odd breach of protocol when SS agents were told not to ride on the back of the Presidential limousine. The Secret Service should have used the steps and handholds on the back of the Presidential limo to offer closer/better protection of JFK—as was their normal procedure. With an agent standing tall on the back bumper, the first shot to hit JFK instead may well have struck the agent—with, hopefully, a non-fatal wound. The agent would have instantly fallen off, which would have alerted the President and his bodyguards to the danger. While it is debated whether or not JFK instructed the agents to stay off the back of the car, Presidents are not dictators and they are required to follow SS protocol. Palamara offers clear documentation of the fact that Presidents must obey Secret Service directives, including this quote from within the WC Report itself, from SS Chief James J. Rowley: "No President will tell the Secret Service what they can or cannot do." Palamara goes further: he cites some twenty Secret Service agents who told him Kennedy did *not* order them off the back of his limo. But obviously, someone did.

    Other mistakes or suspicious breaches of protocol by the Secret Service:

• Windows overlooking the motorcade route should have been

closed, and buildings and rooftops inspected in advance.
- Knowing that the motorcade would traverse through an area with scores of high-rise buildings, with threats having been loudly issued against JFK (such as the "Wanted" poster placed in the Dallas newspaper by a radical rightwing group), security should have been raised, not lowered. Indeed, there had been serious threats to kill the President in the weeks leading up to November 22nd—threats in Dallas and earlier in Miami and Chicago. But security was relaxed, not tightened.
- The follow-up car containing most of the SS agents allowed a much-larger gap between bumpers in the moments before and during the shots. For much of the motorcade, the Presidential limo and the SS follow-up car rode bumper-to-bumper, within three feet of each other... the gap noticeably widened on Elm Street, making it harder for the agents to run up to the limo (after the first shot, Clint Hill barely made it at all to the hand-hold behind Jackie, while the agent on John's side didn't even try.)
- The Secret Service Presidential limo driver, Agent Bill Greer, should have sped up, not slowed down, after the first "backfire" noise, and certainly when he heard passengers behind him cry out in alarm. This was downplayed (and lied about) in the WC Report, but here is what transpired according to witnesses and the Zapruder film: the Presidential limousine had slowed to round the corner, but instead of accelerating going down the hill toward the freeway (the crowds had thinned and were not out in the road), the limo slowed down to less than 15 miles per hour; the first shot was heard (although it missed), and the limo slowed even more; the second shot hit the President in the neck, his elbows flew out and his hands drew to his throat as Driver Greer glanced back; Jackie and Governor Connally both made comments to the effect of "They are killing us!" Greer turned forward and slowed down even more. Many witnesses said the car "stopped" or "slowed down" at that point... throughout much

of the shooting, the car was going less than 10 mph, slower than a walk. Agent Kellerman, in the front seat beside Greer, ordered him to "Get out of line; we've been hit!" Greer disobeyed his superior's order and turned around to glance at the passengers for the second time. Only *after* the fatal headshot exploded in a red halo did he finally try to escape the scene by accelerating. At no time during eight seconds and four shots did he attempt to evade danger by swerving or speeding away.

A point needs to be made here about cover-up. In testimony to the WC, Greer's excuse for slowing was that he did not hear or see things clearly enough behind him, and he paused in a state of confusion. But in SS Agent Gerald Blaine's book, *The Kennedy Detail*, Blaine offers a different excuse, claiming Greer "hit the brakes" to test whether "the tire had a blow-out." Either Greer was lying under oath to the Commission, or someone else fabricated Blaine's cover story regarding the fictional flat tire. The Muchmore film does indeed show a brake-light light up on the limo, but it is right before the fatal shot, thus at least seven seconds after the first shot. Applying the brakes at that point is not justifiable by worrying about a "flat tire," because by then, several people in the limo had already exclaimed they were shot.

Greer claimed he did not hear anyone in the car cry out about being shot until *after* the shots, when Agent Kellerman, in the seat beside him, finally told him to "Get out of here, we're hit!" Even then, he was slow to accelerate. From Greer's testimony to the WC:

```
SPECTER. "Did you hear anyone in the car say anything
from the time of the first shot until the time of the
third shot?"
GREER. "Not to the best of my recollection...."
```

Congressman Hale Boggs came into the hearing later and resumed the questioning about what was said in the car:
```
BOGGS. "Did Mrs. Connally say anything to you?"
```

GREER. "No. Mrs. Connally didn't say anything, either. There is quite a little distance between the front and the back seat of that car. As you know, it is **21 feet long,** and you are quite a little bit away...."

Here I am reminded of the famous monkey who "sees no evil, hears no evil." Despite the fact that Greer glanced back twice at Connally and Kennedy during the first seconds of the shooting, Greer claims he saw nothing to make him think they were shot. Next, Greer claims he heard nothing alarming, and tried to blame this on the *distance*, telling the WC that that the Presidential limo is "21 feet long" and the passengers were "quite a little bit away." But the distance from Nellie Connally's mouth to his ear was less than four feet, and from a hysterical Jackie just six feet. And Kellerman had no such trouble hearing, even though he was the same distance from John Kennedy as Greer was from Jackie (who, according to Nellie Connally, exclaimed, "They have shot my husband" before the last two shots were fired). Kellerman testified to the WC that he distinctly heard the President say "I've been hit!" and that JFK's voice "carried very clearly," Kellerman added. He also heard Jackie in the most distant seat from him but could not recall everything she said. But Driver Greer heard nothing of the sort. Four passengers all reacting audibly and physically to the shots, and Greer claimed to be oblivious.

The inexplicable slowness of Greer to react is in stark contrast to Agent Clint Hill, who immediately upon the *first* shot, looked around, and, though not privy to the exclamations of inside the limo in front of him, still had the instinct to run to the next car and grab hold of the back of the limo—all in less time it took Greer to simply step on the accelerator.

Hill's actions also prove the slow speed of the limo. Hill had time to react, to get down from the running board, dodge a motorcycle, and jog ten feet to catch up to the Presidential limo—in a suit-coat with dress shoes. I don't wish to accuse Greer, but I will say: If you were a conspirator and could have just ONE Secret Service Agent in your cabal, wouldn't you choose the driver of the President's car and ask him to drive slowly through the kill zone?

Could the assassination have been prevented? Any *single one* of the following actions by the Secret Service might have saved JFK's life:

•The aforementioned actions (close building windows, drive faster, ride on limo).

•Install the bubble-top. Agent Gerald Blaine and others have falsely claimed that installing the plexiglass bubble-top on the limo would not have saved JFK. They point out, correctly, that it was not bulletproof. But that is not the point: if the plexiglass top had been in place, it could have *warned* the President. One of the first shots missed JFK by inches, but likely would have struck the bubble. Since most officials were not sure the sounds were shots, had a bullet impacted the bubble, it would have been an obvious alert, giving time for the occupants to duck or be covered and for the driver to be awakened to danger.

•Put more agents on the ground (and mobilize the Sheriff's department, who stood idly by). Agents on the ground (rather than all stuffed into a car) might have discovered suspicious characters in the Dealey Plaza area.

•More thorough advance work. Active solicitation of information by the SS, to enhance communication from the FBI, might have prompted FBI Agent Hosty to share his knowledge of Oswald with the Secret Service. The FBI had received several warnings of assassination plots in November, 1963. This should have caused elevated security standards or even the cancellation of an open-air motorcade entirely—a joint failure by the FBI and the Secret Service (see Lie Number 25).

One Secret Service Agent who tried to pass on a warning was

Abraham Bolden. One of the other personal tragedies of the JFK plot is the story of Agent Bolden, a man who had come up from poverty to graduate with honors from Lincoln University, spent four years of exemplary service as an Illinois State Trooper, with a record so outstanding that in 1959 President Dwight Eisenhower appointed him to the U.S. Secret Service. First based in Chicago, Bolden won commendations for cracking counterfeiting rings. In 1961, President Kennedy appointed him to be part of the White House Detail. Unfortunately, Bolden spent only three months protecting Kennedy, because he complained to Chief U. E. Baughman of the "general laxity and the heavy drinking among the agents who were assigned to protect the President." They metaphorically "shot the messenger": to quiet Bolden, they sent him back to the Chicago office for routine anti-counterfeiting duties. But this did not silence him. In October, 1963, the Chicago Secret Service office received a teletype from the FBI warning of a plot against the President: a four-man Cuban hit squad was planning to kill JFK in the windy city on November 2nd. Bolden tried to raise awareness, but was ignored. The Presidential trip to Chicago was cancelled for other reasons. Abraham Bolden later discovered that the advance information about the Chicago plot had been kept from the Warren Commission. When he complained about this he was told: "Keep your mouth shut." He did not. He travelled to Washington where he telephoned WC Counsel J. Lee Rankin. His reports still fell on deaf ears. Shortly after this, Bolden was arrested and taken back to Chicago where he had been framed or entrapped for bribery. He spent six years in prison, including harsh solitary confinement. Sam DeStefano, an associate of Mafia kingpin Sam Giancana, was one of the men involved in the entrapment of Bolden. DeStefano lived by the sword and died by the sword: like so many criminals involved in the cover-up, he was later murdered.[179]

The plot to kill Kennedy was complex, and in fact, there were contingency plans—in the event the trip to Dallas got cancelled—to kill JFK in Chicago, Miami, or Tampa. But with help from a few elements within the Dallas police, CIA, FBI, and Secret Service involved in the plots to kill or in the cover-up, the plot was guaranteed success.

Lie Number 48: The Mystery Masterminds: We will never know who was behind this. ~the House Special Committee on Assassinations, which found reasons to suspect conspiracy but never named a culprit.

50 years on, with 100 witnesses dead and a 1,000 pieces of evidence destroyed, we could not convict the masterminds behind the *coup* even if they were still alive. We will never identify everyone actively involved in the shooting and cover-up. But the lingering effects of having skeletons in the dark closets of government, the ongoing repression in mainline media on the subject, and the fact that a secret government still exists, these are reasons we must re-open an official investigation.

Any criminal investigation should ask the questions of *Means and Motive*: Who had the most to lose—in money and political power—if President Kennedy had lived another year? Who was driven by jealousy and narcissistic ambition? Who had the means, methods, men and opportunity to do so? Who had a multitude of connections in the state of Texas to arrange matters there? Who was a friend to the owner of the TSBD? Who appointed the Warren Commission and insured the cover-up? Who was close friends with J. Edgar Hoover of the FBI and had private phone calls—now revealed —that speak of the need to limit the scope of that investigation? Who was able to order JFK's limousine cleaned and repaired within days of the shooting, to hide the evidence? Who pressured Captain Will

Fritz of the Dallas police to not dig deeper for conspiracy, because "you have your man" in Oswald? Who chastised Dallas Chief Curry for statements he had made about the FBI's foreknowledge of Oswald? Who had the political power and position to make sure the CIA, Secret Service, Dallas Police, FBI and other government agencies cooperated, focusing on Oswald instead of investigating a conspiracy? Who realized that his political career was being eclipsed by the growing popularity of the young, charismatic Kennedy? Who—with a history of scandal and criminality in his climb to power—rationalized evil actions by quoting Thomas Jefferson, saying: "It is the melancholy law of human societies to be compelled sometimes to choose a great evil in order to ward off a greater"?[180] Who became President instantly when JFK's heart stopped, sworn in with a wink from a Congressman? **There is only one name that can answer ALL of the above questions:**
LYNDON BAINES JOHNSON.

Powerful people in government and the media have a variety of reasons for protecting LBJ's reputation. Ask yourself why the following fact has not been widely broadcast: **Jack Ruby said LBJ was behind the plot**. Ruby is on camera saying, "When I mentioned about Adlai Stevenson [a previous candidate for the White House], if he [had been] Vice-President there would never have been an assassination of our beloved President Kennedy." The reporter asked for more clarification, and Ruby complied: "The answer is, the man in office now." Meaning LBJ. Ruby was calm and deliberate when he said this, and not acting "crazy" (as Posner would claim). On yet another occasion Ruby had said that those with "ulterior motives" in the assassination were at the "highest levels" of government.

Frankly, some scoff at naming LBJ as a mastermind because it seems too obvious. I remember within days of the assassination, my father telling me a not-so-funny joke that was circulating: "Why was LBJ crying after the assassination? Answer: the FBI wouldn't give him his rifle back!" On its face, the accusation that the Vice-President killed the President to steal his crown sounds too obvious, too absurd, too medieval. But is that a reason to reject a proposition? We dismiss an accusation when there is no evidence. And when it comes to LBJ, we have far more than just Jack Ruby pointing the finger.

- **Republican strategist Roger Stone,** who worked for Ronald Reagan, and on Richard Nixon's staff in the seventies, now says that he is sure Johnson "micro-managed" the Dallas motorcade and set-up JFK for the shooting ambush. He also adds when he was a Congressman, Johnson asked Richard Nixon to put Jack Ruby onto the House of Representatives payroll in 1947.[181] Stone recently stated: "I believe that LBJ spearheaded a conspiracy funded by Texas Oil and assisted by elements of the CIA and the Mob.... LBJ's unique relationships with J. Edgar Hoover and the FBI, defense contractors, Texas Oil, and organized crime allowed him to spearhead a conspiracy."[182] Roger Stone (no connection to filmmaker Oliver Stone) adds that Johnson was, "Power hungry, crude, vulgar, abusive, sadistic, vicious and often drunk."[183]

- **The White House Tapes:** The *Atlantic* magazine, books and other media have printed transcripts from Johnson's Oval Office phone conversations. According to the *Atlantic* (and the now-public records), Johnson had set Hoover loose to bug the White House, including his own Vice-President Hubert Humphrey's phones. LBJ was cognizant that his own conversations were being recorded for archival purposes... or if needed, to blackmail any turncoats. Nevertheless, just as with Nixon, he would not always be completely guarded in what he said by phone. In the first pages of this book we related Johnson's conversations with Hoover, which show that they were both privy to the knowledge that someone was impersonating Oswald and in agreement to limit the investigation. In early 1967, Johnson had further conversations about the JFK assassination with Attorney General Ramsey Clark and Governor John Connally (when the CIA plot to kill Castro first began to leak). Reading between the lines, we find that LBJ was not the least bit ruffled by discussions of possible conspiracy in the JFK killing.[184] In fact, he seemed more energized by news that Bobby Kennedy knew about the plot to kill Castro than he did over the accusations that he (LBJ) was involved in the JFK plot. Clark told Johnson: "Hale Boggs was sayin' ...privately around town that it could be traced back to you [i.e. LBJ]." Boggs was a close friend and ally to LBJ (hand-selected by the President to serve on the Warren Commission). One would thus expect Johnson to exclaim in anger or surprise: *That Judas, that backstabber! I had nothing to do with Kennedy's death!!* But instead, the usually-reactive LBJ shows no anger toward Boggs, replying nonchalantly: "Who did he tell?"

•**Barr McClellan, Don Thomas, and Ed Clark:** McClellan was an attorney who had inside knowledge that Lyndon Johnson, Austin Attorney Edward Clark, and their crony, Mac Wallace, were involved in the planning, execution and cover-up of the JFK assassination. In his book, *Blood Money and Power: How L.B.J. Killed J.F.K.*, McClellan makes a strong case that conservative business tycoons (lawyers, oil men, and military contractors) in Texas funded a conspiracy with Johnson and Clark to ensure that LBJ would become President—at any cost. Despite insults hurled at him ("forger, fraud"), Barr McClellen is a very credible inside source: he worked with Austin attorney Edward A. Clark, who watched over LBJ's financial, legal and personal affairs. Barr is not without blemishes, but most high-powered attorneys, especially those involved with politicians, will get mud slung on them—and sometimes self-inflicted mud, the result of wrestling with greedy pigs. But do not dismiss

McClellen; read his book. In it, he documents how Don Thomas, a close friend to LBJ and a full partner in the law firm of *Clark, Thomas and Winters*, confirmed McClellen's previous discoveries: Edward Clark "handled" the events in Dallas, with LBJ's approval and support. Clark/Thomas' firm was allied with Clint Murchison, H. L. Hunt, Wofford Cain, and D. H. Byrd (owner of the Texas School Book Depository), who made fortunes mostly in the defense and oil industries. They needed to remove Kennedy from office for several reasons: to protect their crony-in-power, LBJ; to take a hard stance against communism (in keeping with their political philosophies, but also to thus keep money flowing into the defense industry), and to keep the Oil Depletion Allowance in place, which saved oil companies billions. The depletion allowance remained unchanged during the Johnson presidency, saving the American oil industry over $100 million versus the possible changes Kennedy was considering. Some conspiracy naysayers are good but naive folk, who refuse to believe that persons are routinely killed over a hundred bucks... a few *million* is ample motivation for some "upstanding citizens" to order a killing. Texas oil companies enjoyed some of the highest tax deductions of any U.S. industry—but Kennedy was quietly planning to change that in his next term. As John Kennedy's popularity began to rise in the polls and a second term was looking more like a shoe-in, the Kennedy brothers were poised to take on Hoover, Johnson and Johnson's "Texas Tycoons." McClellen's book is persuasive and by no means a single voice. The Texas crimes of Johnson, Clark and Wallace are corroborated by a long list of witnesses in addition to Estes: Texas Ranger Clint Peoples, Attorney Barr McClellen, Henry Marshall, and Attorney Douglas Caddy. Caddy wrote the Department of Justice, stating that his client, Estes, was willing to testify that Mac Wallace, Cliff Carter and LBJ and had been involved in the murders (discussed below) of

Marshall, John Kinser, George Krutilek... and the President.[185] What follows is a long list of testimony and evidence explaining these connections, as well as LBJ's motives, that ultimately led to the Dallas plot:

•**Evelyn Lincoln**, a highly-credible source as Secretary to both JFK and LBJ, detested Johnson and came to believe that he was involved in killing her favorite boss. In her biographical writings, she later wrote that the Kennedy brothers, with great reluctance, had placed LBJ on the ticket in 1960 mainly because of blackmail by J. Edgar Hoover (who had evidence of Kennedy's womanizing). A few months before his death, JFK confided to Ms. Lincoln that he had decided to replace LBJ on the '64 ticket (by then, the Kennedys had gathered their own blackmail on Hoover's homosexuality and on LBJ's affairs, effectively stalemating their threats). President Kennedy confided to a few others that he wanted Governor Terry Sanford of North Carolina to be the next vice president. When Johnson learned that he would be dumped from the '64 ticket, he sprang into action. According to Attorney McClellen, his law partner, Edward Clark, conspired with LBJ to recruit Malcolm Wallace to be a part of a plot to kill the President. As evil as the motive is, it is understandable. LBJ had only two choices: kill Kennedy and ascend to the Presidency easily and instantly, or give up his lifelong ambition to be President. The latter choice also would have meant the LBJ would face investigation in TWO major scandals: the Bobby Baker scandal and the Billie Sol Estes trial.

•The **Bobby Baker** scandal almost brought down Johnson. Johnson was like a big brother (and criminal partner) to Bobby Baker, who even named two of his children after LBJ (Lynda and Lyndon). In the fifties, Baker had been the most powerful non-elected official in the Senate, working side-by-side with then Senate Majority Leader Lyndon Johnson, and entangled in many of LBJ's nefarious schemes to accumulate votes, money and power. On the day of the assassination, Bobby Baker was being investigated by the Senate Rules Committee for allegations of congressional bribery (offering cash and sexual favors to politicians in exchange for votes and government contracts).[186] LIFE magazine had been given damning evidence (perhaps by Robert Kennedy's staff in the Justice Department) about Baker's and Johnson's malfeasances. According to LIFE writer James Wagenvoord, the popular magazine was planning to run an expose on Lyndon Johnson's corruption in the next issue (due to be mailed out just a week after the assassination). The assassination news bumped the story.

•Another Johnson crony, **Billie Sol Estes**, was involved in various schemes and scams in the fifties and sixties, including bilking money from farmers and the Department of Agriculture via fraudulent sales of ammonia tanks and manipulation of cotton allotments. Johnson got a piece of the action. The May 2013 *This Week* magazine reported Estes' obituary: "He was a fast-talking flim-flam man... [and] when his empire came crashing down in the early 1960's amid allegations of fraud and murder, the shock waves went all the way up to then-Vice President Lyndon Johnson." Estes was being seriously investigated in 1963. Initially, Johnson was able to keep pressure on Estes to remain quiet (using carrot *and* stick). But he knew that the Kennedys would tempt Estes with immunity, turning him into a State's Witness to implicate the Vice-President. Before that could happen, Johnson would steal the seat of power, leaving Estes with little choice but to settle for the limited help Johnson offered. Estes was tried and convicted in 1964 on fraud charges.[187] Not long after JFK's heart stopped, Johnson used the power of the Presidency to lessen the fallout from the Senate investigations into Estes and Baker. Now we go back to look more closely at the entanglements of these Texas bad boys... and one lone White Hat.

•Clifton Carter and Mac Wallace vs. Henry Marshall: The investigation of Billie Sol Estes had begun in 1960 when State Agricultural official Henry Marshall discovered Estes' cotton-allotment profiteering scheme. To side-track Marshall from the Estes case, Johnson ordered Clifton Carter (the same Carter who lied to cover up LBJ ducking prematurely in the Dallas motorcade) to "promote" Marshall out of Texas, to a higher-paying post in Washington. The virtuous Marshall rejected the idea of having his silence bought via a promotion. Estes, Johnson, Carter and Mac Wallace had a meeting in January, 1961 to discuss how to stop Henry Marshall. Johnson purportedly said: "It looks like we'll just have to get rid of him." According to McClellan, Wallace was evolving into a professional hit-man and was paid for the task. It was a sloppy murder *aka* fake suicide. Regarding the Henry Marshall "suicide," even J. Edgar Hoover admitted doubts, writing in 1962: "I just can't understand how one can fire five shots at himself" with a non-automatic rifle. That same year, as the Estes scandal grew, the Feds ordered an exhumation and new autopsy for Marshall's body. After eight hours of re-examination, Dr. Joseph A. Jachimczyk concluded that Marshall had **not** committed suicide. Jachimczyk testified that "if in fact this is a suicide, it is the most unusual one I have seen during the examination of approximately 15,000 deceased persons."

•More "Suicides": Surrounding Johnson was a series of suicides disguised as murders (sound familiar?). On 4th April, 1962, George Krutilek, Estes' chief accountant, was found dead. Despite a severe bruise on Krutilek's head, the Texas coroner decided that he, too, had committed suicide. The next day, Estes and three associates were indicted by a federal grand jury. Two of these men, Harold Orr and Coleman Wade, died before the case came to court. They, also, "committed suicide." Here again, Estes asserts that these were victims of "hit man" Mac

Wallace—to protect LBJ.

- **John Kinser:** LBJ and Mac Wallace's relationship (business and personal) dates back to 1950, when LBJ cohort Edward Clark introduced Wallace to the future President. In 1952, Mac Wallace was involved in a "love triangle" with LBJ's sister and a man named John Kinser, the owner of a golf-putting course in Austin. Wallace shot Kinser in cold blood. According to Barr McClellan, John Kinser was blackmailing Lyndon, and so the killing was encouraged by Ed Clark and LBJ. Billie Sol Estes also asserted that LBJ was involved in this and other murders by Mac Wallace.[188] At the Kinser trial, Wallace was found guilty of murder. But the judge overruled the jury's suggested verdict of life imprisonment, giving Mac Wallace only a five year suspended sentence. Obviously, a powerful politician pressured the judge and saved Wallace... and all the fingers point to LBJ. Two of Johnson's financial supporters, M. E. Ruby and Bill Carroll, posted Wallace's bond.[189] But in 1971, Malcolm Wallace was killed, having fallen asleep while driving, crashing his car. One of Wallace's tools for murder was car exhaust, and in the end, carbon monoxide is apparently what silenced him. Live by the sword, die by the sword.
- Do we have any "hard" evidence linking LBJ's hit man, Malcolm "Mac" Wallace, directly with the events of Dallas in 1963? Yes. A fingerprint.[190] Many scoffed at Estes' claims, until years later, when Mac Wallace's fingerprint was identified as one of the prints from the TSBD "sniper's nest." Oswald's print on a book box on the sixth floor, near the "sniper's nest" does not prove he was involved in the conspiracy: he routinely handled those very boxes as part of his job. However, finding a print there of a non-employee is another matter. The only non-employee fingerprint from the sniper's nest was not identified until 1998, and surprisingly, it matches the ink print of Lyndon Johnson's most nefarious henchman. Fingerprint expert Nathan

Darby signed an affidavit attesting he found a 14-point match between a latent fingerprint found on the cardboard box from the TSBD and Wallace. Several people have gone on record stating that Wallace functioned as a "hit man" for Johnson; if Wallace was present on the sixth floor on November 22nd, there is little doubt it was because LBJ had ordered him to be there.

Naturally, LBJ's defenders have found a few other print experts to question the fingerprint match, who claim there are dissimilarities between the latent and the inked prints. Darby counters the critics, pointing out that Wallace had sustained a finger laceration that caused a tiny bit of scar tissue—which explains the non-corresponding area on his fingerprint. Under further examination, Darby became even more confident of his match, documenting over 30 points of identity-matching. Darby's work was confirmed by another fingerprint expert, E.H. Hoffmeister, and both made their match a "blind" exam (meaning, they did not know in advance they were working on the Kennedy assassination).[191] This cannot be said of the critics, who have an obvious bias—they want to find an imperfection in the match. The only scientifically-accurate tests matched the latent print from the book carton to the inked Wallace fingerprint. This is the kind of concrete, hard evidence critics have long asked for... but now ignore. Despite the fact we have multiple fake suicides and multiple witnesses pointing to Mac Wallace's role as LBJ's "hit-man," and a *fingerprint*, defenders of the *status quo* scoff, regurgitating their same ole' saw about "you can't trust witnesses... where's the evidence?"

•The documentary, "The Men Who Killed Kennedy" is a nine-part British ITV video documentary series produced by Nigel Turner. The now-banned episode, "The Guilty Men," makes a strong case for LBJ's guilt using a variety of witnesses and hard evidence. The History Channel re-packaged the series and showed it widely in the U.S., until it was pressured by high-placed friends of LBJ (including Jack Valenti and Gerald Ford) to air a rebuttal of "The Guilty Men" documentary. Three dubious "historians" were paid to rebut the evidence in McClellan's book and in the History Channel documentary... but instead of discussing any of McClellan's 68 exhibits of courtroom quality evidence, they chose instead to attack McClellan's character and portray him as a disgruntled employee who had been fired from *Clark, Thomas and Winters*... when actually Barr had served over a decade in good standing, where he was treated almost like a partner, with near-partner-level approval and access at the law firm.

•**Richard Nixon** spoke candidly of his low opinion of LBJ's character during an interview with Pat Buchanan on CNN's "Crossfire." Not mindful that the recorder was still rolling when they were off the air in a commercial break, Nixon asked if Buchanan had seen Robert Caro's new-at-the-time biography of Johnson. Nixon whispered that Caro's book made Johnson "appear like a goddamned animal." Then Nixon chuckled and added, "...cuz he was."[192] If a crook like Richard Nixon called him a "goddamned animal," perhaps it is time we stop being shocked that LBJ resorted to a political assassination to preserve his power.

•**Madeleine Brown** (discussed above) confirms the mountain of evidence indicting LBJ as a key part of the plot and cover-up. Critics label Madeleine Brown as a "non-credible" witness. Again, she may be prone to exaggeration, but most of her facts ring true. Newsman Geraldo Rivera presented on television a letter from LBJ's attorney, Jerome Ragsdale, showing that she was being provided hush money from LBJ and, after his death, from his estate.

•**E. Howard Hunt**, proven in a court of law to have been involved in killing Kennedy, and to be a Watergate conspirator and a CIA operative, gave a deathbed confession... on tape. In it, he said that LBJ gave his blessing to a CIA-led hit team, and helped facilitate the Warren Commission cover-up. Debunkers have long asked why key players in the assassination never "leaked," but now that some have begun to confess, they simply dismiss the confessions. Anyone who listens to Hunt's confession tape hears a very believable voice from a person who inarguably was in a position to be involved.[193] (Also see Lie Number 26)

Bugliosi, Posner *et. al.* are quick to discard these facts as lies told by convicted felons—ignoring the fact that the people who would have known the inside story of the crime *were* mostly criminals! A lawyer's adage is: if you wanna convict the devil, you have go to hell to find your witnesses. And never mind that Barr McClellan's conviction was overturned, or that many who are *not* felons corroborate the facts about LBJ: Texas Ranger Clint Peoples, Madeleine Brown, Robert Caro, Robert Kennedy, Nathan Darby, May Newman and others.

•Law enforcement routinely makes convictions based on the testimony of criminals, and often using informants who were *paid* for their convicting testimony. The question for establishing truth is not "Are the witnesses lily-white nuns and boy scouts?" No, the question is, "Is their testimony consistent with all the other facts and evidence known in the case? Is their testimony corroborated by anyone who did not share a common motive in hiding truth?" When we are dealing with crooked, greedy, power-hungry manipulators like Johnson, Hoover and Clark, what sort of testimony can we expect to find? They weren't making a habit of announcing their criminal activities to the local Elks Club. The expectations of Posner and Bugliosi are particularly hypocritical, because as lawyers, they know that the case against Johnson is much stronger than any case against Oswald. If a dozen testimonies, White House tapes, a fingerprint from the sniper's nest, and overwhelming "Means and Motive" logic do not persuade you, then I remind you of a previous point (see Lie Number 7): LBJ ducked. The *only* person in the entire motorcade who was crouched down when the shots began was Lyndon Baines Johnson. (Yet Bugliosi writes in his book, falsely, that after the first shot, other than Connally, no one immediately recognized it as a gunshot and "Johnson was equally puzzled." The Altgens photo disproves that claim.)

We might ask: "If LBJ was the mastermind of the assassination, why would he feel in danger, why the need to duck, when he was two cars behind Kennedy?" LBJ was key to controlling the cover-up, but he was not operationally in charge of the actual shooting.[194] And having stabbed many a friend in the back in his own career, he had learned to trust no one. This gives a context to Connally's exclamation upon being hit by a bullet himself: "They're going to kill us all!" *All!* Connally did not know everything about the plot,[195] but he may have known enough to suspect his buddy LBJ had brought some unsavory characters to Dallas to shoot Kennedy. Apparently, they both feared that when you get the CIA, Hoover and the military involved in a *coup*, anything could happen. So perhaps Connally, like Johnson, had nagging fears that the *coup d'etat* might double-cross them and target him, too. Johnson knew many of the people in the CIA, he knew what they were capable of... he was a redneck outsider to the northern Ivy Leaguers, the Skull and Bones gang that permeated the CIA. LBJ was by no means the only culprit. (But Allen Dulles, Richard Nixon, and George Bush the Elder did a better job of concealing their involvement.[196])

~~~

Our concern now is not to posthumously convict anyone, but rather, to ask the American people to lobby for the case to be re-examined and that more JFK secret documents be released, so that we might once and for all silence the ongoing lies of media and government. Critics may say that I have "stretched" the number of lies in order to arrive at a neat "50 Lies for Fifty Years," but the truth is, I *condensed* the lies! 50 is conservative. With each passing year, the lies multiply and compound. Here's why: several key persons have been giving the equivalent of "deathbed confessions" in recent years, as the clock of ages marches on inexorably, and they approach the twilight of their days. Plus ongoing FOIA requests and other research and interviews with the parties involved have slowly, year by year, unveiled new facts... which always point to more proof of conspiracy. This, in turn, has prompted each critic, in books and websites, to add a new layer of lies trying to explain away the emerging revelations. The case is not dead, the ship has not sunk, it merely has accumulated more barnacles.

Lie Number 49: "Case Closed." ~Gerald L. Posner
"Conspiracy authors.... knowingly mislead and deliberately distort.... [There is] absolutely no substance to their charges." ~Vincent Bugliosi

Case closed? Hardly. The case is not closed until the continued cover-up and lies stop, not until the dark secrets are brought into the light, not until truth flows down like healing waters. *Absolutely no substance?* I have presented here some two hundred references and footnotes from government records, law enforcement and forensic professionals, and other highly-credible sources. We have hard evidence. Debate me, disagree with me, but don't pretend to dismiss these 50 Lies as if they don't exist, or scoff at conspiracists as "kooky" when we have better reputations and credentials than you, Mr. Posner and Mr. Bugliosi. Calling us "kooks," when the bulk of the evidence is on our side, shows your desperation—and makes us wonder who is paying you off.

Only truth can close this case. Oswald was given a death sentence but never a real trial, and the only other accused shooter, E. Howard Hunt, was actually found guilty in court... but left unpunished. (Hunt faced a civil case, not a criminal court: he lost his libel suit against Mark Lane and Liberty Lobby, who accused him of being one of the conspirators for the assassination or the cover-up). Key documents in the JFK investigation have been sealed until 2029 and beyond, and many that were released have been partially redacted/censored. Documents that *have* been released via FOIA show proof of a cover-up and yet more loose ends. Other than Jack Ruby, no one has gone to prison, so how can the case be closed?

In the early Nineties, when a young Wall Street lawyer, Gerald Posner, became a slick-but-verbose defender of the lone gunman theory, he was given ten times the air time as the Warren Commission's critics. With Posner's book, *Case Closed*, the media uncritically jumped on board and praised it as a brilliant exposé of the "nut-cake conspiracy theorists." In its August 30-September 6, 1993 issue, *U.S. News and World Report* endorsed the book, printing two excerpts from *Case Closed* and used that title as the magazine's cover headline, saying this "brilliant new book... proves [Oswald] killed Kennedy." This is strange, considering his work is riddled with errors and omissions and its central thesis rests upon the Magic Bullet Theory —something which has been totally disproved. Anyone who will take the time to read the *WC Summary Report*, or *Case Open* by Harold Weisberg, will have to admit that Posner *et al*. have misled us greatly. Yet supporters of the Warren Commission blindly agree with Posner's lie: that the case is closed, and that Oswald was the lone, unassisted assailant, firing just three magic bullets.

If the case had ever been truly closed (literally or figuratively), we would not have hundreds of books and articles on the subject still being written. We would not have more revealing documents, memos and tapes slowly coming to light. History and public opinion have completely discredited the WC Report, but the exploiters, debunkers and paid spinners continue to support its establishmentarian lie. Even an established newsman as intelligent as pundit Bill O'Reilly jumped on the bandwagon with his recent book, *Killing Kennedy*—with nothing new to say, no evidence or footnotes (but plenty of lies).

I promised to address Posner's work in particular: his Warren Commission apologetic is a litany of outright lies, errors and misrepresentations. He is a proven hypocrite and deceiver. Some examples:

•Posner says that the magic bullet can be seen hitting Kennedy and Connally at the same time because he can see, in the blurry Zapruder film, Connally's coat lapel flap forward by the bullet. He fails to mention that the bullet came nowhere near the coat lapel. The doctor's report, Connally's statement, and the Commission report itself clearly state that the bullet came out near and below Connally's nipple. The hole in his coat is inches away from the lapel!

•In his book and in testimony before Congress, Posner claimed that the JFK autopsy pathologist, J. Thornton Boswell, spoke with him and recanted his problematic testimony about wound positions. But Boswell now denies having talked to Posner! Dr. Gary Aguilar, a practicing pathologist, university professor, and Chairman of Surgery at St. Francis Memorial Hospital, testified before the Assassination Archives Review Board, stating: "JFK's pathologists James Humes and J. Thornton Boswell described the entrance to the President's skull wound as being to the right and just above the external occipital protuberance in the original autopsy report. They repeated that assertion in an interview published in the Journal of the American Medical

Association (JAMA) on May 27th, 1992." Yet, Posner claims to have interviewed both Dr. Humes and Dr. Boswell —with opposite conclusions. Dr. Aguilar was too polite to accuse Posner of lying, but he and I both trust the AMA Journal.

•Posner claims that the Tague Bullet (the one that missed the limo) had been scientifically linked to Oswald's gun using scrapings of metal from the curb near Tague. Absolutely not true. Posner claims FBI Agent Shaneyfelt testified to the WC that the lead found on the curb "came from the bullet's core." Shaneyfelt is not a reliable source... he was one of Hoover's lackeys. And what Mr. Shaneyfelt actually said was, "The lead could [*could*, not *did*] have originated from the lead core of [a bullet from Oswald's rifle], or from some other source having the same composition." In other words, tests show the bullet could have come from any number of guns. The WC made it clear that the FBI was not able to match it conclusively with the bullets purportedly from Oswald, or even say what calibre it might have been. The greater truth is that the metal spectroscopy on the Tague bullet does *not* match Oswald's other bullets. But Posner, as usual, twists the evidence.[197]

•He loves to quote numbers/statistics because they sound scientific. Misrepresented numbers are not science. "Only four witnesses, 2 percent of all the witnesses at Dealey, heard shots coming from more than one location," he states as if pronouncing scientific fact.[198] Nonsense. When someone testified they weren't *absolutely sure* which direction bullets came from, Posner rules them out of the "2 percent." But we find in later interviews with them that most were not saying the shots came from *one* location... they were just saying that because of the many shots and the many echoes, they couldn't pin it down to a single location. Even Police Chief Jesse Curry mentioned two locations for the shooters.

•Posner has been caught plagiarizing in his journalistic work.[199]

And I point that out not to insult him; it is a highly-relevant point of integrity and credibility in this debate, with its history of deceit. [I also refer the reader back to the first few pages of this book—the first portion of Lie Number 50—regarding Posner being sued by Pulitzer Prize Winner Harper Lee.]

•Gerald Posner is not only a plagiarist, he is a run-of-the-mill mud-slinger. He gives his Oswald chapters such *ad hominem* attack-titles as "He Looks Like a Maniac," and "Our Papa is Out of His Mind." He insults those on the other side of the debate. He is only outdone in the childish-insult game by Vincent Bugliosi, whose disrespect toward conspiracy buffs is too vile to repeat. Both of these so-called de-bunkers spout bunk, yet condescendingly condemn conspiracy "buffs" and "nuts" for bias and sins which they themselves commit. They hypocritically attack anyone who disagrees with the WC as money-hungry, yet they made huge sums from their Kennedy books and related personal appearances.

There are hundreds of truth-seeking volunteer researchers who have never made a dime from JFK theories. Posner slurs Sylvia Meagher, one of the best researchers, for her "leftwing" politics and dismisses her as "biased" because she focuses on points of the WC Report that favor her side. The truth is, her website covers the case more comprehensively than anyone in history. And for the record, there is nothing wrong with marshaling the most helpful facts when making a polemical argument.

•Posner smears contrary witnesses with blatant lies, misrepresenting their actual testimony, using out-of-context quotes which he twists at will. For example, he ferociously attacks Arnold Rowland (who saw a gunman in the sixth floor who did not match Oswald's description) and uses a blatant lie to discredit him. Posner complains that Rowland is a poor witness because he stated there were women and children standing on the Triple Underpass. However, Rowland explained that he was accustomed to using the term "triple underpass" as a generic term for the Dealey Plaza area. And indeed, at one point when Rowland was actually referring to the underpass bridge specifically, he used the term "viaduct." Rowland had *correctly* testified that there were a few women and children in that area—on the Grassy Knoll near the underpass. Even when Rowland mentioned seeing people specifically up on the underpass bridge, he qualified his statement by noting that he was about 100 yards away and could not see them "with detailed distinction." Every aspect of Rowland's testimony was consistent with what we know from photos and other witnesses, yet Posner is so desperate to discredit Rowland, the attorney/author uses deceptive tactics that should get him disbarred.

• Posner lies again: "I looked at the original testimony... none of them say there was smoke from a gun fired on the Grassy Knoll... they say instead they saw some smoke from a police motorcycle."[200] That is another outright lie. Smoke at the *fence and trees on the knoll* (**not** on the street near the motorcycles) was seen by S.M. Holland, Lee Bowers, James L. Simmons, Richard Dodd, Austin Miller and others. In a related matter, Senator Yarbrough and others *smelled* gunpowder smoke when they drove past the Grassy Knoll... which smells nothing like engine smoke. Posner also lied about the wind direction, claiming it came from the north (when it was from the west), in order to claim they smelled the gunpowder all the way down from the sixth floor of the TSBD!

• Yet another glaring misstatement: Posner initially dismissed the notion that Oswald knew David Ferrie. This is a strong, and wrong, claim—and for years, Posner and his ilk scoffed at conspiracy "buffs" who made this claim, even though the evidence for it was manifold. Now it has been proven and revealed in the mainstream media. Like so much of the conspiracy evidence, as time unfolds we see the early suspicions of the "buffs" have been proven *more* true, not less (see Lie Number 23, re: Ferrie). But the media remain silent.

Others have documented even more flaws, lies and insults in the "debunking" books of Vincent Bugliosi. In his *Reclaiming History*, he spends several opening pages on a meaningless rant against those of us who have found obvious problems with the WCR. Without citing any specifics to justify his verbal onslaught, Bugliosi calls us "kooky as a three-dollar bill," "paranoid," "deceptive," and like "dogs barking idiotically" and other such hyperbolic, inflammatory and downright ugly insults. Hurling insults is the last refuge of a man who has had his theories publicly rebuffed. But Bugliosi is too smart a lawyer to actually back up his *ad hominem* stone-throwing with an actual example... because if he names names, he'd be sued for libel. It didn't take me long to find that Bugliosi's rant against "wantonly deceptive" "liars" should be directed at himself. He claims conspiracists "knowingly mislead" and omit important facts, but that is exactly what he does himself in retelling the story—conveniently leaving out the "inconvenient" truths.

His bias is particularly exposed when, in those same early pages, Bugliosi calls Allen Dulles a person of "impeccable honor." Allen Dulles tried in the opening hours of the Warren Commission to bias his co-commissioners against a conspiracy, claiming falsely that "almost all" assassinations are done by lone nuts. Once Bugliosi holds up Dulles as his role model for perfect honesty, we have no reason to trust another word out of his pen. Dulles, a man fired by JFK, was the shadowy leader who oversaw the CIA during a time that LBJ referred to the CIA's work in the Caribbean as a "damned Murder Inc." Dulles okayed the plans for the Bay of the Bigs, including the bombing of a ship which killed scores of innocent people, and he initiated the plan to murder Castro, among other leaders south of the border. Dulles ran the CIA's Operation Mockingbird, aimed at controlling the media in direct violation of the Constitution. Before that, Dulles had helped engineer a coup in Iran that put the brutal dictator, Shah Pahlavi, into power.[201] Many of our current problems in the Middle East stem from that criminal coup. You might argue that Dulles committed these crimes with good intent, a product of his patriotism. But his lack of character extended to his personal life. According to his own sister, Dulles cheated on his wife at least "a hundred times," with scores of women, making Bill Clinton look like a boy scout.[202] This man is what Bugliosi defines as having "an impeccable reputation."

There's more: from 1935-1950, while portraying himself as a Nazi-hating friend of the Jews, Allen and his brother, John, enriched themselves with Nazi clients and by laundering money out of Nazi Germany. This included sharing in profits from the I.G. Farben chemical company, a key supporter of the Nazi party, supplying Hitler with money, technology and even Jew-killing poison gas.[203] For siding with Dulles, and a hundred other reasons, we can dismiss Bugliosi.

To sum: Posner and Bugliosi will not own up to their obvious one-sided bias. Worse, they viciously attack the integrity of those of us seeking truth even while their own integrity is in tatters. One has to ask: *Why do the so-called debunkers resort to outright lies and insults, repeatedly, to make their case? Why do they run from an honest debate?* Those of us on the "conspiracy" side are not pretending to be dispassionate, inert historians; we are trying to be honest-yet-vigilant reformers who actively expose lies. It is not our duty to re-tell 26 volumes of the *WCR*. Rather, we look for falsehoods or misleading interpretations within the work of the WC and its later defenders. Posner, Bugliosi, the Warren Commission, and the House Special Committee had, collectively, huge staffs, million-dollar research budgets and unlimited government resources at their disposal—dedicated to one-sided "research." So we conspiracy researchers make no apologies for being passionate in arguing our case... the very-much *open* case.

Lie Number 50, Conclusion: The Impersonators:
"Most of the witnesses [to impersonators] later admitted they were mistaken. There is no credible evidence that there is any impersonation of Lee Harvey Oswald...." ~Gerald Posner in *Case Closed* and in a *PBS Frontline* interview

We began this book with Lie Number 50, as a way to create a "circle of truth," so to speak, making the point that the case for Conspiracy is more circular than linear. The reader might do well to go back and re-read the book's opening, and the details of Lie 50 found there, to see the full context—*the framework of the frame-up*. We have proven that Posner is wrong. We know for a fact there was an impostor of Oswald in Mexico, and in other cities (Chicago, Miami, New Orleans) on other occasions, for the purpose of painting him as a crazy little communist.

Over these fifty years, enough facts have filtered out that most people *do* now know that there had to be a Grassy Knoll gunman. But clinging to a desire to believe the best in our leaders, many folks are not willing to go so far as to see a governmental conspiracy. They are more willing to blame the "bad-guy," the Mafia. The presence of impersonators, however, is not consistent with a Mafia hit. The impostors involved in the case (some mimicking Secret Service Agents and some mimicking Oswald), and the **specific efforts to hide the existence of these impostors**, do not bear the mark of a common criminal. If the perpetrators had no support from elements within the CIA, FBI, Secret Service or other aspect of government, it would have been highly risky to use false identification as a means of escape; what if you flashed your fake Secret Service badge, only to discover the person you just showed it to is himself a Secret Service Agent? You have at least had to know that the Secret Service would stay with the motorcade—every one of them. And you would have had to go to great difficulty to create fake badges that matched up to the real thing well enough to fool seasoned cops. The impersonation of Oswald in Mexico City embassies is even more indicative of a government, not Mafioso, operation.

All these facts point to the CIA, the FBI, and the White House. LBJ was not in the Mafia. The Mafia was not ducking before the shots, as LBJ was. Mafia kingpins had no way to manipulate evidence in FBI crime labs nor could they control the Warren Commission investigation. In fact, no one else had the power that LBJ had, combined with the means, motives and methods to spin the complex web of deceit. No, the cover-up has the markings of a politically-minded operation, a plot that planted a map leading us down a one-way street, where "X" marks the spot of a crazy, lone, communist-leaning assassin. And the ruse worked, albeit imperfectly, for 50 years.

We close with a Number One Truth: "Practically all the Cabinet members of President Kennedy's administration, along with Director J. Edgar Hoover of the FBI and Chief James Rowley of the Secret Service... testified that to their knowledge there was no sign of any conspiracy. To say that these people, as well as the Commission, suppressed, neglected to unearth, or overlooked evidence of a conspiracy would be an indictment of the entire government of the United States." ~Earl Warren, *The Memoirs of Earl Warren*, p. 367.

You said it, Earl! The entire government of the sixties and seventies and beyond is indicted, if not convicted. This "true statement" by Chief Justice Warren, was originally presented as a **hypothetical absurdity**, based on the presumption that all government leaders are honorable men. It is another version of Bugliosi's lie—call it the 51st Lie—that the Warren Commission personnel all had "impeccable reputations." Bugliosi and Warren are perpetuating the great American patriotic myth: that the U.S. of A. is led by flawless, holy men with noble purpose. This naive myth is manifest in the claim that George Washington never told a lie, in the amnesia of 20th Century textbooks about how many "founding fathers" owned slaves, to my own dad's utter shock at hearing Quaker Richard Nixon cursing like a sailor on the Watergate tapes as he talked about ruining people's careers for the sin of criticizing him. There is nothing historically rare about a few evil men conspiring to kill the King, and nothing surprising about a larger number of leaders covering up the unpleasantness for various reasons—some well-meaning, some nefarious. Those who did the killing and those who yielded to the cover-up have two common flaws: the belief that wide-spread deceit in government is justified, and an ego-driven desire to cling to power and wealth. The conspiracy was, like most conspiracies, about *money and power*, not ideology or patriotism or even party-politics. LBJ worshipped at the altar of money and power; politics was only a means to that end. Respected historian Robert Caro describes a young Johnson's path to power this way: "His power was simply the power of money."

The death of JFK was about money and power: it kept the *status quo* in power, and it ensured that a corrupt, pro-military-industrial government continued to favor oil companies and defense contractors with fat profits. On Oct. 11, 1963, Kennedy signed National Security Action Memorandum (NSAM) 263, ordering a reduction in U.S. troops, beginning in December 1963 and to be completed by the end of 1965. The day after Kennedy was buried, on November 26, 1963, newly-anointed President Lyndon Johnson signed his first National Security Action Memorandum, which reversed Kennedy's. NSAM 273 overturned NSAM 263 and started an escalation of the Vietnam War—much to the pleasure of the profiteers in the military-industrial complex. Is it a sheer coincidence that LBJ, Nixon, Ford and Bush all benefitted from campaign contributions from military-industries and/or energy companies, and were all entangled in the JFK crime (either as perpetrators or in its cover-up)? It is almost certain that LBJ, Nixon and Ford would never have been made President if the Kennedy Dynasty had lived on. The corruption is bigger than partisan ideology. LBJ and Earl Warren were liberals, but the cover-up enabled their careers to move forward and to see their aims achieved. And for conservatives, the deaths of John and Robert Kennedy assured that the Vietnam War and the later Middle East wars would escalate, insuring giant profits for cold-war and defense contractors like General Dynamics, Bell Helicopter, Boeing, Bechtel, and Halliburton. Oil companies benefitted because Kennedy had threatened to take away part of their oil depletion allowances (raising taxes on oil giants), and a progressive Kennedy regime might have been quicker to encourage efficient automobiles, mass transit and thus less fuel consumption. Besides the personal loss to the Kennedy family, the American people lost, as the Federal debt and deficits began to soar shortly after Kennedy died... and now is trillions higher than in 1963, and higher as a percentage of GDP. The cost of war, the cost of energy, and the cost of debt interest all inflated in ways that would not have happened if the Kennedys had remained in power another four or eight years under Jack and Bobby's peaceful leadership.

If the Kennedys had not been shot, it is almost certain that LBJ and J. Edgar Hoover would have been out of a job by 1964— and likely facing criminal investigations. The CIA would have been reduced in size, scope and secrecy. The mega-contractors and tycoons of Texas would have been poorer, and in jail. The Mafia would have been harassed further. The defense industry would have been shrinking. It was a "perfect storm." The very people who had the most to gain by Kennedy's death are the very people who left their fingerprints at the scene. Oswald, however, had nothing to gain. Fifty years later, fifty lies later, we have found the Patsy, the Sucker... and he is *us*.

Verdict:

Pro-conspiracy "buffs" debate pro-Warren Commission "lone-nutters" in online forums, and it often seems like a game of egos, arguing over trivialities. This is not a game of nitpicking. It is a search for truth. And if I'm only 50% right, that would be enough to achieve my goal: to convince Americans to press for a re-examination of the evidence, including an **exhumation of John F. Kennedy's remains**. Anyone who views this as distasteful or disrespectful is forgetting that for "Jack" to have died in vain, to be buried with the lies, is the greater disrespect.

What happened in Dallas in 1963 is not a "fun mystery" to be solved, nor is it an academic question to be answered for mere intellectual curiosity. It cuts to the core of our now-rotten Republic, to the tattered principles of democracy that beg for restoration in our land. Like it or not, we need our dysfunctional government, we even need the CIA, but we also need to be able to **trust** that our "public servants" (who, by the way, are paid with *our* tax dollars and empowered by *our* votes) serve the public and not themselves. This is a battle between vice and virtue, a war between the arrogance and lust for power of a few versus an infinitely wider, universal value of Truth for the many.

In assessing truth, we need **not** raise the level of acceptable evidence to the standard of the most skeptical judge or doubting jury. This is not a trial. The bar set by Posner and Bugliosi for conspiracy theorists is not reasonable: fifty years on, we cannot prove *every* point with scientific certainty (although many points have, indeed, been proven by science). Our star witness was killed shortly after the crime, and his interrogation notes were destroyed by the police. The original autopsy notes were burned. The postal records for Oswald's "A. J. Hidell" P.O. Box are missing. Thousands of documents have been labeled "Top Secret" and hidden away or redacted. A note from Oswald to the FBI was torn up and flushed. JFK's brain is missing. White House and CIA tapes were erased. Scores of witnesses died in mysterious circumstances, and others were threatened, coerced into changing their story. The government marshaled all its massive resources to control the evidence and shape the story from the start. **Considering the coercion, the altered and lost evidence, and the constant misinterpretation of the evidence by the powers-that-be, it is miraculous that we have any case at all.** Yet, we do. We have persuaded the majority of Americans there was indeed a conspiracy, which is a testament to the dedicated, diligent work of hundreds of conspiracy researchers and the bravery of witnesses who came forward with the truth in the face of intimidation. 50 years later, we finally have an ironclad case. We have a good outline of what likely transpired around the tragedy of November 22nd, 1963. I won't waste words speculating on *exactly* who shot JFK. I don't have to. It was not Oswald, nor even Mac Wallace, shooting a fourth or fifth shot from the sixth floor. We have proved a second gunman fired a final, frontal, fatal shot, which in turn proves a government cover-up, which warrants an exhumation of JFK's body. A new autopsy (with honest, independent observers) would then prove the autopsy photos were forged. We would no longer have a "closed case." But forget courtrooms and irrelevant details and the inevitable mistakes that "buffs" have committed—that is now unrelated to the challenge before us. The challenge is to make our democracy transparent and our media honest.

Returning to the metaphor of a jigsaw puzzle: the conspirators have managed, by deception, to hide away many of the pieces of the puzzle, but these 50 Lies were the ones that failed to obscure the truth. We have revealed enough pieces to see the big picture. There is no longer a shadow of doubt: we see clearly the shape of a conspiracy that includes a second shooter, five or more shots, and a vicious government cover-up at the highest levels. It is time to fully expose the lies, to cease the nitpicking and get serious: release *all* JFK-records now, and exhume the incontrovertible evidence remaining underground in Arlington.

"For there is nothing hidden that will not be disclosed, and nothing concealed that will not be known or brought out into the open.... Then you will know the truth, and the truth shall set you free." *~Jesus, in Luke 8:17 and John 8:32*

About the Author:

Dr. Lance Moore is an ordained United Methodist minister. He holds a doctoral degree from Emory University, a masters degree from Candler School of Theology, and an English degree from Auburn University. He has been a preacher, rock guitarist, and author of six nationally-published books; repeat panelist/guest on TV and radio talk-shows, (Naomi Judd's *Hallmark Channel* show, "Naomi's New Morning," Christian family TV, and others); six time contributor to the Abingdon Preaching Annual; contributor to various magazines/journals.

As for credentials in the JFK case, his expertise is not in

forensics, but in human behavior, logic, and problem-solving. In addition to academic study in the fields of human nature, psychology, sociology, and pedagogy, being a parish minister for 30 years yields an understanding of human motivation and behavior— good and bad.

Other Books by Dr. Moore include:
- *Class Crucifixion: Money, Power, Religion and the Death of the Middle Class*
- *Majestic Twelve... Minus One*
- *The Neurotic's Guide to God and Love*
- *Outdoors with God*
- *Firm Foundations: An Architect and a Pastor Guide Your Church Construction*

More info at www.Sky-Fy.com or **www.Amazon.com**

The low price on *JFK: 50 Years, 50 Lies*, is sponsored by Sky-Fy Publishing... please consider buying another Sky-Fy book (fiction and non-fiction). For those interested in public policy and justice, try:

Class Crucifixion:
Money, Power, Religion & the Death of the Middle Class

- Available at www.Sky-Fy.com and at www.createspace.com/3991040

quality, large softcover: for **$14.99** and on Kindle for **$7.99** at www.Amazon.com/Class-Crucifixion-Religion-Middle-ebook/dp/B007CEJN5A

- "Timely, intelligent, and well-researched, this provocative book is an examination of the growing gap between rich and poor. Dr. Moore applies theology to political ethics, reviewing what world religions have to teach us about greed, poverty and human worth. He argues that U.S. executives are vastly overpaid compared with other developed countries, but goes further to

argue that society grossly undervalues blue-collar workers."
~from the publisher

• "This is a significant work... well-crafted, painstakingly researched, a book people need to read... a Great Book."
~Edward Wesley of Third Coast Media

• "Every responsible and virtuous citizen should read three things: the Scriptures, a daily newspaper... and this book!"
~author, pastor and radio/TV personality Dr. Thomas L. Butts

The Rev. Dr. Moore has been an ordained minister in the United Methodist Church for over 25 years, including six years as pastor to Pulitzer Prize-winner **Harper Lee** (*To Kill a Mockingbird*). Ms. Lee praised his previous work, writing,

• **"Reads awfully well...a fine job...a beautiful book in every way."**

~~~

For those interested in a thoughtful science fiction thriller, try:

Majestic Twelve Minus One
What lies hidden in an underground government lab?

FACT: In 1947, the Army Air Force recovered strange debris in the sands of New Mexico. According to a leaked memo from President Truman to President-Elect Eisenhower, a dozen top scientists and military leaders were chosen to form a task force to process, and hide, the most momentous event in modern history: an actual crash of a flying saucer. *Operation Majestic-12* changed over the next 60 years, yet as each of the original twelve "Majestics" took the secret to their graves, the U.S. government continued to glean technology from alien hardware... and continues to mask the truth.

FICTION: *Majestic Twelve Minus One* is a riveting tale spun from the longstanding cover-up of UFOs. The greatest conspiracy of silence since the JFK assassination unfolds around the family of one honest scientist caught in a life-and-death ethical dilemma. Will Dr. "Blue" Bellew steal alien technology to keep his daughter alive, or will he honor his patriotic pledge of confidentiality? Will desperation and curiosity lead Jessica Bellew to dark and dangerous alliances? A brainy techno-thriller in the Michael Crichton/ James Rollins genré includes palindromes, numerology and subterfuge... all underground, all awaiting the light of day.

- "A gripping tale, cleverly and masterfully crafted." ~G.K. Robinson
- Available at www.Sky-Fy.com and at www.amazon.com/Majestic-Twelve-Minus-One-ebook/dp/B008ZQU60K

Majestic Twelve Minus One (free sample excerpt):

"There is a great secret at the center of the U.S. government, and the government is guarding that secret with a fanatical zeal...."

~Whitley Strieber

Dr. Franklin Stanton lay dying. Life did not flash before his eyes. Regret did. Was his life a waste? Should he have been more bold in revealing the secret? Had he left enough clues for his successor? His only remaining hope was that his replacement might have more courage, and more aptitude, at rending the curtain in two, at revealing the one behind the veil. With that, his thoughts blurred into a dreamlike reminiscence of The Wizard of Oz.

The words *Ignore the man behind the curtain!* reverberated in his mind. Through one eye that was not filled with blood, he stared at the white headliner of his Audi, his field of vision not taking in the bullet hole through the roof or the red speckles aft of his mortally-wounded head. So at least it was a pleasant hallucination. The Wizard, the Tin Man, and Franklin Stanton, all smiling, all safe in the basket of a hot air balloon. Their balloon floated upward over an emerald city, up into a cobalt sky, up through a white billow swallowing them. And then, in that dreamy state of mixed metaphor, he mumbled his parting words: "I hear the angels singing...."

~~~

Blue was agitated at his wife. "Aliens!? Come on, we've had this conversation before. It's ridiculous."

Indeed, they had. Jessica had an active imagination, and long before Blue had taken a job at the Defense Advanced Research Projects Agency (DARPA), she had read books on the Kennedy assassination-conspiracy theories, pyramid power, tales of Atlantis, and flying saucers. She readily admitted that many of her interests were akin to reading fairy tales. Blue knew she was grounded in reality. As a scientist, he would not have married a crack-pot, even if she did have remarkable cleavage. Jessica was level-headed.

"Just because I bought a book on aliens doesn't mean I believe in them." Though she did. And she was a true believer in conspiracies—the JFK assassination conspiracy in particular. She believed in a grassy knoll assassin, five bullets not three, a high-level government cover-up. Early in their marriage, in a tedious presentation over wine and cheese and firelight, Jessica had ruined a perfectly-wonderful romantic evening convincing Blue that the Warren Commissioners, not Jessica, were the ones outside of mainstream rational thought. Blue's only remaining objection to the plot she had articulated was, "How could government keep a secret so big?"

To which Jessica had answered matter-of-factly: "They didn't."

It was such a good retort, she let it settle on him a moment. Just before he began to speak, she drove the point further, punctuated with a finger playfully poking his ribs: "Let's see, how would a scientist put it: 'The evidence is clear and compelling that the government made every effort to cover-up the assassination conspiracy.' Yet we're sitting here discussing it by the fire. So don't act like they succeeded in keeping things secret!" At that moment, Dr. William "Blue" Bellew fell even more deeply in love with his gorgeous wife.

"Pretty and smart," he said as a concession speech.

He knew her views were informed and reasonable. In another context, Blue had joked with friends that his wife was the more "normal" of the two, possessing a calm and strong mental peace.

So now, Jessica was surprised and perplexed that he verbally attacked her for bringing home a book about a UFO crash in New Mexico. Surprised... yet after a breath, she knew the reason: DARPA.

Blue had only been working for the secretive inner core of DARPA for a few weeks, but he had changed. Rather than laughing about her light fancy of "fairy tales," Blue now fired off a litany of derisive remarks about "flying saucer fanatics" as he read the back jacket.

"Where'd you get this?" he interrogated.

"Books-a-Million."

He mumbled "Crap." Then after a pause, "Did you use the VISA?"

"Yes... what's wrong with that?"

Blue paused again to chide himself mentally: No one's taking the time to monitor credit cards. He tried to muster indignation in his reply, "Well, I wish you'd quit wasting money on stupid books like that."

Here he added name-calling and put-downs of "so-called Ufologists" and "shysters trying to make a buck off gullible people."

Jessica was miffed. Early in their marriage, they'd had a minor fight over her cavalier use of the credit card... but since then, she'd become frugal. Plus, Blue's lucrative promotion had made money a moot subject, no longer the slightest source for marital discord. So she discarded puzzlement about the VISA question and became defensive of her whole "aliens and pyramids" interest.

Jessica came back at him: "You know, your problem is you have no imagination."

She immediately caught the irony of her own barb—Blue worked for the most creative, cutting age research agency on the planet. As he mulled a reply, she continued: "Seriously, how do you know flying saucers aren't real?"

As soon as the words "flying saucers" left her lips, she felt silly. Most Americans tell pollsters they believe in UFOs, but in public, they snicker. Years before, Jessica had felt the condescension directed at her, when she had brought the topic up at a dinner party and her guests did, literally, laugh at her suggestion that flying saucers were real. Ever since, she'd been more restrained. Except around Blue. And now, with his odd response, the words "flying saucer" seemed again as childish as drinking invisible tea from a doll's tea cup and saucer.

Her fast-talking husband shifted into an abnormal stance: visibly tense, slow with words, parsing. "Okay, obviously, I can't disprove UFOs... but if word got back to my coworkers that you had books on these wacky topics, I'd be a laughingstock.... Just promise me you won't buy a book like that again."

This made Jessica even more disturbed.

"Oh, I'm the wacky one? I've met your geeky coworkers."

She had attended employee parties where the "geniuses" from DARPA told juvenile jokes, fawned over stupid sci-fi movies, and demonstrated not one whit of shame in childish pranks and lampshade-type behavior.... No, that's not the right metaphor. Those geeks aren't even cool enough to get "wild and crazy" with liquor and lampshades. Just days before, at a backyard barbecue, Blue's friend, Nathan, had walked over to the mini-bar for a gin and tonic, and the host, Blue's new boss Jackson Menzel, had put his hand gently on Nathan's wrist and said, "Haven't you already had your third?"

Jessica, having witnessed what seemed to her as strangely-parochial behavior between two office-nerd colleagues, had even mentioned it afterward to Blue. He was not reluctant to tell her: "We're not allowed—even on a weekend, even in the privacy of home—to ever have more than five beers in a day, or three stiff drinks. It's policy. National security. You know the deal."

Which had made sense to Jessica. Liquored lips are loose lips.

But now, this outsized concern about buying a UFO book. It had the same kind of feel as seeing Menzel's restraining hand on Nathan. Just to confirm where her mind was headed, Jessica added, half a test and half a tease: "Okay, I promise never to buy UFO books again... I'll just check them out at the library for free."

Blue looked even more tense, if that were possible: "Jessi, I'm serious... not even the library... if they saw the book lying around the house, they might think you're some kind of UFO fanatic."

And before she could carry the conversation further, he abruptly walked to the bathroom and shut the door. No man had ever walked out on her in the middle of a conversation.

Jessica sauntered to the patio and stretched out by the pool. She fretted over the word Blue had used: "they." Us and them. Or is it me and them? She studied a honeybee working the chrysanthemums that bloomed in the large clay pot near her chaise lounge. The afternoon sun bleached the blue out of the sky around it, its haloed brightness forcing her eyes down to the bee. The bee took on the look of burnished metal in the sun, and the flower likewise shined vivid with brightness and color, and the hot air, made softer by a steady breeze, was as pleasing to her skin as the flower and bee were to her sight. A beautiful day, a beautiful woman, a beautiful spot by the blue pool, a beautiful life. And yet, a horrible gnawing presence, and prescience, within her.

Something loomed.

She could almost put her finger on it... some of it still future, some of it still iceberg-hidden, some of it bobbing above the surface, like the red pool toy that now pulled her eye away from the honeybee. She could identify only the tip of the gnawing anxiety: the deteriorating health of her daughter, Kelty. Partly a definite thing, not just a mother's paranoia—Kelty was not well—and partly a mystery, as yet undiagnosed. And likewise, with her husband and DARPA, another mystery... or maybe a figment of her "active imagination." But in her mind's eye, as vivid as the honeybee, and the flower, and the blue sky, and the red toy bobbing in the pool.

The reality that stabbed at her: a large part of her husband's life was now a secret. He had just hidden away a bigger part of something. She decided then and there to call it "the iceberg," and with that came a mind-flash of a polar bear harpooned on an ice flow, bright red blood on white fur and gray ice.

She closed her eyes. As that image faded from her imagination, an event from a month prior crawled up from her subconscious, tugging at her conscious thoughts for immediate attention....

~~~

ENDNOTES:

1 *The Warren Commission Report*, Marboro Books, Barnes & Nobles Edition, 1992, p. 19.
2 *WCR*, p. 22.
3 *Newsweek*, October 13, 1997, p. 57-58.
4 In 1967, Johnson had a White House phone conversation (which we also have taped) with Ramsey Clark. Clark was warning Johnson that Congressman Hale Boggs was saying "privately around town that it [the assassination] could be traced back [to you, LBJ]." Johnson does not seem the least bit surprised, but after a few more sentences on the topic, Johnson tell Clark "you have to call me direct." This seems to be a hint to avoid the White House phone lines and the recorder.
5 from the LBJ Library archives, and in the *Lopez Report*, a long-suppressed House Select Committee on Assassinations (HSCA) report on Oswald's alleged trip to Mexico City.
6 Read it here: www.jfkassassination.net/russ/testimony/smith_j1.htm
7 Summers, Anthony, *Conspiracy: The Definitive Book On The JFK Assassination*, (New York: Paragon House, 1989), p. 50.
8 *WCR*, p. 640.
9 quoted on PBS *Nova*, 1988, and in Jack Anderson's film, *American Expose: Who Murdered JFK?* (New York: Journal Graphics Transcript)
10 Ed Hoffman and Ron Friedrich, *Eyewitness*, (1998, JFK Lancer Publications).
[11] WC testimony... read it here: www.jfkassassination.net/russ/testimony/bowers.htm
12 *The House Special Committee on Assassinations*. Referenced herein using the acronym "HSCA". (Government Printing Office, U.S. National Archives, 1979.) This quote is from the HSCA Report summary, p. 184, (referenced at the Assassinations Archive and Research Center).
13 HSCA Report, Book 7, p. 535, and Book 6, p. 312.
14 Jim Marrs, *Crossfire: The Plot That Killed Kennedy*, (Carroll & Graf Publishers, 1993), p. 330 AND www.acorn.net/jfkplace/09/fp.back_issues/06th_Issue/r.craig.bio.html
15 see the *WC Report*, page 640.
16 www.history-matters.com/archive/jfk/lbjlib/phone_calls/Nov_1963/audio/LBJ-Hoover_11-29-63.htm
17 *Inquest*, Edward Jay Epstein, (NY: Viking Press, 1966), p. 28.
18 "Findings of the Select Committee on Assassinations in the assassination of President John F. Kennedy," U.S. National Archives, 1979.
19 see the various Senate and House investigations of the CIA, or HSCA "Book 5: The Investigation of the Assassination of President John F. Kennedy: Performance of the Intelligence Agencies."
20 Epstein, a very gentle, reluctant critic of the WC, gave ample citations of Ball and Lieberer's complaints, and of how the WC swept them under the carpet, in *Inquest*, pp. 129-145.
21 see Newman's live interview, filmed within minutes of the shooting, on WFAA TV here: www.youtube.com/watch?v=3fPpLegSn1k
22 *The Warren Commission Report*, Volume II, pp. 135-142.
23 Sylvia Meagher, "The Curious Testimony of Mr. Givens," *The Texas Observer*, August 13, 1971.
24 *WCR*, p. 161
25 Barry Krusch, *Impossible: The Case Against Lee Harvey Oswald,* Vol. 3, (The Intelligent Community, 2012).

26 *The Warren Commission Report*, Volume II, pp. 135-145.
27 www.acorn.net/jfkplace/09/fp.back_issues/01st_Issue/rr.html
28 from the UK Independent Television Company documentary, "The Men Who Killed Kennedy," also re-broadcast on "The History Channel".
29 FBI report is found in the *WCR*, Volume 27. Video with Dodd's actual statement is found here: www.educationforum.ipbhost.com/index.php?showtopic=17168
30 The bullet hit a window frame, but the sniper could have easily gotten off another shot if he was as fast as claimed at bolt-action reloading.
31 *WCR*, p. 250-252.
32 Internet sites sometimes change. If the link fails, then search for "Algens 6 uncropped"
33 Some of Youngblood's testimony is found in the WC Summary Report, pages 51-52, but for more detail, read the full-volumes.
34 *WCR*, p. 52.
35 This is detailed in *LBJ: The Mastermind of JFK's Assassination*, Phillip Nelson, (Xlibris, July 23, 2010)... I do not agree with every theory Nelson puts forward, nor do I uncritically accept the words of witnesses as readily as he does. Nevertheless, much of his well-written book is thoroughly documented, and he deserves credit for more thoroughly developing the Altgens "missing LBJ" issue.
36 www.jfkassassination.net/russ/testimony/euins.htm
37 *The Warren Commission Report, Volume II*, pp. 144-145.
38 see *WCR* testimonies or for a quick summary of 50 such witnesses, see *Assassination Research, Vol. 5, No. 1*, John P. Costella, 2007, pp. 48-50
39 *WCR*, p. 116.
40 ibid
41 *WCR*, or find it here: www.jfkassassinationforum.com/index.php?topic=1641.5;wap2
42 www.oswald-is-guilty.blogspot.com
43 *Reclaiming History*, Vincent Bugliosi.
44 "To Steal a Mockingbird," *Vanity Fair* magazine, August 2013 issue.
45 During the first Gulf War, DoD stats report about 110 battle-related deaths by enemy fire... about 35 more were killed by so-called "friendly fire," and 145 U.S. military died in non-combat accidents during that period.
46 Sibert, in an interview with William Matson Law, found in Law's book, *In the Eye of History: Disclosures in the JFK Assassination Medical Evidence* (2005).
47 see *High Treason 2*, by Harrison Livingstone, 1992, and David Lifton's persuasive work.
48 an easy to locate copy of the FBI report is found in the book, *Inquest*, by Edward Jay Epstein, (NY: Viking Press, 1966), p. 182.
49 FBI Report, as shown in the book, *Inquest*, by Edward Jay Epstein, (NY: Viking Press, 1966), p. 182 and 196.
50 *WCR*, Vol. 15, p. 700.
51 "Proper Assessment of the JFK Assassination Bullet Lead Evidence from Metallurgical and Statistical Perspectives," by Dr. Erik Randich and Dr. Patrick M Grant, July *2006 Journal of Forensic Science*, Vol. 51, p. 722.
52 ibid
53 *Washington Post*, Thursday, November 22, 2007.
54 www.washingtonpost.com/local/crime/justice-dept-fbi-to-review-use-of-forensic-evidence-in-thousands-of-cases/2012/07/10/gJQAT6DlbW_story.html
55 *WCR*, p. 116.
56 *WCR*, p. 76.

57 *WCR*, p. 93, and FBI Report found in the book, *Inquest*, by Edward Jay Epstein, (NY: Viking Press, 1966), p. 199.
58 *WCR*, p. 60.
59 ibid.
60 www.spot.acorn.net/jfkplace/1-hold/05-Reviews/05-05-TV/cbs-news.review
61 for those who don't speak Cajun, this means he was later pressured to back-off his emphatic, definite statements about which bullet hit him... Posner claims that when he showed Connally the (fake) medical "proofs" that the same bullet hit JFK, Connally back-pedaled (as crayfish are famous for doing) and purportedly said it was "possible."
62 TIME magazine, Nov. 25, 1966.
63 Harry A. Yardum, *The Grassy Knoll Witnesses: Who Shot JFK?*, p. 45.
64 *WCR, Volume II*, pp. 140-142.
65 *WCR, Volume II*, p. 124.
66 www.jfkassassination.net/russ/testimony/kellerma.htm
67 Charles Crenshaw, *JFK: Conspiracy of Silence*, (Signet Books, 1992).
68 *WCR*, pp. 90-91
69 *WCR*, 521.
70 Robert Groden, Harrison Livingstone, *High Treason*, (NY: Berkley Books, 1990), p. 45.
71 Harrison Livingstone, *Killing the Truth*, p. 718.
72 video interview on "The Men Who Killed Kennedy, Part 5," *The History Channel*.
73 *WCR*, page 540.
74 *WCR, Volume 6*, p. 136, and Harrison Livingstone, *Killing the Truth*, 1993, p. 180-192
75 Horne's table lists the witnesses and the sources of their statements; see *Inside the ARRB*, Volume IV, pp. 989-992.
76 Lifton, David (1988), *Best Evidence*, (New York: Carrol & Graf Publishers).
77 Part 1 of "CBS News Inquiry: The Warren Report," broadcast June 25, 1967.
78 Fred Newcomb and Perry Adams, *Murder From Within:Lyndon Johnson's Plot Against President Kennedy*, p. 213 (AuthorHouse, republished November 3, 2011).
79 The quotes here are from Kinney, as reported to Vince Palamara in 1994, and published in *JFK: The Medical Evidence Reference*, Vincent Palamara, 1998.
80 ibid
81 Groden/Livingstone, *High Treason,* p. 27.
82 HSCA Book 6, pp. 299-300
83 *Case Closed: Lee Harvey Oswald and the Assassination of JFK,* Gerald Posner, (New York: Random House, 1993), p. 304.
84 HSCA Book 6, pp. 301-302
85 HSCA Book 10, pp. 313-356
86 Dr. Mantik discusses this important finding in a chapter on the medical evidence in his book: *ASSASSINATION SCIENCE: EXPERTS SPEAK OUT ON THE DEATH OF JFK* (Chicago: Catfeet Press, 1998).
87 United States of America Assassination Records Review Board: Public Hearing. Washington, D.C.: U.S.Printing Office. November 18, 1994, pp. 25-26, 41-43.
88 American Bar Association, *Mock Trial of Lee Harvey Oswald*, August 10, 1992; Martin Shackelford, *Case Closed: A Preliminary Critique*, "The Investigator," August-September, 1993.
89 Noel Twyman, *Bloody Treason*, (1997), p. 160.
90 www.jfklancer.com/pdf/Jet_Effect_Rebuttal_II_(4-17-2012).pdf
91 www.mcadams.posc.mu.edu/oncebuff.htm
92 Ray and Mary La Fontaine, *Oswald Talked* (Pelican: Gretna, LA, 1996), p. 351.

93 *WCR*, p. 326
94 John Newman, *Oswald and the CIA,* (Carroll & Graf Publishers, 1995)
95 *WCR*, cited here: www.jfkassassination.net/russ/testimony/oswald_r.htm
96 La Fontaine, pp. 352-353, 357
97 These connections have been documented by a number of witnesses and writers, the most recent and indisputable being La Fontaine's work (see above); and Robert K. Tanenbaum's writings and public statements (he served on the HSCA); also see Robert D. Morrow, *First Hand Knowledge* or Anthony Summers, *Conspiracy*.
98 www.pbs.org/wgbh/pages/frontline/shows/oswald/glimpse/index.html#ferrie, and La Fontaine, p. 54.
99 see Thomas Hartmann's solid research, mostly from declassified government documents, detailed in his book with Lamar Waldron, *Ultimate Sacrifice: John and Robert Kennedy, the Plan for a Coup in Cuba, and the Murder of JFK*, (Carroll & Graf; 2006).
100 Top Secret *Report on Oswald's Foreign Activities*, by Coleman and Slawson, to Warren Commission Counsel Rankin, p. 55. See the original manually-typed report here: www.history-matters.com/archive/jfk/wc/wcmemos/Oswald_Foreign_Activities/html/180-10096-10364_0073a.htm
101 www.jfkresearch.freehomepage.com/minox.htm
102 informal talks by the author with Megrez Sheldon Rudolf in April 2013.
103 *History Channel* Documentary, "JFK: 3 Shots that Changed America," and on YouTube at www.youtube.com/watch?v=Cp_eOBEXqs0
104 La Fontaine, p. 300.
105 ibid, pp. 78-79.
106 ibid, pp. 148-150.
107 ibid, p. 200.
108 *The Ends of Power*, by H.R. Haldeman, (Dell Publishing, 1978) p. 39.
109 United States District Court, Southern District of Florida, Miami, Florida, case number 80-1121-Civ-JWK, 1983, cited in Mark Lane's book, *Plausible Denial*.
110 *The Last Confession of E. Howard Hunt*, (*Rolling Stone* magazine, April 4, 2007.
111 Chapter 19, *Rockefeller Commission Report*.
112 *Boston Globe*, July 9, 1976.
113 www.jfkmurdersolved.com/nixonruby.htm
114 www.secretsofthefed.com/former-nixon-aide-claims-he-has-evidence-lyndon-b-johnson-arranged-john-f-kennedys-assassination
115 One photo of Sturgis shows an expression matching that of the "tramp's," squinting in the sunlight, but Sturgis' jaw is wider and more square than the tramp jaw; Mary La Fontaine's review of Dallas Police records later proved Sturgis was not one of those arrested... though this did not rule out Sturgis' presence elsewhere in Dallas.
116 *Florida Sun Sentinel*, December 4, 1963.
117 This was reported by researcher Jim Marrs, and was widely known for years without any protest from Allan Tippit. In 2004, "debunker" Dale Meyers claimed to have interviewed Allan and that Allan denied the last words by his father. However, to my knowledge, there is no tape or affidavit to prove Meyer's claim.
118 HSCA document, Book 23, p. 855.
119 www.jdtippit.com/html/intro_faq.htm
120 John Armstrong in *Probe* magazine, January-February, 1998 issue (Vol. 5 No. 2), and www.jdtippit.com/html/intro_faq.htm
121 www.history-matters.com/archive/jfk/wc/wcvols/wh26/pdf/WH26_CE_2781.pdf.
122 HSCA document, Book 24, p. 263.

123 HSCA document, Book 24, p. 415.
124 HSCA document, Book 24, p. 414.
125 Seth Kantor, *Who Was Jack Ruby?* (Everest House, 1978).
126 www.jfkresearch.com/morningstar/killgallen.htm
127 Kantor, *Who Was Jack Ruby?*
128 John H. Davis, *Mafia Kingfish*, (Signet, 1989), pp. 449-451.
129 Kantor, p. 215-217.
130 Interview with Harry Kendall, included in "The Men Who Killed Kennedy" TV documentary and in "The Plot to Kill JFK" video by Sterling Entertainment, 1993.
131 www.druglibrary.org/schaffer/lsd/marks4.htm
132 This is well-documented by airline records and other files... see Kantor's book and La Fontaine's book.
133 *High Treason*, Groden and Livingstone.
134 *WCR*, Volume 14, p. 429 and Volume 15, p. 321; Also, Lamar Waldron with Thom Hartman, *Ultimate Sacrifice: John and Robert Kennedy, the Plan for a Coup in Cuba*, and *The Murder of JFK*, (New York: Carroll & Graf. 2005), Chapters 24 and 28.
135 Seth Kantor, *The Ruby Cover-Up*, (New York: Zebra Books, 1978), 58-63.
136 in *Oswald Talked*: see Chapter One, "Follow the Guns," and pp. 395-397
137 HSCA Report, Book 7
138 www.history-matters.com/essays/jfkmed/How5InvestigationsHow5InvestigationsGotItWrong_6.
139 www.hum.uchicago.edu/~jagoldsm/Papers/JFK/11_HCSA.pdf
140 Blakey's 2003 Addendum to his interview on the PBS *Frontline* episode, "Who Was Lee Harvey Oswald?"
141 www.dcdave.com/article5/120608.htm
142 www.giljesus.com/jfk/alibi.htm
143 www.maryferrell.org/wiki/index.php/Essay_-_Rewriting_History_-_Bugliosi_Parses_the_Testimony
144 FBI report, Dec. 6, 1963, contained in Warren Commission Exhibit 2089, pp. 35-36.
145 see *WC Summary Report*, p. 152-153.
146 www.jfkassassination.net/russ/testimony/adams_v.htm
147 *The Girl on the Stairs: My Search For A Missing Witness To The Assassination Of John F. Kennedy*, by Barry Ernest, (March 13, 2011), p. 176.
148 *WCR*, p. 151.
149 *WCR*, pp. 149, 151, 152, respectively.
150 HSCA, Book 6, p. 109.
151 quoted by Jim Marrs in *Crossfire*, p. 26.
152 from the *WCR*, and found at www.jfkassassination.net/russ/testimony/baker_m1.htm
153 see the original FBI report from 11-22-1963, warning of Brennan's inaccurate line-up "I.D.", here: www.giljesus.com/jfk/brennan.htm
154 www.spartacus.schoolnet.co.uk/JFKcarrR.htm
155 www.acorn.net/jfkplace/09/fp.back_issues/06th_Issue/r.craig.bio.html
156 Belin's rejected draft of Chapter 6, *Warren Commission Report*, August 7, 1964.
157 www.jfklancer.com/morley.html
158 www.commondreams.org/views06/1019-21.htm
159 www.spartacus.schoolnet.co.uk/JFKmeyerM.htm
160 a partial list can be found in *Crossfire* by Jim Marr and here: www.spot.acorn.net/jfkplace/09/fp.back_issues/34th_Issue/fear.html
161 found on CNN.com, August 2, 2013, online here:

www.thelead.blogs.cnn.com/2013/08/01/exclusive-dozens-of-cia-operatives-on-the-ground-during-benghazi-attack/?hpt=hp_c2
162 *Dallas News*, January 14, 2013.
163 www.ctka.net/2013/The_MSM_and_RFKJr.html
164 David Talbot, *Brothers: The Hidden History of the Kennedy Years*, (Free Press, 2007), p. 359.
165 Anthony Summers, "The Secret Life of J. Edgar Hoover," *The Guardian*, January, 2012.
166 www.surftofind.com/document
167 *Newsweek*, October 13, 1997, p. 58.
168 *Newsweek*, October 13, 1997, p. 57.
169 Anthony Summers, *Official and Confidential: The Secret Life of J. Edgar Hoover*, (G.P. Putnam, New York, 1993), and www.oswald-not-guilty.blogspot.com/2011_12_01_archive.html
170 see Jim Marrs, *Crossfire*, pp. 57-58, and *The New York Times*, November 24, 1963.
171 *Newsweek*, October 13, 1997, p. 57-58.
172 ibid.
173 Associated Press article cited from the *Dothan Eagle*, Thursday, July 3, 1997.
174 Thursday, July 3, 1997, editorial column of *The Dothan Eagle*.
175 www.nytimes.com/2013/08/10/us/mystery-from-the-grave-beside-oswalds-solved.html?pagewanted=2&_r=0&ref=general&src=me
176 For whatever reason, Donahue was reticent to concede a conspiracy and instead blamed the fatal shot on a misfire from a Secret Service agent carelessly wielding an automatic weapon in the SS follow-up car. No one in that car heard a shot from that weapon, no spectators observed it, and the fatal wound on JFK was clearly a frontal shot. Despite Donahue's crazy speculation about the origin of the last bullet, his expertise as a professional marksman and gun expert still makes his doubts about the difficulty of the sixth floor shots relevant.
177 *Discovery* show, "JFK: Inside the Target Car"
178 www.geocities.ws/jfktruth/MOORMANPIX.jpg
179 Much of Bolden's sad tale can be found in the book by Lamar Waldron, *Ultimate Sacrifice*, and confirmed by Journalist Edwin Black, who investigated the Chicago JFK plot for the *Atlantic Monthly* (and had his life threatened as a result).
180 Lyndon Johnson, *State of the Union Address, 1967*. He was quoting Thomas Jefferson, in defense of the murderous Vietnam War... it is not a stretch to imagine LBJ using this same quote to rationalize the plot against JFK.
181 www.secretsofthefed.com/former-nixon-aide-claims-he-has-evidence-lyndon-b-johnson-arranged-john-f-kennedys-assassination/#ShhTbWSmlCJVMGq5.99
182 www.jfkfacts.org/assassination/poll/why-roger-stones-jfk-book-cant-be-dismissed/
183 ibid
184 www.theatlantic.com/past/docs/issues/2004/06/holland.htm
185 Phillip Nelson, *LBJ: Mastermind*
186 Evan Thomas, *Robert Kennedy: His Life*, (NY: Simon and Schuster, 2000), pp. 254-270.
187 Reported in *Time* magazine, *The New York Times*, in historian Robert Caro's work etc.
188 See *The Austin Statesman-American*, (27th February, 1952) and Phillip Nelson, *LBJ: Mastermind*
189 www.spartacus.schoolnet.co.uk/JFKwallaceM.htm
190 www.viewzone.com/lbj/
191 Barr McClellan, *Blood, Money & Power: How LBJ. Killed JFK*, (Hannover House, New York, 2003; paperback used here, by Skyhorse Publishing, 2003), p. 323-329.
192 CNN's "Crossfire," November, 1982.
193 *The Last Confession of E. Howard Hunt*, (*Rolling Stone* magazine, April 4, 2007).

194 Sources revealing LBJ's actual behind-the-veneer character include:
- Robert A. Caro, *The Years of Lyndon Johnson: The Path to Power* (1982), *Means of Ascent* (1990), and *Master of the Senate* (2002) (Alfred A. Knopf, New York)
- J. Evetts Haley, *A Texan Looks at Lyndon: A Study in Illegitimate Power* (Palo Duro Press, Canyon, Texas, 1964)
- Joachim Joesten, *The Dark Side of Lyndon Baines Johnson*, (Peter Dawnay Ltd., London, 1968)
- Barr McClellan, *Blood, Money & Power: How LBJ. Killed JFK*, (Hannover House, New York, 2003; paperback by Skyhorse Publishing, 2003)
- Harry Middleton, *LBJ: The White House Years* (Harry N. Abrams, New York, 1990)
- www.reformation.org/president-lyndon-johnson.html
- Phillip Nelson, *LBJ: The Mastermind of JFK's Assassination*, (Xlibris, July 23, 2010)

195 On a White House tape dated March 2, 1967, Texas Governor John Connally engaged LBJ in a conversation about the attempted Castro assassination, the JFK assassination, and how DA Jim Garrison might be digging deep enough to cause LBJ grief. LBJ reassures Connally, in part, by saying "Hoover and 'em [will] watch it very carefully." Connally concludes, "I don't want to know anything. I don't need to know...."

196 Richard Nixon and George H. W. Bush have a rare commonality: they are about the only Americans who can't remember where they were when Kennedy was shot... both have given changing stories across the years. I know exactly where I was at 12:30 November 22nd, 1963: in my elementary school first grade classroom.

197 Harold Weisberg, *Case Open: The Omissions, Distortions and Falsifications of 'Case Closed'*, (Carroll and Graf: NY, 1994), pp. 151,186,187; also see *WCR*, Vol. 15, p. 700.)

198 Gerald Posner in a PBS *Frontline* Interview.

199 www.slate.com/articles/news_and_politics/press_box/2010/02/more_posner_plagiarism.html

200 In the video, *The Secret KGB JFK Assassination*, narrated by actor Roger Moore.

201 Tim Weiner, *Legacy of Ashes: The History of the Central Intelligence Agency*, (New York: Doubleday, 2007).

202 www.nytimes.com/2012/11/10/opinion/when-a-cia-director-had-scores-of-affairs.html?_r=0

203 see Charles Higham, *Trading with the Enemy: An Expose of the Nazi-American Money Plot 1933-1949*, (Delecorte Press, NY, 1983) and John Loftus and Mark Aarons, *The Secret War Against The Jews: How Western Espionage Betrayed The Jewish People*, (St. Martin's Press, NY, 1994)